Effective Writing
for the
Business World

Effective Writing for the Business World

Thelma D. Kantorowitz

Community College of Rhode Island

Catherine R. Ott

Community College of Rhode Island

HarperCollins*Publishers*

To our daughters: Karen, Jo Ann, Debra

Library of Congress Cataloging in Publication Data

Kantorowitz, Thelma D.
  Effective writing for the business world.

  1. English language — Rhetoric.   2. English language —
Business English.   3. Commercial correspondence.
4. Report writing.   I. Ott, Catherine R.   II. Title.
PE1479.B87K36 1983   808'.066651   83-16270

ISBN 0-673-39271-6

ISBN 0-673-39271-6

90 - 5

Preface

This book represents the best efforts of our combined thirty-four years of teaching writing at the Community College of Rhode Island. In our classes we lead our students step-by-step through the process of writing effectively for the business world. Our goal has always been to prepare successful business communicators. For these reasons, we have developed the following organization for *Effective Writing for the Business World*:

Technique, including some basic grammar and punctuation review
Format
Letters, divided according to types
The memo
The formal report
Other forms of communication, both oral and written

Effective Writing for the Business World is practical, clearly written, and well organized. We devote not one or two, but nine complete chapters to letter writing. Too many books use too many pages to discuss formal report writing, visuals design, library research, or basic composition. Too many books are too theoretical and often stale. Every chapter of our book uses examples to make our discussions clear, checklists to review major points covered, and a generous number of exercises to test understanding. These exercises have been developed and used successfully in our classrooms.

For those teachers who teach the formal written report, we have two chapters. Chapter 14 contains a complete sample feasibility report. Students are led step-by-step through the writing process — from assignment to format. Each report element is discussed and illustrated.

We appreciate the encouragement of the many people who helped us with this book. Thanks go to members of the English Department at the Community College of Rhode Island. We are also grateful to Robert Benoit, Postmaster, East Greenwich, Rhode Island, for his information on postal services; to Isabella P. Goldberg, for her proofreading skills and invaluable suggestions; to Robert L. Shaffer, whose business acumen and mathematical ability enhanced many sections, especially those concerning the formal report; and to Bernice Whitaker for her help and information on the job process. Last, but far from least, we are grateful to Irene Miller for her help and encouragement during the entire process.

For their helpful advice and contributions — textbook writing is a truly collaborative effort — we would like to thank the following teachers of business writing: William J. Buchholz (Bentley College), Helen L. Cropley (West Virginia State College), John T. Dever (Thomas Nelson Community College), Stanley J. Kozikowski (Bryant College), Daniel Lynch (LaGuardia Community College), Robert E. Mehaffy (American River College), Kathleen O'Shaughnessy (Coastal Carolina Community College), and Marguerite P. Shane (Illinois State University).

Thanks, too, to the following Little, Brown staff members: Peter Shepard, for giving us the initial shove; Molly Faulkner, for having more faith in us than we had in ourselves; and Sally Stickney, for her patience and guidance.

T. K.
C. O.

To the Student

All students at one time or another have wondered why they must take various writing courses. "Why must I take Composition, Business Writing, or Technical Writing? After all, English is my native tongue. I learned it in the cradle and have been speaking and writing it all my life! What difference does it make whether I use good grammar? As long as I make myself understood, who cares?" But do you really make yourself understood? The answer is no if you have ever been asked, "What do you mean?" or "Whatever are you trying to say?" Is your writing always clear? The number of "not clear" notations on your work will supply the answer. Writing courses teach the skills you need to know in order to write correctly and clearly.

Clarity in business communications is vital. Unclear letters and contracts can not only cost money, but may even create legal problems. The first step in avoiding such problems is realizing that language is a tool easily adapted to fit all your communication needs whether they be writing letters to friends and family, business letters, or even love letters. Unlike social letters, which may have no definite purpose, business letters have a specific goal. They are written to get results and must make a good impression on the reader if you want to stimulate action. It makes sense, therefore, for anyone going into any aspect of business whether as a corporate executive, a secretary, or pool typist to learn the fundamentals of business communications. In fact, writing good letters is so important that a growing number of companies offer courses in business communications to employees on site during working hours. Such courses may include top-level executives, clerk-typists, and bank tellers as well as secretaries and sales personnel and are often taught by local college faculties, usually for college credit. Where such on-site courses are unavailable, some businesses encourage employees to take evening courses by paying the cost and/or offering incentive raises.

As with any skill, writing business letters requires learning certain techniques and rules, among them the "Seven C's of Communication."

1. *Completeness* — Say all that must be said.
2. *Clearness* — Say it clearly so there is no mistaking your meaning.
3. *Concreteness* — Be specific and choose your words carefully.
4. *Correctness* — Know your facts and use proper grammar.
5. *Conciseness* — Be brief.

6. *Courtesy* — Be polite, treating your reader as you would like to be treated.
7. *Character* — Let your personality show in a natural, unstilted writing style.

While the styles and rules for writing business letters have changed over the years, the basic concepts have not. To realize some of these changes, look in the Appendix at the "Directions for Letter Writing" circa 1800, origin unknown, printed at Old Sturbridge Village in Massachusetts. How does it stand up to the "Seven C's"? While we may smile at the wordiness and some of the suggestions, one rule still holds true today: legibility of address.

As recently as the 1970s, many businesses, banks in particular, still clung to the old trite, pat phrases such as "Yours of the 10th inst.," "Your esteemed favor," "We beg to inform you," and "It has come to hand." Today the writer uses simple, everyday language naturally and easily.

Hand-in-hand with changes in style and vocabulary have come changes in technology. The typewriter replaced the quill pen, and the telephone made communication almost instantaneous. Why, then, write when talk is cheap? Surely the telephone is the way to go when you can dial directly virtually anywhere in the world in seconds! Some people point out that it is much easier talking in a face-to-face conversation or over the telephone than writing a letter. Oral communication has an intimacy and immediacy not found in letters. The instant feedback of facial expressions, body language, and tone of voice is nearly impossible to duplicate in written communication. But, in many instances, the disadvantages of conversation outweigh the advantages. The major drawback is the lack of permanent records of conversations, orders, or agreements. Time differentials must also be considered when using the telephone. Thus, despite the ease of direct dialing and the WATS line, letters must still be written for verification and for records.

Written communications have numerous advantages. The preciseness of the good letter helps avoid misunderstanding or misinterpretation. The content is permanently recorded, and information is readily available for study at any time. Thus letters are convenient, economical, permanent records of transactions and may serve as legal evidence in the event of civil suits.

Unfortunately, most people dislike writing letters. To combat this problem, some organizations develop a collection of form letters covering various situations. For example, an executive may receive a number of unsolicited job applications and would need form letters designed to cover the following situations:

1. No positions now open or anticipated in the near future.
2. No full-time positions open but occasionally have part-time positions. If interested, call for an interview.
3. Letter referred to personnel department.
4. Letter from earlier applicant. Situation unchanged since first communication.

Each letter is individually typed, and the typist simply refers to the files for the kind of answer required. This procedure not only saves the busy executive time for other more important work, but also creates good will on the part of the applicant because someone took the time to acknowledge his or her letter.

One disadvantage of correspondence is the lack of immediate feedback. While domestic mail is quick, overseas mail can be unbelievably slow depending on the individual country and whether the letters are sent by surface or air. For detailed information on the many types of United States mail service, see the Appendix.

Good letters are the wheels of business, while bad letters are like sand and sugar in the gas tank of a car. They gum up the works, sabotage the machinery, cause delays, and cost money. In the United States, the cost of business letters, which includes not only the paper and postage but also the dictator's and typist's time, runs into billions of dollars per year. Bad letters increase that cost.

Letters with the right information, the right tone, the right point of view, the right attitude toward the reader, and the right opening and closing can make the difference between success and failure. The reward of a good letter comes when the reader either buys what you are selling, does what you have requested, or develops a feeling of good will toward the writer.

Successful writers of business letters realize the importance of thinking before writing and know that the ultimate goal of the letter is to stimulate action or good will on the part of the reader. The good writer carefully considers the reader when determining the attitude and tone of the letter, keeping in mind two questions. "Would I like to receive this letter?" "Would I be offended by this letter?"

Writers of business letters can also look to modern technology for help. Computers, word processors, even typewriters with memories all speed the composing process, eventually paying for themselves and lowering the cost of communication in time saved. Last but not least are texts like this, which teach the beginner the basics of business communications.

Look through the text. Familiarize yourself with the contents. Notice that each chapter deals with a particular problem, type of letter, type of report, and language use. Notice the additional useful information in the Appendix. When you have completed the text, you will be familiar with many of the situations requiring written communication in the world of work and even in your private life. You should be able to do the following:

1. Apply in writing the basic principles involved in business letters and reports.
2. Write clear, concise, interesting, and mechanically correct business letters.
3. Write a comprehensive formal business report in proper form.
4. Write effective telegrams.
5. Write correct minutes of a meeting.

6. Summarize written material concisely and accurately.
7. Understand the problems involved in business communications and some of the laws governing the content.
8. Use the telephone correctly.
9. Make oral presentations.
10. Write a suitable job application letter and prepare a proper résumé.

Although you may never be called upon to write all the different types of letters you will learn about, to make speeches, or to preside at meetings, should such occasions arise you will be familiar with the basic principles governing these activities.

Contents

建立 relationship.

14   *The Formal Report*   *298*

15   *Other Forms of Communication: Oral and Written*   *336*

Effective Writing
for the
Business World

1

Establishing Rapport with Your Reader

All letters are written *to* someone *from* someone. The pattern is:

$$\text{Sender (Writer)} \longrightarrow \text{Recipient (Reader)}$$

First, put yourself in the sender's place and ask, "Why am I writing this letter?" Aren't you writing usually because you want something from the recipient? Maybe you want information or the answer to a question. Maybe you want a prospective customer to order from you or to pay an overdue bill. Or perhaps you just want the reader to think well of you or to like you. Thus, we must first acknowledge that the writer of a letter generally has a self-centered motive for sending a business letter.

Now, put yourself in the recipient's place. Would you react favorably to a letter that is obviously motivated by the self-centered interests of its sender? No, probably you would be turned off, and you would tune out the sender. Now, think about a letter that would cause you to have a positive reaction — naturally it would be one that emphasized *your* interests or your point of view.

The "You" Attitude and Reader-centered Letters

As a sender, how can you write letters to which recipients will react positively? You must phrase the wording of the letter so as to make them feel important. This positive reaction can be accomplished by using the "You" attitude.

The "You" attitude is a simple but effective method for gaining and keeping attention. Always stress the positive effects for readers — how they will benefit by doing what you ask.

For example, would you say, "Please buy the new Wonder Lady washer because I will make a good profit"? Of course not!

How about, "The new Wonder Lady washer will save you time and money. No more annoying trips to the laundromat, long waits for a machine, or hunting for change. And the average load of wash in the Wonder Lady costs you only 12 cents — compare that with your coin-op charge!"

Notice that the "You" attitude emphasizes *you* (the reader) instead of *I* (the writer). Check over your letters after they are written. If they contain too many *I*'s, they probably sound very selfish and probably do not strongly emphasize *reader* benefit. Letter recipients want to know, "What's in this for me?" If you can convince them that they will profit, that their needs or desires will be met, or that what you suggest is in their best interests, they will like what you say and will react favorably to your requests. If they think you are concerned with what their responses will do for *you,* they will react unfavorably and may not follow your suggestions.

How can you write sentences that emphasize the "You" attitude? First, think about what you want and then think about what your reader might want. For example, if you try to collect an overdue payment by saying, "I need your money because I, too, have to pay my suppliers for merchandise," your reader will only see how a payment will meet *your* needs. This sentence should be rewritten to emphasize how payment will benefit the reader: "Surely you want to keep your fine payment record and credit standing in our community. Prompt payment of this bill will ensure continuation of your A+ rating." Wouldn't the second message make the customer more eager to send a check than the first one?

Let's consider another example. You operate a discount store where prices are kept as low as possible because you sell for cash only; you have no charge accounts and thus eliminate the cost of billing and collecting. This saving is passed on to your customers. You have just received an order from a customer who asks you to send merchandise and charge it on his VISA card. How would you explain, using the "You" attitude, why you are unable to accept this payment proposal? Remember to emphasize how your policy benefits the buyer's pocketbook.

Using Words with Appropriate Positive Connotations

Word choices also play an important role in establishing good relationships with your readers. In order to choose the best possible words, you must consider both their denotations and their connotations. The *denotation* of a word is its dictionary meaning, factual and unemotional. The *connotation* of a word is its emotional meaning, the negative or positive response that it invokes.

In business letter writing try to choose words that will convey a positive message to the reader. Some words are objective; that is, they have little emotional impact. Some examples of words that have denotations but little connotation are *house* and *automobile*. Change the word *house* to *mansion* or *shack* and notice that these words convey an emotional meaning. How about *limousine* or *jalopy* rather than *automobile?* Don't offer to sell a line of dresses made for *fat* women; direct your sales pitch to those with a *fuller figure*. Don't sell *cheap* furniture to *tightwads*; sell *budget-wise* furniture for the *smart buyer*.

Word choice also involves the ability to communicate your message without using negative or insulting words. How would you react to being called *dishonest* or a *deadbeat?*

For Class Discussion

Try your hand at changing the following words into synonyms with positive connotations:

mutt	silly	smell
bum	claw	rotten
filthy	sloppy	ugly
skinny	flimsy	old hag
lazy	stupid	shack
selfish	liar	sneaky

Also avoid the negative approach by accentuating the positive. Tell your reader what you can do, not what you can't do, by emphasizing *yes*'s rather than *no*'s. Write optimistically, not pessimistically. If an order is going to be delayed for two weeks, say, "Your order will arrive at your store on June 15," not, "Your order has been delayed and will not arrive until June 15."

Other examples are: "We can repair your radio for a small fee" rather than "We can't repair your radio free." "Your payment was expected on May 4" rather than "Your payment is late." "I can come for an interview any afternoon after 2:00 p.m." rather than "I cannot come for an interview in the morning." "Selling for cash only saves you, the customer, 25 percent" rather than "We do not accept charges."

Being Tactful

It isn't always easy to be tactful, especially when you are angry or dissatisfied. You want to use harsh, bitter words and blow off steam. An old trite saying goes: "You catch more flies with honey than with vinegar." Think about that. Will nasty, negative words convince the recipient of a letter to do what the writer wishes? No, the reader will probably react angrily and negatively. He or she may even decide that there is no point in trying to satisfy because the situation is beyond repair. Certainly you should state the facts and present the problem in a calm, fair, and unemotional way. Most likely, your reader will react and answer in the same manner.

What should you do if you just *have* to be nasty? Try the following: First, write a nasty letter, letting out all your anger. Second, throw the letter in the wastebasket. Third, now write a new, tactful letter.

For Class Discussion

Study the following letter and its revision. Which letter would you rather receive? To which would you give a more favorable hearing?

```
Gentlemen:

That radio you sold me three weeks ago is a piece of junk.
And you cheated me, too. I saw it advertised in last
Sunday's paper for $5.00 less at the Blythe Store. If you
don't give me my money back immediately, I'll take you to
court!
```

Wouldn't the next letter do a better job?

```
Gentlemen:

Three weeks ago I bought a Liteline radio from you which I
am now returning by United Parcel Service. I cannot get
any stations clearly. Also, I feel that I overpaid as this
radio was advertised in last Sunday's paper for $5 less at
the Blythe Store.

Please refund my $89.95.
```

Give specific reasons why the second letter is better than the first one. What words are offensive in the earlier letter? Are there other reasons why the second letter is more satisfactory?

Discuss with your classmates how you might phrase tactful letters for the following situations:

1. You recently had minor surgery and have received a bill for $200 from the surgeon. His secretary had told you that your health insurance policy would cover his services in full. Thus, you believe that you should not have to pay this bill.

2. You ordered a book from a publisher, specifying that it must be delivered by the 5th of June as it was to be a birthday gift for your father. It is now the 8th of June and the book has not arrived although you have already been billed for $10.95. You want to cancel your order, as you had to buy another present when this one did not arrive on time.

Using Passive Verbs and Subordination to Communicate Bad News

First, we shall define *active* and *passive* verbs. Use *active* verbs when the doer of an action is the subject of a verb.

> Jon rewrote the report.

Jon is the subject of the verb *rewrote*; he performs the action on the object, the *report*. When the subject acts, the verb is active.

Now, let's rearrange the above sentence to make the verb passive. A verb becomes passive when the subject receives the action or is acted upon.

> The report was rewritten by Jon.

Here *report* is the subject of *was rewritten*, but it does not perform the action; rather, the action is performed upon it.

Note the differences between the first and second sentences.

1. The second sentence uses more words.
2. The second sentence is more roundabout and less direct.
3. Jon seems less important in the second sentence.

A sentence with a passive verb is much weaker, less forceful than a sentence with an active verb. Do you think that you would say, "I just won one thousand dollars" or "A thousand dollars was just won by me"?

Sentences in good business letters should generally use active verbs to express ideas more emphatically and concisely. However, if writers wish to deemphasize bad news, they would often achieve their purpose of tactful conveyance more effectively through the use of passive verbs.

Compare the following sentences:

> You cannot have a charge account at our store.
> A charge account at our store cannot be granted at present.

or

> You have not made your monthly payment.
> The monthly payment on Account #5532 has not been received.

Note that we have eliminated the *you* in the above examples. Here the *you* emphasizes the negative rather than the positive ideas. The "You" attitude, therefore, would not be appropriate here because these sentences are not reader-benefit oriented.

A letter cannot always convey good news or tell the reader what he or she wants to hear. In order to lessen its impact, disappointing news should be deemphasized or subordinated. Placement in both sentence and paragraph can aid in minimizing the force of the negative message. One successful technique is to subordinate the bad news in a dependent (subordinate) clause, while conveying the best possible information in the main clause. Note how the following sentence stresses the positive idea:

> We have arranged with Acme Electric Supply to honor our service contracts, although we are closing our Houston service facilities.

Also, if you blurt out the bad news in the very first sentence of your letter, the recipient will probably read no further. He or she will be left with a negative feeling toward the writer or company represented. Therefore, you must organize the message so that it will receive a complete reading. Provide a buffer before giving the negative information. This can be done by delaying the bad news until at least *the second sentence of the second paragraph*. First, get in step with the reader in a cordial opening paragraph. Provide an introductory sentence for the second paragraph, giving the reason for what follows. Finally, deemphasize the bad news by using the passive voice in a subordinate clause.

Note how this letter follows the above suggestions:

```
Dear Mrs. Jones:

Thank you for your interest in the New Age Children's
Store. We offer fine clothing for the younger set at
discount prices.

Because we combine large-volume buying with low overhead,
we are able to sell top-quality merchandise at close-to-
wholesale prices. We help to keep our overhead down by our
no-refund policy. We shall be glad to exchange the blue
spring coat for a credit slip, although it cannot be
returned for a refund.

You will, we are sure, enjoy using your credit toward
items from our huge selection of clothing for the little
people in your life. We look forward to seeing you in our
store soon.
```

How would you react to this letter if you were Mrs. Jones?

Writing Complete Letters

Being reader-oriented, positive, and tactful all help to create successful letters. However, the best-written letter is ineffective if it does not completely and adequately cover the intended subject matter. If the reader must reply with an inquiry about missing facts or ideas, the letter has not done its job.

To ensure completeness, you must first be sure that you understand the situation about which the letter is written. If you are not entirely clear about what must be included, ask questions! Ask for more information or clarification of the problem and do not begin writing until you are *sure* that you know exactly what is expected.

Next, jot down those points that must be included. Make an outline that you can follow and reread it to be certain that the letter will provide enough information to satisfy your recipient. Put yourself in the reader's place and make certain that he or she does not have to assume anything or read between the lines in order to receive the full message.

However, be sure not to go overboard by saying more than is necessary. Don't include irrelevant matters or dwell upon what your reader already knows as indicated by previous correspondence. For example, don't waste precious space saying:

```
I have received your letter of May 15 (obviously you have if
you are answering it!) and shall be glad to give you the
dealer's price on our Model X-32 radio, which retails for
$79.95. (If all of this was in the letter, don't repeat it, answer it!)
```

Instead, begin with new information as follows:

```
The dealer's price for the Model X-32 radio is $48.78
each. We have them in brown and in white for immediate
delivery.
```

To summarize this chapter, use the following Checklist to review the methods by which you can establish rapport with your readers. Next, apply your knowledge by doing the exercises on the following pages.

CHECKLIST

Establishing Rapport with Your Reader

- Use the "You" attitude.
- Use words with positive connotations.
- Be tactful. Avoid words that will antagonize.
- Communicate bad news through subordination and passive verbs.
  a. Write a buffer first paragraph.
  b. Write an introductory sentence for the second paragraph, giving reasons for what follows.
  c. Deemphasize the bad news through passive verbs in dependent clauses.
- Write complete letters.
  a. Ask questions if necessary.
  b. Outline.
  c. Recheck.

EXERCISES

1. Rewrite the following sentences so that they will reflect the "You" attitude.
   a. Pay your bill for $32.50, which is three months overdue.
   b. We are the most successful local manufacturer of high-fashion sports apparel.
   c. Our sale of dining room sets has been caused by the fact that we overbought last spring.
   d. Please send me the following information about your sales policies as I am writing a report for my business writing class.
   e. I would like a job with your company because it is near my girlfriend's home.
   f. We cannot refund your money because of our company policy.
   g. Because we sell to wholesale customers only, you will have to purchase your restaurant supplies from a local dealer.
   h. We cannot open a charge account for you because you already owe us too much money.
   i. We would like to open a charge account for you.
   j. We are having this sale because our business is doing poorly.

2. Reword the following sentences to eliminate negative wording or tone.
   a. We must assume that you are dishonest because you have failed to send your monthly payments on schedule.
   b. We sell appliances more cheaply than our competitors do.
   c. We can't send your order because you filled in the order blank incorrectly.
   d. The blouse I bought was made of a sleazy material and washed terribly.
   e. We cannot refund your money because you obviously dropped the radio.
   f. We cannot send you this confidential information because we don't trust you.
   g. Employees must stop taking advantage of their privileges by too long lunch hours.
   h. We cannot hire you because your college grades were lousy.
   i. You can no longer charge at our store because you are a deadbeat.
   j. The old geezer had better give us his Social Security number.
   k. I cannot make an appointment this week.
   l. Your order will be three weeks late.

3. Rewrite the following sentences so that they are more concise and forceful. (*Hint*: Change them from passive to active voice.)
   a. The refund will be sent to you sometime next week.
   b. People who want the best merchandise at the lowest prices are catered to by the Smith and Jones Furniture Store.
   c. The letter will be written by me this afternoon.
   d. Forceful teachers are appreciated by students who are eager to learn.
   e. The following items that come from your latest catalogue are desired by me.
   f. Can an appointment be made with you soon for a meeting?
   g. A reliable product is desired by all of our customers.
   h. A speech about lateness was made by the personnel manager.
   i. Overtime pay is appreciated by most of the office staff.
   j. You will be assisted in the new job by my secretary, Robin French.

4. The following excerpts from bad-news letters need to be rewritten so that the bad news is handled as clearly and inoffensively as possible. (*Hint*: Use the passive voice and subordination.)

a. Dear Ms. Rolle:

We are sorry but we cannot refund the purchase price of the chair you bought last week. Because it was marked down, it was sold "as is" and "all sales final." You can surely overlook the slight scratch on the leg because you got such a bargain.

b. Dear Mr. Dole:

We cannot grant you a charge account because you already owe too much money to other stores. But we shall be glad to have you as a cash customer.

c. Dear Dr. Simmons:

We cannot send the dress you ordered because we ran out of your size in blue. Do you want us to send your money back?

d. Gentlemen:

That washing machine that you sold me is no good. Take it out of my house immediately and send my money back.

e. Dear Mr. Glidden:

We are not interested in hiring you because you want too much money. Also, Mr. Smith wrote a very poor recommendation for you.

5. The following letters are incomplete. What facts or points would you add so that the recipients would have enough information?

a. Gentlemen:

Please send me one of the blouses that you advertised. I must have it by next week at the latest. Charge it to my account.

b. Dear Mrs. Williams:

Thank you for your order. The blue skirt, size 12, that you requested is no longer in stock. However, we have some other nice ones. What do you want us to do about this matter?

c. Gentlemen:

Please tell me all about your resort as I am thinking about spending my vacation there soon. I hope to hear from you soon.

d. Dear Miss Pullen:

Your bill is now long overdue. Send us your check immediately.

e. Gentlemen and Ladies:

I don't want one of the lamps that I bought the
other day. Please refund my money.

f. Dear Mrs. Cole:

We can't refund your money.

2

More Technique: Getting the Message Across

Using the Correct Word, Correctly Spelled

The basic unit of writing and speaking is the word. Thus, using the correct word in the best way is of utmost importance if you are to get a message across successfully. In the previous chapter you learned how word choice can affect a reader's reaction either positively or negatively. Review what was said about choosing words with positive connotations that do not antagonize.

Choosing the best possible correct word plays an important role in communication, especially written communication. If you choose an incorrect word in conversation, your listener may not hear it or may forget about it. If you use an incorrect word in a letter or report, it will remain there to be read and reread as an indelible witness of your inability to handle the English language successfully. Your errors may be used as ammunition against you when you are eligible for a promotion or a salary increase. Your best friend is a good college-level dictionary that you consult whenever you are not *positive* about the precise meaning of a word.

Not only must you use the correct word, but you must also spell it correctly. Spelling in English is especially difficult because our vocabulary is derived from several languages with diverse spelling/pronunciation systems. For example, the *gh* spelling for the *f* sound as in the word *rough* comes from Germanic origins; the *ti* spelling for the *sh* sound as in the word *nutritious* comes from Romance languages. Also, many words in our language sound alike but are spelled differently and have different meanings. Some examples of these words (called *homonyms*) are *there, their, they're; meat, meet, mete; been, bin;* and *right, write, rite.* Again, use your dictionary whenever you have any doubt about spelling.

Troublemakers

Study the following list of thirty troublemakers that cause frequent errors in writing. Because the list is incomplete, think of five of your own problem words. Look them up in your dictionary and add them to the list along with those suggested by others in the class.

accept, except

Accept is a verb meaning "to take" or "to receive": He *accepts* my gift.

Except may be used as a verb meaning "to exclude": The new rules *except* freshmen. It is more often used as a preposition meaning "other than": They were all here *except* John.

advice, advise

Advice is a noun meaning "opinion": He gave us his *advice*.

Advise is a verb meaning "to recommend": I *advise* that you rewrite that letter.

affect, effect

Affect is a verb meaning "to influence, change, or stir the emotions": His advice *affected* my decision.

Effect is a noun meaning "result," or it can be used as a verb meaning "to cause or accomplish": The *effect* of the child's illness was deafness. They *effected* a compromise.

all ready, already

All ready means "completely prepared": The secretary was *all ready* to take dictation.

Already means "by or before the given time": The office was *already* empty when he called.

all together, altogether

All together means "in a group": The officers are *all together* at the meeting.

Altogether means "wholly, completely": Overtime pay is *altogether* unnecessary.

a lot, alot

A lot is an informal way of saying "a great number or amount." It is generally too informal for use in business writing.

Alot is incorrect.

among, between

Among is a preposition used when three or more are referred to: The commissions were divided *among* the three salesmen.

Between is a preposition used when two are referred to: The commissions were divided *between* the two salesmen.

amount, number

Amount refers to bulk and is followed by a singular noun: They spilled a large *amount* of ink.

Number refers to countable units and is followed by a plural noun: We have a large *number* of pens in the drawer.

any one, anyone

Any one refers to a specific person or thing in a group and is followed by a prepositional phrase beginning with *of*: *Any one* of those letters can be sent.

Anyone means "any person at all" and is not followed by a prepositional phrase: Can *anyone* help me?

Everyone, every one and *someone, some one* are used in the same manner.

conscious, conscience

Conscious is an adjective meaning "aware" or "in a normal waking state": He is *conscious* of the need to be honest.

Conscience is a noun meaning "moral sense": A man's *conscience* should bother him if he lies.

continual, continuous

Continual means "repeated often": His *continual* coughing disturbs the office.

Continuous means "going on without interruption": The alarm rang for five hours *continuously.*

disinterested, uninterested

Disinterested means "impartial": A judge must be *disinterested.*

Uninterested means "indifferent": John is *uninterested* in learning his father's business.

emigrate, immigrate

Emigrate means "to move away from": He *emigrated from Canada to the United States.*

Immigrate means "to go to": He *immigrated* to the United States from Canada.

eminent, imminent

Eminent means "prominent, distinguished": The *eminent* philosopher was in great demand as a speaker.

Imminent means "about to happen": The philosopher was worried about the *imminent* loss of his teaching position at the university.

fewer, less

Fewer is an adjective used to refer to that which is countable: There are *fewer* cookies to be baked because our guests are not coming.

Less refers to that which is not countable such as an amount or a collective quantity: There are fewer cookies to be baked because we have *less* sugar than we need to make a whole batch.

in, into

In is a preposition meaning "enclosed by": He is *in* his office.

Into implies motion from outside to inside: He walked *into* his office.

incredible, incredulous

Incredible means "unbelievable": He told an *incredible* story about his adventures.

Incredulous means "unwilling or unable to believe": We were *incredulous* about the truth of his incredible story about his adventures.

its, it's, its'

Its is the possessive form of the pronoun *it*: The dog lost *its* sight.

It's is the contraction for *it is*: *It's* unusual for a dog to lose its sight.

Its' is not ever correct.

later, latter

Later means "subsequently": The board meeting will be *later* than scheduled.

Latter means "last mentioned of two" (use *former* to denote the first mentioned of two): We shall discuss the *latter* proposal when we meet.

likely, liable

Likely means "probable": It is *likely* that the executives will get pay increases next month.

Liable means "legally bound" or "obligated": He is likely to be *liable* for the damage caused by the accident.

lose, loose

Lose is a verb meaning "to mislay": He will *lose* his briefcase if he is not careful.

Loose is an adjective meaning "free, unbound": He will lose his *loose* papers if he is not careful.

may be, maybe

May be is a verb phrase expressing possibility: He *may be* wealthy some day.

Maybe is an adverb meaning "perhaps": *Maybe* he will earn some large commissions.

precede, proceed

Precede is a verb meaning "to go before": His speech will *precede* the president's.

Proceed is a verb meaning "to go on, advance," especially after stopping: After his speech, we will *proceed* with the meeting.

principal, principle

Principal is an adjective or noun meaning "chief" or "most important": The *principal* speaker at the meeting was an efficiency expert.

Principle is a noun meaning "fundamental truth" or "rule": The principal discussed the *principles* by which an honest man must live.

raise, rise

Raise is a verb meaning "to lift or cause to move up": We *raise* a flag before the start of the business day.

Rise is a verb meaning "to get up": He must *rise* from his seat when his supervisor calls him.

respectfully, respectively

Respectfully means "with esteem": He *respectfully* thanked the president for the promotion.

Respectively means "in regard to each of two or more, in the order named": He respectfully thanked the president and then shook hands with the manager and his assistant *respectively*.

Never end a letter with the incorrect complimentary close *Respectively yours*. Be sure that you use *Respectfully yours*.

than, then

Than is a conjunction used to introduce the second element in a comparison: He is taller *than* she is.

Then is an adverb meaning "at that time": He is taller than she was *then*.

there, their, they're

There is an adverb indicating location: He went *there* yesterday.

Their is a possessive pronoun: Do all the children have *their* books?

They're is a contraction for *they are*: *They're* going there with their friends tomorrow.

to, two, too

To is a preposition indicating direction: They will go *to* the director's meeting.

Two refers to a number: There are *two* directors at the meeting already.

Too is an adverb meaning "also" or "more than enough": They *too* think that the paperwork takes too long.

who's, whose

Who's is the contraction for *who is*: *Who's* coming to the company picnic?

Whose is a possessive adjective: *Whose* house shall we meet at?

Choosing Specific, Concrete Words and Expressions

The use of specific, concrete words will also help to get the message across successfully. A general word is one that is indefinite and does not appeal to the senses. A concrete word, on the other hand, appeals to the senses; it is a *precise* word that gives the reader an exact picture, often through the visual sense. Avoid using vague generalities; turn the general words into specific ones. Words such as *good, pretty, ugly,* or *nice* tell the reader nothing. A sales letter trying to get orders for "pretty dresses" wouldn't get much response. But how about "V-neck, puffed sleeved sheaths of loosely woven cotton in subtle sherbet tones"? Good adjectives can make your ideas come alive.

Now try your hand at choosing some good descriptive words. How many colors can you think of that begin with *b*? What features would cause you to call another person pretty or ugly?

Don't forget that verbs can also be concrete. Instead of saying, "Betty walked down the street," use a word that tells *exactly* how she moved. Did she stroll, prance, stagger, or hobble? Remember our previous discussion about connotation and also apply it to word choices. Allow a few well-chosen words to do the job; if you select a specific word, it can carry the force of several nonspecific ones.

Avoid trite, worn-out expressions. When they were originally used, they were fresh and descriptive, but they have lost their force through repetition and have become flat, dull, and undescriptive clichés. Look at the following examples and change them to fresh and concrete expressions:

smooth as silk
clear as crystal
pretty as a picture
slow as cold molasses
sly as a fox
smart as a whip
good as gold
ugly as sin
cute as a button
big as a mite
brown as a berry

Using Plain English

Jargon

Unless you are writing for a specific, knowledgeable audience, clear writing requires that you avoid technical jargon or "shop talk." Speak simply unless you know that your reader is familiar with your terminology. If your doctor tells you that you have catarrh caused by an ultramicroscopic or submicroscopic infective agent, he's using technical jargon to tell you that your stuffy nose is caused by a virus. Would you have understood his diagnosis? Probably not — and that's how a reader will react if you use the specialized vocabulary of your job or profession in a communication to an outsider.

Jargon can also be long, overstuffed words used when short, simple words will express your ideas better. Pompous (and poor) writers believe that the bigger and fancier their words, the more they'll impress their audience. They couldn't be more incorrect! Never use a long word when a short one will do the job. The only thing you'll succeed at is straining your reader's patience. Look at the following list of synonyms and note how well the short, simple words convey the same meaning as the longer, more complex ones. Can you think of additions to this list?

Short, simple	Long, pompous
face	countenance, visage
agree	acquiesce
will	volition
tail	appendage
try	endeavor
get	procure
show	demonstrate
rural	pastoral
fire	conflagration
think	cogitate
leafy	foliaceous

Slang

Slang is another type of specialized vocabulary that should be avoided by the competent business writer. According to *Webster's New World Dictionary of the American Language,*★ "slang is a "highly informal language that is outside of conventional or standard usage." Thus, slang is not only unprofessional but also may create misunderstanding between a communicator and audience. Therefore, use standard American English at all times and beware of using words and terms such as:

blow one's mind (impress)
gross (disgusting)
unreal (pleasant, enjoyable)
out to lunch (confused, unaware)
right on (informed)
okay (fine)
sharp (attractively dressed)
pot (marijuana)
bread (money)
blue (depressed)
booze (liquor)
super (very good)
dish (pretty woman)
grind (drudgery)
knock (find fault with)
milk (exploit)
to queer (to spoil)
guys (men)
gals (women)

★*Webster's New World Dictionary of the American Language* (Cleveland, OH: William Collins Publishers, Inc., 1979).

Being Concise

Avoid using more words than necessary to convey your ideas, or you may strain your reader's interest to the breaking point. Replace a long-winded phrase with one or two well-chosen words that carry the meaning. Don't be roundabout; be direct and concise and make it easy for your reader to receive and digest your message.

Instead of	*Use*
in the same place	there
at that time	then
sometime in the near future	soon
in the neighborhood of	near
in relation to	about
make a decision about	decide
call a meeting	meet
with the result that	so
call your attention to	show you
in the amount of	for
under separate cover	separately

Caution: Never sacrifice meaning or completeness by being overbrief. Do not leave out necessary information or vivid details, but do leave out every word that can be spared without reducing the effectiveness of your message.

Learn, too, to avoid redundancies — word pairs that do the work of one word and, thus, should be reduced to one word. Some examples are *exactly identical, finish up, cancel out, honestly truthful, close proximity, fully completed,* and *return back.* Revise your writing if necessary to eliminate this type of deadwood.

Writing Proper Sentences

In good writing, appropriate word choices must be combined to write clear, forceful sentences. The sentence is the conventional unit of connected speech or writing and is the basic unit of all written business communications. Essential parts of the sentence are the *subject* and the *predicate.*

Subjects and Predicates

The subject is the noun, noun phrase, or noun substitute that does something, has something done to it, or is identified or described.

    a. The *boy* runs. (*boy* is the subject of *runs.*)
    b. The *typewriter* was broken. (*typewriter* is the subject of *was broken.*)
    c. *Jane* is Mrs. Robb's secretary. (*Jane* is the subject of *is.*)

The predicate is the verb or verb phrase that comprises what is said about the subject; i.e., the predicate expresses action, occurrence, or existence.

In a. *runs* is the predicate.
In b. *was broken* is the predicate.
In c. *is* is the predicate.

A complete sentence must have both a subject and a predicate. Sometimes the subject is understood rather than stated: "Go to the file cabinet." In this command, *you* is the understood subject, for the full meaning of the sentence is, "You go to the file cabinet."

Phrases and Clauses

Phrases and clauses are building blocks of sentences. A phrase is a group of related words that does *not* have both a subject and a predicate. Thus, a phrase can never be a complete sentence; it functions as a part of speech — a noun, adjective, verb, or adverb.

a. *Writing business letters* is my main task. (*Writing business letters* is a phrase used as the subject of the verb *is*; this phrase is used as a noun.)

b. The manager *of our office* is out today. (*Of our office* is a phrase used as an adjective modifying *manager*.)

c. She *has been typing* for three hours. (*Has been typing* is a verb phrase; it is a group of words used as a verb.)

d. He wrote *with great speed*. (*With great speed* is a phrase used as an adverb modifying the verb *wrote*.)

A clause is a group of related words that has both a subject and a verb (predicate). There are two types of clauses — *independent*, or main, and *dependent*.

Independent clauses.   An independent clause can stand alone because it is a grammatically independent unit. It also may be joined with other clauses to form a compound or complex sentence.

Both of the following sentences are independent clauses; the subject and predicate of each are italicized. Can you identify them?

Bob called.
The tall, slender *girl* in the blue dress *called* our president last week.

Dependent clauses.   Dependent clauses are marked by introductory words that make them dependent on main clauses to complete their meaning. These dependent clauses act as nouns, adjectives, or adverbs and are, therefore, only part of a complete sentence. They are introduced by either:

1. Subordinate conjunctions — such words as *after, although, since, because, if, when, while,* and *that*

or

2. Relative pronouns — such words as *who, whose, whom, which,* and *that*

That his work was good was well known in the office. (*That his work was good* is a dependent clause that functions as a noun, i.e., as the subject of the verb *was.*)

My supervisor, *who is very temperamental,* does not work well with others. (*Who is very temperamental* is a dependent clause that functions as an adjective modifying *supervisor.*)

He will arrive *before the meeting begins.* (*Before the meeting begins* is a dependent clause that functions as an adverb modifying the verb *will arrive.*)

Classifying Sentences

The four major classifications of sentences are:

1. *Simple* — one independent clause.

   The secretary typed a letter.

2. *Compound* — two or more independent clauses.

   The secretary typed a letter, but he made too many errors.

   The secretary typed a letter; he made too many errors.

3. *Complex* — one or more independent clauses combined with one or more dependent clauses.

   After the secretary finished typing the letter, he realized that he had made too many errors.

   The secretary, who is a poor typist, made too many errors.

4. *Compound-complex* — two or more independent clauses combined with one or more dependent clauses.

   The secretary must correct the errors, and he must retype the letter before he leaves for lunch.

   After he returns from lunch, the secretary must finish the bills; he must also start typing the memo on his desk.

Sentence Errors

Sentence errors occur when we do not handle one of the four classifications correctly.

Error: The *sentence fragment* (SF) occurs when we use a phrase or a dependent clause as a complete sentence:

> With her head held high . . .
> Running down the street . . .
> After I complete my work . . .

If you have a sentence fragment, either include it in a preceding or following sentence or rewrite it to make it a complete sentence. Be sure that it is transformed into at least one independent clause.

> She smiled with her head held high.
> I was running down the street.
> After I complete my work, I'll leave.

Error: The *comma splice* (CS) occurs if we use a comma when a comma plus a coordinating conjunction or stronger punctuation, the semicolon, is needed. Note the following patterns for compound sentences:

1. _____i_____ , __c__ _____i_____ .
    i = independent clause
    c = coordinating conjunction (and, or, but, for, nor, yet)

The following sentence is punctuated correctly:

I like to type, and I like to write letters.

When two independent clauses are joined by a coordinating conjunction, a comma precedes the conjunction.

2. _____i_____ ; __b__ , _____i_____ .
    i = independent clause
    b = conjunctive adverb (words such as *however, therefore, thus, whereas*) or transitional phrase (phrases such as *in the meantime, for example, on the other hand*)

The following sentences are punctuated correctly:

I like to type; however, I do not like to take dictation.
I like to type; on the other hand, I do not like to take dictation.

When a conjunctive adverb or a transitional phrase comes between two independent clauses, it must be preceded by a semicolon, indicating a longer pause than that required by a comma. (These elements are usually followed by a comma.) When the semicolon is incorrectly replaced by a comma, we have a comma splice (CS).

Note: Both conjunctive adverbs and transitional phrases function as adverbs used to connect or relate independent clauses. They do not have a fixed place in the sentence as do coordinating conjunctions. If a word or phrase can be moved around within its clause without distorting meaning, use the semi-colon. For example:

> He will attend; however, he will stay only an hour.
> He will attend; he will, however, stay only an hour.

Error: *Run on* (RO) or *fused sentence* (FS). This error occurs when no punctuation is used between two independent clauses that require separation by the semicolon. Thus, the RO or FS occurs at the same place as the CS.

> (RO)
> I like to type however I do not like to take dictation.

To correct this sentence, place a semicolon between *type* and *however.*

> I like to type; however, I do not like to take dictation.

Arranging Sentences

Effective sentences must also be coherent; their parts must be arranged so that they make sense to your reader and convey the *exact* message you intend. Meaning in English is very dependent upon word placement. Avoid needlessly separating related parts of a sentence; if you distort meaning, you may be held liable for what is said, even though it is not what you intended to convey! Rewrite any sentence that does not clearly say what you want it to.

Avoid misplaced modifiers (danglers). A phrase or dependent clause, especially one beginning with a relative pronoun, should be placed so that it is clear what it modifies. If a modifier is placed so that it does not clearly refer to the specific word or word group intended, an incorrect or ridiculous message may result.

> The boy saw a car walking down the street. (Can a car walk down a street?)
>
> Walking down the street, the boy saw a car. (Isn't this clearer — and more sensible?)

When a verbal phrase or elliptical clause (one with an implied subject and verb) comes at the beginning of a sentence, it should immediately precede and clearly refer to the subject of the sentence.

> Typing rapidly, the chair was uncomfortable. (Can a chair type?)
>
> Typing rapidly, I found the chair uncomfortable. (Doesn't this make more sense?)
>
> When a baby, my father often rocked me. (When your father was a baby, he rocked you?)
>
> When a baby, I was rocked by my father. (Better.)

Adverbs such as *almost, only,* and *just* are usually placed immediately before the words they modify. Note how word placement affects meaning in these sentences:

I almost won $1,000 in the lottery.
I won almost $1,000 in the lottery.

Finally, avoid the squinter — a word placed between two words, either of which it might modify. Place it before the first word or after the second word to clarify meaning.

The assistant who was writing slowly arose. (Was he writing slowly or rising slowly?)

Change this to:

The assistant who was slowly writing arose.

or

The assistant who was writing arose slowly.

Sentences may also be incoherent if the parts do not agree clearly and logically. The most common troublemakers are verbs and their subjects, also pronouns and their antecedents.

Pronouns, Subject-Verb Agreement

	Singular	*Plural*
1st person	I	We
2nd person	You	You
3rd person	He, She, It	They

A verb must always agree with its subject in number (singular or plural) and person (first person — I, we; second person — you; third person — he, she, it, they). We rarely have problems when the verb immediately follows its subject.

The *typist* (third person singular) *sees* her error.
The *typists* (third person plural) *see* their errors.

A problem can arise when there are words between a subject and its verb so that we lose sight of the word with which the verb must agree. These intervening words often form dependent clauses or prepositional phrases that must not influence the verb form chosen.

The *captain* of the cheerleaders *is* clapping.

not:

The *captain* of the cheerleaders *are* clapping.

Captain, the subject, is a third-person singular noun; therefore, *is,* the third-person singular form of the verb *to be,* agrees with this subject.

Also correct is:

The *cheerleaders* of the school *are* clapping.

Cheerleaders, the subject, is a third-person plural noun; therefore, *are,* the third-person plural form of the verb *to be,* agrees with this subject.

Interrupting word groups introduced by expressions such as *in addition to, together with, as well as,* and *and not* do not influence the form of the verb.

The *president,* together with the board members, *oversees* all plant operations.

President, the subject, is a third-person singular noun; therefore, *oversees,* the third-person singular form of the verb, agrees with this subject.

The *secretaries,* as well as the file clerk, *perform* many tasks.

Secretaries, the subject, is a third-person plural noun; therefore, *perform,* the third-person plural form of the verb, agrees with this subject.

Note: An exception is made here if both words denote one person or unit:

The president and chairman of the board (this is one person with two titles) is coming to the meeting on Thursday.

The following words are singular and, therefore, if used as a subject are followed by singular verbs: *either, each, everybody, anybody, anyone, one, nobody, every, a person.* When these words are antecedents of pronouns (the word to which a pronoun refers), the pronouns must also be singular.

One of the salesmen *is* calling.
Everybody is taking a two-week vacation.
Does anyone want *his* lunch hour early today?
Each executive *has her* own office.

Choose all pronouns with care so that they agree with the word to which they refer (their antecedent). Pronouns must agree with their antecedents in both number (singular or plural) and gender (male, female, or neuter).

The *lady* (antecedent) in the blue gloves has *her* (feminine singular) ticket.

The *stenographer* will arrive early and *he* (or *he or she*) will prepare for the meeting.

Every man has *his* favorite sport.

All *presidents* believe that *they* have excessive responsibility.

One can relax during *his* (or *his or her*) spare time.

We can use *our* coats this morning.

Alternatives to Sexist Language

Sexist writing uses language that stereotypes functions or characteristics on the basis of sex. Contemporary business writers avoid terms that suggest discrimination in role or inequality between male and female.

Some suggestions for eliminating sexism in business communication are:

1. Avoid using *man* or *woman* or other word endings that imply one particular sex in words that denote certain occupations or levels not pursued exclusively by either male or female.

Nonsexist	*Sexist*
chairperson	chairman
charperson	charwoman
innkeeper	host, hostess
businessperson	businessman
householder	housewife
flight attendant	steward, stewardess

2. Use the phrase *he or she* when referring to a singular noun that may denote a member of either sex.

   A company president is responsible to his or her stockholders.

3. Change the subject of a sentence from singular to plural to eliminate a third-person singular pronoun that is gender-oriented.

   Company presidents are responsible to their stockholders.

4. Reword to eliminate a sexist pronoun. Change:

   A company treasurer wants his balance sheet to be accurate.

   to:

   A company treasurer wants an accurate balance sheet.

Writing Effective Sentences

Arrange sentences to emphasize important ideas. Put the important words at the beginning or the end; the middle of a sentence should contain less emphatic material.

The vice president called to discuss my promotion in his office. (weak)

The vice president called me to his office to discuss my promotion. (more emphatic)

Arrange your ideas in a climactic order with the strongest ones last.

Yesterday I had an accident on the way to work after I overslept and forgot my lunch. (unemphatic order)

Yesterday I overslept, forgot my lunch, and had an accident on the way to work. (climactic order, more emphatic)

Use parallel structure to emphasize a listing of parallel points.

> All employees are instructed to sign in, go to their desks, and then the new daily figures should be delivered by them. (nonparallel, lacks emphasis)

> All employees are instructed to sign in, to go to their desks, and then to deliver their daily figures. (parallel structure, more emphatic)

Use periodic sentences rather than loose ones for special stress. A loose sentence is one that makes a statement and then adds the details; the important ideas come first. The majority of sentences should be loose. A periodic sentence holds the reader in suspense by keeping the major details for the end. Periodic sentences should be reserved for situations that merit special emphasis.

> I resigned from my job because I was tired. (loose)
> Because I was tired, I resigned from my job. (periodic)

In business writing, sentences should be kept relatively brief without excessive detail and subordination. However, this does not require a series of simple, choppy sentences reminiscent of a first-grade reader. Do not always begin with the subject; instead, sometimes begin with an adverb, adjective, or phrase.

> Ms. Steadman, our attorney, argued loudly with the judge.
> Loudly, Ms. Steadman, our attorney, argued with the judge.
> Arguing with the judge, Ms. Steadman, our attorney, spoke loudly.

Use compound sentences only when two or more statements deserve equal emphasis.

> I like to type; I also like to file.

Often relationships can be shown more clearly through subordination, using complex sentences to demonstrate dependency of the elements.

> After the Board of Directors meets, several officers will be asked to resign.

Short sentences can also be effective if used sparingly to produce an emphatic effect.

> Do this immediately!

Variety in both length and structure will add spice to your communications.

Writing Appropriate Paragraphs

A paragraph is a unit of thought concerned with developing a single idea. The average paragraph in an essay is six to ten sentences in length. Paragraphs in business letters, memos, and reports are generally shorter. Often business paragraphs are one, two, or three sentences long. Surrounding them with white space makes the writing seem less formidable and increases the probability that the material will be read. Put each point in a separate paragraph, and your reader will get the entire message more easily.

Organization and planning are important in a business letter. First, jot down what must be included for completeness. Next, outline the ideas in the order of presentation. Finally, plan your letter to include the following parts:

1. *Introduction* — This will generally be a brief first paragraph, usually one or two sentences. Here you will indicate the purpose of your letter. Always use complete sentences, never outdated participial phrases such as "Referring to your letter of May 18 . . ."
2. *Body* — This may be one or several paragraphs. Here you will develop all the specific details and information necessary for the purpose of the letter.
3. *Conclusion* — Again, this is usually one brief paragraph consisting of one or two sentences. You may state or restate the action you wish taken, or you may conclude with a statement of appreciation. (But never thank in advance for a request that has not yet been granted!) End with a complete sentence, never an outdated participial such as "Hoping to hear from you, we remain . . ."

Notice how the following letter is organized.

```
Dear Mrs. Smith:
```

(Introduction)

```
Welcome as a new Lifetime Associate of the Wonder World
Health Spa.
```

(Body)

```
Your membership entitles you to use our facilities from
9:00 a.m. to 9:00 p.m., Monday through Friday and 9:00
a.m. to 3:00 p.m. on Saturdays. We are closed on Sundays
and holidays.

    Take advantage of our sauna and swimming pool as well
as our hourly classes and top-rated equipment. Instructors
are always available to answer questions or help with
individual diet and exercise requirements.
```

(Conclusion)

```
We look forward to seeing you often at the Wonder World
Health Spa.
```

Using the following Checklists, review this chapter, which has demonstrated how words, sentences, and paragraphs can help to get your message across. Then apply what you have learned by doing the exercises on the following pages.

CHECKLISTS

Good Word Usage

- Use the correct word.
- Spell correctly.
- Choose specific, concrete words and expressions.
- Use short, clear, simple words.
- Avoid slang.
- Be direct and concise.

Writing Proper Sentences

- Write complete sentences.
- Punctuate correctly.
- Provide for coherence through proper word placement.
- Check subject/verb and pronoun/antecedent agreement.
- Avoid sexist language.
- Emphasize important ideas through word arrangement.
- Vary sentence length and structure.

EXERCISES

1. Choose the correct word, correctly spelled, in the following sentences, using your dictionary or the list in the text unless you are positive of your choice. (Some of these words were not previously discussed.)
   a. Will he (accent, assent) to the agreement?
   b. (Who's, Whose) coming to the party tomorrow?
   c. They will (recieve, receive) (their, there) awards tomorrow.
   d. The (affect, effect) of the pollution will (affect, effect) our water supply.
   e. The city (council, counsel) will listen to the lawyer's (council, counsel).
   f. He had (alot, a lot) of time to spare.
   g. Will you eat (dessert, desert) after dinner?
   h. (Its, It's) (too, to, two) bad that the dog hurt (its, it's) paw.
   i. They (excepted, accepted) a/an (number, amount) of awards for (their, they're, there) bravery.
   j. He (complemented, complimented) her (disinterested, uninterested) help in solving the conflict.
   k. When (writing, writting) to an older person, you could sign the letter "(Respectively, Respectfully) yours."
   l. They made a (conscious, conscience) effort to obey the (principals, principles) of their religion.
   m. Because of the general's (advice, advise), the colonel (adviced, advised) his men to stop fighting.
   n. Will they be (all ready, already) for the spelling quiz (among, between) the three finalists?

o. The (eminent, imminent) scientist assured his fellow workers that a new discovery was (eminent, imminent).

p. Tell them to (precede, proceed) with the work even though one of the windows is (lose, loose).

q. If you come (than, then), I will have more time (than, then) I had planned on.

r. Many Russians want to (emigrate, immigrate) from the Soviet Union and (emigrate, immigrate) to the United States.

s. They want to (elicit, illicit) some information because they are (incredible, incredulous) about his story.

t. It is (likely, liable) that the driver is (likely, liable) for the damage he caused.

2. Rewrite the following sentences so that they are clear, concise, and brief.

a. I am writing with regards to your epistle which was concerned with the fact that you were about to make an announcement in the early part of the forthcoming month.

b. The incendiary blaze within the last few days has made us reach the conclusion that we must mete out retribution to the recidivists who have not ceased and desisted pursuant to their agreement with this organization.

c. Sometime in the near future we should come to a decision in relation to how we should be advised of the information that they have in their files.

d. I am happy to inform you that at this time we are sending you our newest current catalogue under separate cover.

e. Pursuant to your request in the normal course of events, we shall be totally able to conduct an interview with you in the course of the next few days subsequent to our meeting which takes place once a year.

f. I wish to acknowledge receipt of your request for a meeting at my earliest convenience. I regret to inform you that at the present writing I will be unable to meet and visit with you until in the neighborhood of about the date of the middle of next month.

g. It is my personal opinion that it is the responsibility of the department that deals with human resource development to take action upon the matter of the indigent recipients of our largesse.

h. The process of application for systems of employment for upwardly mobile employees of this very organization is absolutely complete at this point.

i. He is acquiescent with my tentative suggestion that he should be able to entirely finish the job as completely as possible by the hour of two o'clock in the normal course of events.

j. I wish to take this opportunity to give thanks to you for reducing all the extraneous verbiage in the report which was brought to my attention after it was perused by higher echelon company officials.

k. That pothead will need some bread or he'll be off the walls.

3. Improve the following sentences by eliminating clichés and making vague words and expressions more concrete and specific.

a. He is a good choice for the position.

b. His office is as pretty as a picture.

c. The report is as dull as dishwater.

d. The vase is ugly.

e. Is your supervisor nice?

f. Our product is selling like hotcakes.

g. You will find our new stove inexpensive.

h. That new salesman is as sly as a fox.

i. His speech was unenjoyable.

j. The new employee is as slow as cold molasses in January.

4. Identify the errors (SF, RO, CS, dangler, squinter, misplaced modifier) in the following sentences. Rewrite or correct the sentence as necessary. Two sentences are correct as written.

a. After running, the couch is a comfortable resting place.

b. You may take a one-week vacation however you cannot leave during August.

c. After I am through typing.

d. Will you be here tomorrow?

e. I cannot come tomorrow, on the other hand, I am available on Wednesday.

f. The boy walked quickly putting his hands in his pockets.

g. The car was driven by a driver with a broken windshield.

h. However I can come.

i. Sailing down the narrow river.

j. She is ready therefore let's leave.

k. She typed four hours, and thus she finished all the letters.

l. And I will be available later.

m. The typist at the typewriter in the blue dress is available now.

n. Are you available, can you come right now?

o. Almost I can finish the book.

5. Rearrange the words in the following sentences to make important ideas more emphatic.

a. I will make the presentation as soon as I am prepared.

b. Today I have to read all the proposals and choose one after deciding which I like best.

c. Before you begin, get your equipment together, think through the problem, and make sure you have chosen a comfortable chair.

d. I will dismiss that employee after I have informed him of his rights.

e. The document was signed willingly by the president and then unwillingly by the vice president.

f. Your suggestion will increase efficiency I am sure.

g. Please bring the ledger to me, show me the current totals, and then you should correct the errors.

h. Either call your friend or you should be writing him a letter.

i. They voted for the union president after much discussion, I guess.

j. You should analyze the problem, a decision should be made by you, and then the appropriate officers should be notified.

6. Choose the correct words in the following sentences.

a. John and his friends (has, have) (his, their) books.

b. (Do, Does) everybody know (his or her, their) part?

c. All officers of the company (knows, know) the regulations.

d. The file clerks, as well as Mary White, (is, are) in the front office.

e. Each of the students (has, have) (his or her, their) class schedules.

  f. The president and his assistant (is, are) in Cleveland this week.

  g. Your aunt called to say that (her, their) train will be late.

  h. Mary, together with Bob, (is, are) taking (her, his, their) lunch hour now.

  i. One of your friends (is, are) waiting outside the office.

  j. Bill, and not the others, (thinks, think) the report is too long.

  k. Many typists have cushions on (his or her, their) chairs.

  l. Each person may call (his or her, their) home.

  m. Every female dancer has (her, their) costume.

  n. Do writers type (his or her, their) manuscripts?

7. The following letters need paragraph division. Indicate with the symbol ⁋ where you would begin each new paragraph.

  a. Gentlemen:

    I am hoping to vacation at your new resort, Seadown, on Seaview Island, the first week in July and would like some information about rates and transportation. My wife and I would like a room with a double bed, near an elevator, and with an ocean view. We also plan to eat brunch and dinner daily at Seadown and hope to use the golf course daily. Please tell me what these accommodations would cost and if use of the golf course is included. We plan to fly from Boston via Universal Airlines arriving at the Seaview Airport at 3:05 p.m., E.D.T. Do you provide transportation from the airport; if not, are taxis available? Please send us any brochures that might be helpful. I look forward to hearing from you soon so that I may book my reservation by May 1.

  b. Dear Ms. Robbins:

    We are sending today by United Parcel Post the Super Hostess carafe for your Ominex electric coffee pot. It should arrive within a week. The Super Hostess carafe goes elegantly from kitchen to company table. Note the beautiful tracery design in fourteen-karat gold as well as the subtle shadings of brown and blue. Your entertaining will be enhanced by this lovely accessory. Enclosed is the newest catalogue of Ominex electric appliances. Just fill out the order blank, and your selections will immediately be sent postpaid. We appreciate your interest and look forward to adding to your Ominex collection soon.

  c. Gentlemen:

    I am very dissatisfied with the couch that I purchased from you on May 19. One of the legs wobbles badly, and the left seat cushion is larger than the right one. As I am planning a large party next month, I would like a new couch as soon as possible. Please let me know when you can deliver a replacement.

3

Form and Parts of the Letter

Making a Pleasing Presentation

When we wish to say that something is correct in every aspect, we often use the phrase *letter perfect*. Keep this compound adjective in mind when you write messages that you expect to be seen by others. Your presentation may be the only indication of your ability to the recipients. Therefore, the letter, memorandum, or report must represent you as positively as possible.

For comparison, think about the care that you would take with your appearance before meeting someone you want to impress, perhaps a prospective employer. Your personal hygiene would be faultless and your clothing clean, pressed, and appropriate for the occasion. If you were outwardly less than pleasing, you might not create interest or approval. Remember to be as careful with the appearance of letters, memos, and reports as you would be with your person, or you may lose the attention of or even credibility for a reader. He or she may think, "If this person couldn't even take the time to write something that looks professional, why should I take the time to read it?"

Create a good first impression by observing the following rules:

1. Use appropriate stationery and envelopes.
2. Provide a balanced, symmetrical arrangement.
3. Follow a consistent format.
4. Include all necessary parts.
5. Check for flawless mechanics.

Using Appropriate Stationery

Paper

When appropriate paper stock is used, the first overall glance makes a good impression. Generally, business stationery is 8½ by 11 inches, a size that fits most office files. Although brightly tinted paper may be used for special situations such as sales messages, white or conservatively colored sheets typed with black ribbon are traditional and still most popular. For letters, wise businesspeople select a good-quality, rag-content bond paper with matching envelopes. Number 10 (9½-by-4⅛-inch) envelopes are most commonly used because of the ease of folding and placing the 8½-by-11 sheet in them. Nevertheless, sometimes the smaller #6¾ (6½-by-3⅝-inch) envelope is preferred. Memos with preprinted guide words may use full-sized sheets or half sheets (8½-by-5½ inches).

An attractive letterhead, usually created by specialists, is at the top of most business and professional stationery. Although graphic design is not within the scope of this book, note the basic facts that should be presented. A letterhead should answer the questions:

1. Who? (the name of the organization)
2. Where? (the address)
3. What? (the nature of the business)

Additional facts such as telephone numbers and cable code names, as well as date of establishment, may be included. If letterhead stationery is used, the date must be added; if not, a complete return address must head the letter.

Folding and Placing in Envelopes

Carefully fold and place letters in their envelopes so that they will open into a readable position. (See Figures 3–1 and 3–2.)

If using the larger-sized (#10) envelope, do the following:

1. Place the letter so that the writing faces you, with the letterhead at the top.
2. Neatly bring the bottom edge up to ⅓ of the distance from the top of the sheet. Be sure that it is even across and make one sharp crease.
3. Bring the top edge down to about ¼ inch above the first crease and make another sharp crease.
4. Hold the envelope in your left hand with the back facing you and the flap pointed toward your right hand.
5. Insert the edge of the second crease, open edge at the right, in the envelope. (The first crease is nearest the flap.)

When using the smaller-sized (#6¾) envelope proceed as follows:

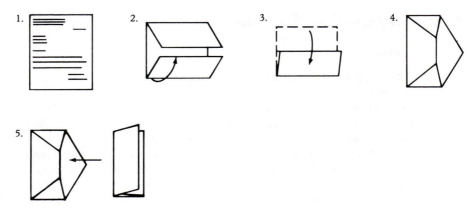

FIGURE 3–1   Folding and Placing the Letter in a #10 Envelope

1. Place the letter so that the writing faces you in an upright position.
2. Neatly bring the bottom edge to within ¼ inch of the top edge and make one sharp crease.
3. Fold from right to left to within ⅓ of the distance from the left edge. Make one sharp crease.
4. Fold from left to right to within ¼ inch from the second crease and sharply crease again.
5. Hold the envelope in the left hand with the back facing you and the flap pointing toward your right hand.
6. Insert the edge of the third crease, open edge at the right, in the envelope. (The second crease is nearest the flap.)

Providing a Balanced, Symmetrical Arrangement

Appropriate layout makes a letter or memo stand out on the page. Be sure to provide for centering and adequate side margins. Notice the placement of the sample letters in this chapter. Arrangement should be guided by length, that is, the number of words. Study the following chart and use it as a standard for placement.

Words in Letter	Line Length	Margins (left and right)	Lines Between Date* and Inside Address
0–99	4 inch	2¼ inch	8
100–199	5 inch	1¾ inch	6
200–300	6 inch	1¼ inch	4

*Begin date on line 15

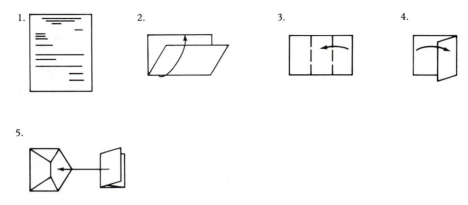

FIGURE 3–2   Folding and Placing the Letter in a #6¾ Envelope

Other than the distance between the date and inside address, double spacing is used between the units (such as salutation, body, paragraphs, and complimentary close) and single spacing within the units (inside address and paragraphs).

Envelopes

On envelopes, the United States Postal Service (USPS) optical scanning machines (OCR) require that certain procedures be followed. Both the complete return and outside addresses including zip codes should be single spaced in block style. The USPS also suggests using all capitals and no punctuation on the envelope. However, it is still acceptable to use lowercase letters and traditional punctuation.

The return address, unless preprinted, should be typed in the upper left-hand corner, leaving a one-inch margin at the side. The outside address must agree with the inside address of the letter. On #10 envelopes, first put a light pencil dot in the center. Place the envelope in the typewriter, backspace one-half inch, and begin the address. On the #6¾ envelopes, both backspace one-half inch and start one-half inch above the center dot. The entire outside address, if it is to be read by optical character recognition, must observe the following boundaries. It must be at least one inch from the left and right margins, ⅝ inch from the bottom edge, and must begin no more than three inches from the bottom edge. The rectangle enclosed by these restrictions defines the OCR read area. Nothing other than the appropriate parts of the address may appear within this area. There must also be no printing in the Bar Code read area, which is a 4½-by-5⅛-inch area at the right bottom of the envelope (see Figure 3–3).

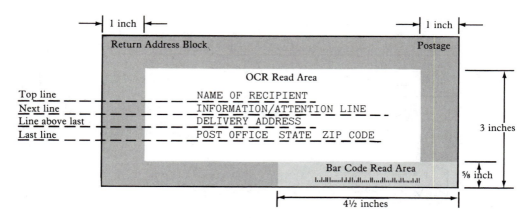

FIGURE 3–3   Information to Be Placed on Envelopes

The required address format is:

1. Top line — name of recipient.
2. Next line — information/attention line.
3. Line above last — delivery address.
4. Last line — post office, state, zip code.

Unit, apartment, mail receptacle, and office or suite numbers belong at the end of the delivery address line (line above the last) or, if there is insufficient room, on the line above. The only abbreviations acceptable are the new two-letter state ones (see the appendix). The first digit of the zip code should be separated from the state name by between two and five spaces. Special delivery instructions (e.g., Registered, Certified, Air Mail, or Special Delivery) should be placed in the upper right corner below the postage. Other notations such as *Personal, Confidential,* or *Hold for Delivery* should be placed at the upper left, two spaces below the return address. These may be in all capitals or with the first letter capitalized and the word underscored.

See samples of completed #6¾ and #10 envelopes in Figure 3–4.

Letter Format

During the past century, the punctuation of the address sections of a modern business letter has become simplified. Closed punctuation, in which the ends of all lines in the return and inside addresses have either a comma or a period, is obsolete in the United States although still used in the British Isles. It has been replaced by *mixed punctuation,* which requires a colon after the salutation and a comma after the complimentary close, but nothing at line ends in the addresses. Another, more contemporary, choice is *open punctuation*; in this style all punctuation after the parts of the letter is omitted. To more conservative

```
#6¾ ┌─────────────────────────────────────────────┐
     │                                             │
     │      SENDER'S NAME                          │
     │      STREET ADDRESS                         │
     │      CITY, STATE  ZIP CODE                  │
     │                                             │
     │                                             │
     │              NAME OF RECIPIENT              │
     │              INFORMATION/ATT. LINE          │
     │              DELIVERY ADDRESS               │
     │              P.O.  STATE  ZIP CODE          │
     │                                             │
     │                                             │
     │                                             │
     │                                             │
     │                                             │
#10  └─────────────────────────────────────────────┘
   ┌───────────────────────────────────────────────────┐
   │                                                     │
   │    SENDER'S NAME                                    │
   │    ADDRESS                                          │
   │    CITY, STATE  ZIP CODE                            │
   │                                                     │
   │                                                     │
   │                                                     │
   │               NAME OF RECIPIENT                     │
   │               INFORMATION/ATTENTION LINE            │
   │               DELIVERY ADDRESS                      │
   │               POST OFFICE  STATE  ZIP CODE          │
   │                                                     │
   │                                                     │
   │                                                     │
   │                                                     │
   └───────────────────────────────────────────────────┘
```

FIGURE 3–4   Completed #6¾ and #10 Envelopes

writers, the lack of a colon after the salutation and the omission of the comma following the complimentary close look like errors. The choice depends upon an individual or office style; either is correct.

Four styles of letter format are currently used in the United States. They are: (1) full block, (2) block, (3) semiblock, and (4) simplified.

Full Block Style

The full block style is popular because it saves typing time. As all lines in this format are blocked or begin at the left margin, no counting or centering is required, and there are no changes of margin. Some writers object to the left-leaning, rather unbalanced, appearance of this style. Open punctuation is often used in full block style; mixed punctuation is also acceptable. Example 3–1 shows the full block style.

EXAMPLE 3–1 Full Block Style Letter with Open Punctuation

Lazy Days Store
352 Whitcomb Street
Dover, OH 00000

May 18, 198–

Mr. Robert Smith
Rotman's Inc.
140 Mesa Street
Pawtucket, RI 00000

Dear Mr. Smith

This is a model of a full block style letter with open
punctuation. Notice that all lines, including the date and
the complimentary close, begin at the left margin.

Open punctuation does not require a colon after the
salutation or a comma after the complimentary close.

This letter can be typed more quickly than the other block
styles. It has grown in popularity recently.

Sincerely

Samuel R. Black

Samuel R. Black
Personnel Manager

SRB:tk

Block Style

The block style contains three elements placed in different positions from their counterparts in full block style. These are:

1. The date (or date and return address if there is no letterhead), which is placed either centered under the letterhead or to end at the right margin.
2. The complimentary close.
3. The signature lines, which are placed at or slightly to the right of the center under the date.

Either mixed or open punctuation is appropriate with this style. To some correspondents, this style presents a more balanced appearance than the full block form. Example 3–2 shows the block style.

Semiblock Style

The semiblock style is a bit more traditional than the two styles previously discussed because it requires indentation of paragraphs, generally four to seven spaces. It is the same as the block form in all other respects. Mixed punctuation is usually used with this style. Example 3–3 is in semiblock style.

Simplified Letter Style

This style is recommended by the Administrative Management Society as an important step in improving business correspondence. It saves time and, therefore, cost. Like the full block form, every line begins at the left margin. In addition, the salutation and complimentary close have been omitted. A subject line in all capital letters is placed three spaces below the inside address and three spaces above the body of the letter. The writer's name is typed in all capitals three spaces below the body. Example 3–4 shows the simplified letter style.

Necessary Parts of the Letter

Return Address

The return address is the first element to appear on a letter, twelve or thirteen spaces below the top edge. This section is omitted if letterhead stationery is used. It gives the address of the writer and must be complete so that the reader can reply if he or she wishes. Placement may be at the upper left (full block) or the upper right (block and semiblock), establishing both the top and side margins. No abbreviations may be used except for the two-letter state code.

EXAMPLE 3–2   Block Style Letter with Mixed Punctuation

15 Waverley Street
Worcester, MA 00000
February 18, 198–

Red Rock Soda Company
82 Broad Street
Waverley, MA 00000

Gentlemen:

This is a model of a block style letter with mixed punctuation. There is a colon following the salutation and a comma
after the complimentary close.

Notice that the complete return address precedes the date because this is not letterhead stationery. A two–line address
is placed approximately thirteen lines from the top of the
paper.

This style appeals to many because of its neat and balanced
appearance.

Yours truly,

Roderick P. Hunter

Roderick P. Hunter
Correspondent

RPH:enh

EXAMPLE 3–3 Semiblock Style Letter with Mixed Punctuation

400 East Avenue
Plattsville, WV 00000
October 15, 198–

Research Writing Associates
200 Wisdom Way
San Christophe, CA 00000

Ladies and Gentlemen:

This letter is in semiblock style with mixed punctuation. Notice that each paragraph is indented a consistent number of spaces.

Some writers prefer this style because of the traditional indentation of paragraphs as in essays, books, and periodicals. They also usually prefer the long-established custom of punctuating after both the salutation and the complimentary close.

This style requires a little more typing time but is well worth the added effort to those who choose to use it.

Sincerely yours,

John B. Anthony
Professor of English

JBA/rwt

EXAMPLE 3–4 Simplified Style Letter

Batway Writers
Long Cove Road
Laguna, TX   00000

December 15, 198—

Mr. Robert Anthony
Time Saver Systems
123 Laurel Lane
Grover, CT   00000

THE SIMPLIFIED LETTER STYLE

This style is popular with correspondents who wish to save
both time and money. It eliminates two formalities, the
salutation and the complimentary close.

The subject line in all capitals is placed above the body,
and the writer's signature goes above the name, which is
typed in all capitals immediately below the body.

To some this approach seems too cold and impersonal. Do you
feel that it looks distant or unfriendly?

Alene C. Hutchinson

ALENE C. HUTCHINSON

Two or three single-spaced lines are customary.

```
164 Medway Street      (number and street,
Wills, NH  00000       no additional identification)
                       (city, state  zip)
```

or:

```
Suite J                (extra information)
359 Silk Way           (number and street)
Milo, WY  00000        (city, state  zip)
```

Note that a comma is placed between city and state but not between state and ZIP code.

Date Line

The date line records the date of the letter. If a typed return address is used, the date line will appear on the space immediately below it. If on letterhead paper, the date line will be placed two spaces below the last line of print, on the left or right depending upon the letter format used. Some writers center the date under the letterhead design.

Again, no abbreviations may be used, nor such additions as *st, nd, th, rd*. The customary order is: *month — day — comma — year* although the military and some government agencies often use a slightly different format: *day — month — year* with no commas. This style is gaining in popularity because time, and thus money, can be saved. The following are examples of the two different styles:

```
May 15, 198—
```

or:

```
14 October 198—
```

Inside Address

The inside address, which must be the same as that on the envelope, gives all necessary information about the recipient of the letter, ensuring correct delivery. It is placed below the date line a number of spaces dictated by the length of the letter (see the chart on page 34). Blocked, single spaced, and beginning at the left margin in all formats, it contains a minimum of three lines: (1) name, (2) number and street, and (3) city, state, and zip code.

More lines are added, usually after the first one, if the information is too extensive to be contained in three sections. If a recipient has no special title,

Mr., Miss, Mrs., and Ms. are used. If two people with different last names are addressed, put the names on two separate lines:

```
Mr. and Mrs. James Wilton
```

but:

```
Miss Sally Rome
Miss Grace Welby
```

Be sure to spell names correctly and to follow a company's usage or logo in addressing it. Do not use both a title and a degree if they are the same. Use either *Dr. Thomas Rogers* or *Thomas Rogers, M.D.* (note the comma before *M.D.*), but not *Dr. Thomas Rogers, M.D.* If a name is followed on the same line by a title, separate the two with a comma:

```
Mr. Sylvester Sims, Vice-President.
```

The comma is unnecessary if two lines are used:

```
Mr. Sylvester Sims
Vice-President
```

Study these examples:

```
Dr. Philip Somersby, Jr.
1234 Bridge Road
Norton, PA   00000

Dr. Philip Somersby, Jr.
Director of Research
1234 Bridge Road
Norton, PA   00000

Brandon Associates, Inc.
14 Merrywood Boulevard
Strongwood, MD   00000
```

Attention Line

Though not an essential element in a letter, the attention line is often used when the writer is uncertain about whom to contact within an organization. It also is useful when one wishes to contact a person who has handled a particular matter previously, especially when the writer is not sure that this is still the appropriate addressee. The attention line can also direct a letter to the correct department in a large company and thus save delivery time.

The attention line is placed two lines below the inside address and two lines above the salutation. It may be placed at the left margin or centered on the sheet. Either all capital letters or capitalization of first letters of each word may be used. The word *Attention* is followed by the name; usually no punctuation separates the two, although some writers use a colon.

1. ```
   The Rothberg Company
   15 Witton Avenue
   Media, OH  00000

   Attention Credit Manager
   ```

2. ```
   The Rothberg Company
   15 Witton Avenue
   Media, OH  00000

            ATTENTION CREDIT MANAGER
   ```

3. ```
   Sims Furniture Company
   109 Broadway
   Yarmouth, MO  00000

   Attention: Mr. Harold Casey
   ```

Salutation

The salutation or formal greeting begins at the left margin two spaces below the inside address or the attention line if it is used. It is followed by a colon in mixed punctuation; no punctuation follows if open punctuation is used. The first word and all titles and names are capitalized. *The salutation must always agree with the first line of the inside address.* Its form is not influenced by the inclusion of an attention line.

If a name is given on the first line of the inside address:

```
Miss Susan Lacey
15 Long Court
Mobile, AK  00000
```

the correct salutation will be as follows:

```
Dear Miss Lacey
```

If a title without a name appears on the first line:

```
Credit Manager
Bradley's
432 Wilde Corner
Bandie, MI  00000
```
```

the correct salutation is one of the following:

```
My dear Sir
Dear Sir or Madam
```

If a firm or company name appears on the first line:

```
Bradley's
432 Wilde Corner
Bandie, MI  00000
```

the correct salutation is either:

```
Gentlemen
```

or:

```
Gentlemen and Ladies
```

("Dear Sirs" is considered obsolete; do not use it.)
If there is an attention line:

```
Bradley's
432 Wilde Corner
Bandie, MI  00000

ATTENTION: MR. PAUL FARRELL
```

the correct salutation is:

```
Gentlemen
```

or:

```
Gentlemen and Ladies
```

Use *Gentlemen* or *Gentlemen and Ladies* when writing to a box number. *Gentlemen* is correct when writing to an all-male organization. *Ladies* is appropriate when writing to an all-female group. Usage of *Gentlemen* versus *Gentlemen and Ladies* has not crystalized. The feminist movement decries the use of *Gentlemen* when addressing a mixed group; however, it is still preferred by some who find *Gentlemen and Ladies* (or *Ladies and Gentlemen*) wordy and awkward.

Subject Line

The subject line, an optional element, can help get a letter off to a fast start by elimination of the need for an introductory sentence explaining what the letter is about. If used, it is placed two spaces below the salutation and two spaces above the body of the letter. It may be placed at the left margin or centered, may be in all capitals, or may have only the first letters of the words capitalized. The words *Subject* or *Re* are usually followed by a colon. The subject line should be brief and very specific.

1. Gentlemen:

   SUBJECT: OUR INVOICE #3215

2. Dear Ms. Gill

   Re: Homeowner's Policy #678432

Body

The body of the letter contains the message. The first paragraph begins two spaces below the salutation or subject line. In full block and block styles, the paragraphs begin flush with the left margin. The first line is indented four to seven spaces in semiblock style. Single space within paragraphs and double space between them. Never write a one-paragraph message. Review the discussion of paragraph organization and division into three identifiable parts in Chapter 2.

Complimentary Close

The complimentary close is the formal leave-taking or farewell at the end of a letter. It is placed two spaces below the last line of the final paragraph at the left margin in full block style and centered or under the date line in block and semiblock formats. The first word is capitalized. If a colon follows the salutation (mixed punctuation), a comma follows the complimentary close; otherwise both are without end punctuation (open punctuation).

Sincerely, Sincerely yours, Yours truly, and *Cordially* are some of the most common choices. *Respectfully yours* may be used when addressing someone much older or of high rank in government or in an organization.

Sincerely   (full block, open punctuation)

Respectfully yours,
(block or semiblock,
mixed punctuation)

Signature Section

The signature section consists of a pen-written signature, a typed name, and several optional additions. Placement depends upon letter style; this section is at the left margin in full block style and centered or aligned with the date in the other styles. First, the company name may be in all capitals two spaces under the complimentary close. This placement indicates that company policy is the dominant factor in the message and that the writer is following established procedure rather than being individually responsible for the contents. Four spaces are left below this for the writer's signature. If the company name is omitted here, four spaces are left below the close to accommodate the pen-written signature. When the signer takes more individual responsibility for the message, the company name may appear below the signature or signature and title.

All letters should be hand signed in ink after the signer has carefully read the contents for completeness and correctness.

The pen-written signature should be the correspondent's full given name as he or she customarily chooses to be known. Titles, such as Mrs., Mr., Dr., or Ms. are not used before the signature, nor does the signer add degrees or titles after the name.

The typed signature appears next. Below it may be typed a title and/or the company name (especially if this is not clearly indicated in the letterhead or return address) on one or more single-spaced separate lines. The typed signature adds the necessary information for appropriately addressing a letter to the sender. If the first name is one that might indicate either a male or female (Terry, Dale, Lee, Jay), *Mr., Miss, Mrs.,* or *Ms.* is helpful. Otherwise, *Mr.* is not proper. A woman may, if she wishes, indicate her marital status here. Current practice is to address as Ms. any woman who does not indicate her preference of *Mrs., Miss,* or *Ms.* If a woman wishes to be addressed by her husband's name preceded by *Mrs.,* she would type this form below the signature using her own first and last name. Titles such as *Dr.* or *Reverend* may precede the typed name. Degrees such as *M.D., D.D.S.,* or *Ph.D.* follow the name.

1. Sincerely yours,

   THE ROBERTS BOX COMPANY

   Robert J. Doe

   Robert J. Doe
   Personnel Manager

2. Cordially

   Terry Bradley

   Mr. Terry Bradley
   Vice-President
   Bradley Tool and Die Company

3. Sincerely

Mary Wilkins

Miss Mary Wilkins
Assistant Manager

4. Truly yours,

Rebecca Stone

Mrs. Samuel Stone
Credit Department

5. Sincerely,

Nancy Brownless

Nancy Brownless
(Nancy would be addressed as Ms. in this case.)

6. Respectfully

Richard S. Leff

Richard S. Leff, M.D.

Identifying Initials

The initials of the dictator and typist or just one set (either typist's only or one set indicating that one person performed both duties) follow the signature section. Placed two lines below the signature section at the left margin in all styles, they are especially helpful in a large office where the transcriber can be quickly located if a question or problem arises. Sometimes these are shown only on the file copy. If both sets of initials are used, the transcriber's initials customarily follow those of the dictator. Acceptable arrangements include:

    TDK:emh
    TDK/emh
    emh

Enclosure Notices

When additional items are included with a letter, an enclosure notice must appear at the left margin two spaces below the identifying initials. The word *Enclosure* or *Enc.* may be used if a single item is inserted; *Enclosures 2* or *Enc. 5* indicate that more than one item is present.

    Enclosure
    Enc.

```
Enclosures 5
Enc. 5
```

Some writers list the additional contents:

```
Enclosures: Monthly Report
            Dividend Statement
```

This notice serves as a check of completeness both before mailing and upon receipt. Note that only checks are placed on top of a letter; all other enclosures are arranged at the back in the order of mention or of importance.

Copy Distribution Notations

If used, a copy notation is at the left margin two spaces below the item preceding it (usually either the identifying initials or the enclosure notation). This notation indicates that one or more duplicates of the message are being distributed. If *cc* is used, the names of the additional recipients are given in alphabetical order. Sometimes carbon copies are sent to various persons without the knowledge of the addressee. This is indicated by typing *bcc* and any pertinent information on the copies only. Thus, copy recipients know that the recipient of the original message is unaware of the existence of duplicates in the possession of others.

```
cc: Order Department

cc: Mrs. Alice Ames
    Mr. John Carr

bcc: Mr. Robert Lima
```

Postscripts

Postscripts generally do not belong in business correspondence because they indicate disorganization. A letter properly planned should not need to add information in this fashion. However, there are occasions, especially in sales letters, when a postscript is intentionally included to emphasize or reemphasize an idea that might have been overlooked in the body of the letter. Use this element wisely, well, and rarely. It should be the last item to appear on a letter and is placed at the left margin. The initials *PS* may or may not appear.

```
PS: Remember, you must return the enclosed card by May 15
    in order to take advantage of these spectacular
    savings.

Send for your sample TODAY. Be sure of receiving this gift
while our limited supply lasts!
```

Continuation Page Headings

When a letter is extremely long, it is necessary to use two or more pages. These pages should be typed on plain, non-letterhead stationery of the same quality as the first sheet. The left and right margins are retained; the continuation page heading starts one inch from the top edge, two spaces above the first line of the continued letter. The heading should contain the name of the addressee, the page number, and the date in one of the following styles:

```
Miss Debra G. Kay
Page 2
October 8, 198—
```

or:

```
Miss Debra G. Kay            2          October 8, 198—
```

Never carry fewer than three lines over to a continuation page and leave at least two lines of a new paragraph at the bottom of a previous page. Be sure that there is a bottom margin of at least one inch. A paragraph carried to a following page must contain at least two lines on that page; also, do not hyphenate the last word at the foot of a page. Some of these restrictions may require retyping or realignment.

Checking for Flawless Mechanics

Now that your letter has been written and typed, it must be carefully checked before it is signed and mailed. *Remember*: If it is not letter perfect, redo it until you are completely satisfied. Using the following Checklist, critically examine your work. If you can answer yes to all the questions, your letter is ready to be mailed.

CHECKLIST

Pleasing Presentation

- Are all words spelled correctly?
- Are all word choices clear, exact, and concise?
- Are tact and a positive attitude present?
- Are sentences grammatically correct, complete, and coherent?
- Is punctuation correct?
- Is the information complete?
- Is appropriate stationery used?
- Are all necessary letter parts included?
- Are paragraphs short and informative?

- Is the format appropriate and consistent?
- Is the placement balanced and pleasing to the eye?
- Is copy clean and fresh looking with no holes, smudges, strikeovers, or poor erasures?
- Are the enclosures actually enclosed?
- Is the envelope properly set up and typed?
- Would you react favorably if you received this letter?

EXERCISES

1. Answer the following questions. If you have problems, reread Chapter 3.
   a. Why is the perfect appearance of a letter so important?
   b. What size and quality of stationery and envelopes should be used for a business letter?
   c. According to United States Post Office requirements, what belongs on each line of the outside address on an envelope?
   d. Where should special instructions be placed on an envelope?
   e. How does full block style differ from block style? From semiblock style?
   f. How do mixed and open punctuation differ?
   g. How does the simplified letter style differ from a more traditional format?
   h. What is the only element that may be abbreviated in addresses?
   i. What is the first typed part of a letter written on letterhead stationery?
   j. The salutation must always agree with what element?
   k. What is the correct placement of an attention line?
   l. What is the correct placement of a subject line?
   m. If the company name is typed after the complimentary close and before the pen-written signature, what message is conveyed to the reader?
   n. If the pen-written signature immediately follows the complimentary close, what message is conveyed?
   o. Must a woman indicate her marital status in the signature section?
   p. Where is the enclosure notice placed in a letter?
   q. What does *bcc* mean and how is it used?
   r. When are postscripts appropriate?
   s. Should continuation pages be typed on letterhead stationery?
   t. What questions should you ask yourself about a letter before you sign and mail it?

2. What would be the appropriate salutations in letters with the following inside addresses?

   a. Mr. John Jones
      Wyler Manufacturing Company
      Williston, NV 00000

   b. Credit Department
      Wyler Manufacturing Company
      Williston, NV 00000

      Attention Mr. John Jones

    c. Miss Catherine Simpson
       Miss Sally White
       148 Terrace Drive
       Minot, FL 00000

    d. Mary Drake
       Blake's Eatery
       14 Ware Street
       Tungsten, UT 00000

    e. Personnel Director
       Soames Department Store
       Wylie, OK 00000

3. **Make any necessary corrections to the following:**

    a. Dear Miss Wade;

         . . .

       Sincerely yours

    b. Respectively yours,

    c. Dear Gentleman and Ladys:

    d. Dr. John J. Holmes, M.D.

    e. May 31st, 198–

    f. Sincerely Yours

    g. 115 Boone St.
       N.Y., N.Y., 00000

    h. Truly Yours,

       Mrs. Aester Rock

       Ruth M. Rock

    i. Butler Associates
       15 Hawthorne Drive
       Butler, HI 00000

       Subject: Monthly Report

    j. Dear Mrs. Rowe:

       Attention Mrs. Rita Rowe

    k. Enclosure

       ABH/der

4

Letters of Inquiry
and Replies

Letters asking for information and letters replying to these requests are often required in both business and personal correspondence. Writers have questions about many matters; the most common subjects are products, services, and prices. A clear and reasonable inquiry letter deserves a prompt answer, even when the request cannot be satisfied.

Letters of Inquiry

A good letter of inquiry is both brief and specific. Avoid boring the recipient with an unnecessarily long-winded message. If the questions are vague or incomplete, more correspondence may be required. Letters are costly in both time and money; prevent wastefulness by checking your inquiries for clarity and completeness. If your reader knows *exactly* what information is desired, he or she will be able to write a satisfactory reply.

Courtesy is also important. Some of your letters will be eagerly welcomed because reader benefit is evident, such as when you ask about an intended purchase. Other letters are obviously more self-seeking, such as those asking for information for a student paper. Emphasize benefits to readers by using the "You" attitude whenever possible. It helps to justify your request when you appeal to the self-interest of the person or firm to whom you are writing. If you cannot appeal to financial gain, appeal to good will, which most progressive business and professional people recognize as a precious commodity. Make your letter courteous; ask, don't demand. On the other hand, do not use a timid, humble, self-effacing approach.

Invited Letters of Inquiry

The invited letter of inquiry is written in response to an invitation (usually advertised in one of the media) to send for information. The ad may appear in a newspaper or magazine, may be sent in the mail, or may be conveyed on radio or television. If in printed form, it may include a coupon or a stamped, addressed postcard, making reply easy. If there is no ease-of-reply provision, a brief, specific letter, mentioning exactly what is wanted and where you learned about it is usually all that is necessary. Be sure that here, as in all letters, you include your address if you write on non-letterhead stationery so that you will receive the material.

Note how short and complete Examples 4–1 and 4–2 are.

Uninvited Letters of Inquiry

The uninvited letter of inquiry is one written "cold turkey," that is, unsolicited. It is necessarily longer and more detailed than the invited response. Again, be sure to provide a return address. If you are writing to an individual or to a very small organization, especially when you are asking a favor, include a stamped, addressed envelope. Briefly mention this enclosure either in the last paragraph or in your enclosure notice. When you are writing to a larger group or when there is potential reader benefit, the stamped envelope is not as essential. In fact, most large firms prefer to use their own envelopes and mailing procedures.

The following format will help ensure the appropriate reply:

1. A brief first paragraph identifying the subject of your request and explaining why you want or need it. Answer "who?" "why?" and "when?" Remember the time factor is important. Stress reader benefit where possible.
2. A middle section in which separate specific questions or areas are itemized. Try to phrase the questions so that answers will require only a few words or a sentence. Indent and number each item and separate the questions by double spacing. Be sure that you are clear and precise.
3. A final paragraph in which you express anticipation or appreciation. Never thank in advance, however; for you will seem presumptuous, taking for granted that your request will be honored. Here you may also mention an enclosure such as an envelope or questionnaire. If you are asking for confidential information, assure the reader that you will be discreet.

Read Example 4–3, a letter from a student. It is an uninvited inquiry asking for a favor. Example 4–4 is an easier uninvited reply to write because a prospective sale is involved.

EXAMPLE 4–1   Invited Letter of Inquiry

15 Lilly Drive
Moulin, ME 00000
August 18, 198—

The Moulin Electric Company
800 Circuit Street
Moulin, ME 00000

Gentlemen:

Please send me the booklet <u>Saving</u> <u>Energy</u> <u>Through</u>
<u>Good</u> <u>Air</u> <u>Conditioning</u> <u>Maintenance</u> that you adver-
tised in today's <u>Moulin</u> <u>Times</u>.

Sincerely,

James Ring

James Ring

EXAMPLE 4–2   Invited Letter of Inquiry

```
                                   Apartment 2C
                                   592 Washington Drive
                                   Fairbanks, WY  00000
                                   May 27, 198—



The Relamont Insurance Company
80 Mutual Place
Hartsville, UT 00000

Gentlemen and Ladies:

Please send me your pamphlet, Insuring Your Children's Col-
lege Education, which you advertised in America magazine on
May 25, 198—.

I am also interested in purchasing the type of tax—deferred
annuity available to staff members of teaching institutions,
hospitals, and home service agencies. I would appreciate your
sending me any pertinent pamphlets about your offerings in
this area.

                              Yours truly,

                              Lucy Rankin

                              Mrs. Lucy Rankin
```

EXAMPLE 4–3   Uninvited Letter of Inquiry

1420 Ticonderoga Avenue
DeWitt, SC 00000
February 26, 198–

Ms. Mirabel Mason
Langley, Simms and Hughes, Inc.
400 Hospital Trust Tower
DeWitt, SC 00000

Dear Ms. Mason

Would you, one of the city's outstanding stockbrokers, help me by answering the following questions? I am writing a paper on sexism and sexual equality in your profession for my Management 101 class at the Community College of DeWitt.

1. How many female stockbrokers work in your office?

2. How many male stockbrokers work there?

3. Are unsolicited inquiries from potential new customers referred to brokers (1) in turn, (2) by sex, (3) by seniority?

4. Are your clients (1) mainly women, (2) mainly men, (3) equally divided?

5. Is there a stated dress code for women? If so, briefly, what are the restrictions?

6. Is there a stated dress code for men? If so, briefly, what are the restrictions?

I should appreciate your confidential replies in the enclosed envelope. If you wish, I shall gladly send you a copy of my report, which is due on April 2.

Sincerely

Rita V. Molloy

Rita V. Molloy

Enc.

EXAMPLE 4–4   Uninvited Letter of Inquiry

13 Mountway Street
Newington, MA 00000
October 14, 198—

Olean Realty Company
14 Oceanview Drive
Merry Estates, FL 00000

Gentlemen:

I am planning to buy a condominium in Florida this winter and would like information about the complex you are building in Pointview Estates. Please send me your prospectus and answer the following questions.

1. When will your units be ready for occupancy?

2. What is the price range of a studio apartment?

3. What appliances are included?

4. Would my cat be welcome?

5. What is the anticipated monthly fee for a studio unit, and what does the fee include?

6. Does your company offer preferred mortgage rates to purchasers?

As I plan to be in Florida during the last two weeks of next month, I would appreciate hearing from you by November 1.

Sincerely,

Ben F. Setts

Ben F. Setts

Ease-of-Reply Inquiry Letters

One way to ensure a speedy reply to an inquiry is to use an ease-of-reply letter — a letter that provides space for reply and usually has an envelope in which it can be sent back to its source. These letters are efficient for both sender and recipient because:

1. The recipient does not have to spend time composing and writing an answer; he usually fills in blanks, checks boxes, or uses the bottom section of the letter.
2. The inquirer knows immediately what questions are being answered because he or she has the original letter along with the answers.

The growing popularity of this type of message is well deserved, although its usefulness is limited to brief replies. Examples 4–5 and 4–6 illustrate two possible formats for ease-of-reply letters.

Replies to Inquiries

Every logical and understandable inquiry deserves a prompt and gracious response. Courteous responses build good public relations whether or not the requested information can be given. If the answer reflects good will and a desire to be of service, friends are made or kept. On the other hand, a perfunctory or rude response is the written equivalent of a snub. A non-answer is even more offensive to one who is eagerly awaiting a reply.

Letters Satisfying the Request

Because these are "good news" or "yes" letters, they are relatively easy to write. But just because they are not difficult, don't answer them in a careless, routine manner. Make the effort to "walk the extra mile" by writing more than a form reply whenever possible. Make your letter reflect warmth and a willingness to go beyond the basics. Sell yourself or your organization. If you are including printed material that will answer the questions, don't just say in effect, "Go find the answers yourself"; tell where the specific facts can be located. Add information that you think might be of interest. Offer further assistance. If material is being sent separately, do more than just mention it. Tell how and approximately when it should arrive.

Answering invited letters.   Compare the replies to an invited letter of inquiry shown in Examples 4–7 and 4–8. Would you rather receive Example 4–7 or Example 4–8? Why?

EXAMPLE 4–5   Ease-of-Reply Letter of Inquiry

Office of the Registrar
Community College of Sayles
322 West View Avenue
Sayles, VT   00000

November 20, 198—

Mrs. Irene Miller
40 Wells Street
Sayles, VT 00000

Dear Mrs. Miller

Because you are currently a student at our Weekend
College, we would appreciate your opinions about
this program. Please help us to make Weekend College meet your requirements by answering the following questions.

Their return by December 15 in the enclosed
stamped, addressed envelope will be greatly appreciated.

Sincerely

Susan Dean

Susan Dean, Registrar

Enc. Questionnaire

EXAMPLE 4–5   *(continued)*

1. In the last five years have you taken any courses at the college during weekdays or weekday evenings?
   YES_____
   NO_____

2. Are you currently enrolled in a degree program?
   YES_____
   NO_____

3. If the answer to Question 2 was YES, what program?

4. When are you taking courses this semester?
   Friday afternoon_____
   Friday evening_____
   Saturday morning_____
   Saturday afternoon_____

5. Would you like to have courses offered on Saturday evening?
   YES_____
   NO_____

6. Would you like to have courses offered on Sunday?
   YES_____
   NO_____

7. Are you satisfied with the choice of courses offered at the Weekend College?
   YES_____
   NO_____

8. What other courses would you like offered?
   First choice_____
   Second choice_____
   Third choice_____
   Fourth choice_____

9. Further comments:

EXAMPLE 4–6 Ease-of-Reply Letter of Inquiry

Reynaud Corporation
1000 Murray Road
Gates, MI   00000

March 15, 198–

Mrs. Jane Smithers
302 Rounds Avenue
Gates, MI   00000

Dear Mrs. Smithers:

Last month the Board of Directors offered to buy six vans to be used for employee carpooling. As this purchase will be made only if there is sufficient interest, please complete the following questionnaire and return it to the Personnel Office by April 15.

1. Would you be interested in driving one of the carpool vans in return for use of the van during your free hours?

2. Would you be willing to pay $8.00 a week for transportation to and from work? (You would be picked up at a corner within 3 blocks of your home.)

3. In what section of the city do you live?

4. What hours do you work?

5. Would you be willing to spend approximately one hour per day in the van coming from and going to work?

Your prompt answer placed in the enclosed envelope will be appreciated. Tentative starting date for the service is July 1.

Sincerely,

Robin Thomas

Robin Thomas
Assistant to the Personnel Director

Enc. Envelope

EXAMPLE 4–7   Letter Satisfying The Request

Finton Investors Service
1732 Robinson Place
Tuscany, CT   00000

August 4, 198–

Dr. Daniel Lattimer
4 Greenwood Road
Rowell, CT   00000

Dear Dr. Lattimer

Here is the booklet you requested, "Investment Alternatives for Today."

We hope it is helpful.

Sincerely

John R. Bisson

John R. Bisson
President
Finton Investors Service

Enc.

EXAMPLE 4–8   Letter Satisfying the Request

Finton Investors Service
1732 Robinson Place
Tuscany, CT   00000

August 4, 198–

Dr. Daniel Lattimer
4 Greenwood Road
Rowell, CT 00000

Dear Dr. Lattimer

We are happy to send you the booklet you requested,
"Investment Alternatives for Today." It gives you a
quick, but comprehensive, idea of what Finton
Investors Service believes are the best current investment opportunities.

Notice the list, on pages 4–6, of stocks we feel
are currently underpriced. Our research staff constantly updates this group. A call to your local
branch office (456–1900) will put you on its
monthly mailing list of recipients of our newsletter, "New Buying Opportunities."

If tax reduction is a priority, section 2, page 16,
shows how you can get more income through tax-de-
ferred strategies approved by the Internal Revenue
Service.

Please call if you have any further questions or
would like help with your financial planning.

Sincerely

John R. Bisson

John R. Bisson
President
Finton Investors Service

Enc.

Answering uninvited letters.   When an uninvited inquiry with a list of specific questions is received, a clear and complete reply must be sent. A good format would be:

1. A brief introductory paragraph indicating willingness to be helpful and mentioning any additional material that is enclosed or being sent separately.
2. A specific answer to each question. The setup may be just like the inquiry letter with each item numbered and separated by double spacing. Write a complete sentence for each answer and rephrase each question so that the reader will know exactly to what inquiry you are responding.

Another format would organize your replies in paragraph form, again clearly stating to what questions your answers refer. Put separate ideas into separate paragraphs.

3. A concluding paragraph that offers further assistance or motivates further action.

Examples 4–9 and 4–10 show the two possible formats.

Letters giving instructions.   Sometimes a letter of inquiry asks for instructions, such as how to make or repair something. Or it may ask for directions to or from a specific location. Here the first paragraph would follow the suggested arrangement given previously for replies to inquiries. The next section would supply the requested information in a clear and simple manner. The step-by-step format may be developed in paragraphs, or each step may be separated and numbered in logical sequence. The proper sequence of steps in chronological order is usually extremely important. At times, the writer may have to pause to clarify the instructions by an explanation or a description. A brief concluding paragraph either offers further help or conveys assurance of success.

Example 4–11 gives travel directions in playscript form. Example 4–12 uses paragraph format. Which of these do you find easier to follow? Explain your choice.

Letters Not Satisfying the Request

Sometimes an inquiry cannot be granted, either because the respondent does not have the requested information or because he or she is unwilling to share it. These letters are "bad news" or "no" letters and, thus, require special tact and a positive attitude. (See Examples 4–13 and 4–14.)

Never solve the problem by simply not replying; reply in a manner that will demonstrate fairness and honesty. Also, never hide behind the vague excuse called "company policy"; at least tell what the company policy is and the reasons for maintaining it. You may not be able to make the inquirer like what

EXAMPLE 4–9   Response to an Uninvited Inquiry

Bolger Electronics
234 Peyton Place
Wills, MD   00000

January 15, 198—

Mrs. William Chatterton
15 Meni Court
Lewiston, PA   00000

Dear Mrs. Chatterton:

I am pleased to answer your questions about our new Electric
Plus the Works stove. I am also enclosing our new brochure
containing pictures and facts about how this wonderful new
appliance can revolutionize cooking.

1. The stove retails for $1,069.50.

2. Yes, you can use both the microwave and baking elements at the same time.

3. All parts are guaranteed for one year.

4. After one year, a policy, covering both service and
   parts, can be purchased for only $45.00 yearly.

5. As our brochure shows, the stove comes in white, almond, yellow, pink, and green.

The Girl in White at the Woodriver Electric Company will be
happy to demonstrate the amazing features of the Electric
Plus the Works and answer any further questions. Or, just
call me toll-free at (800) 439-0999 from 9:00 a.m. to 5:00
p.m. weekdays. Once you see this stove in action, it will be
the only one you will ever want!

Cordially,

Roland Bowler

Roland Bowler
Customer Sales Representative

Enc.

EXAMPLE 4–10   Response to an Uninvited Inquiry

Faulkner Industries, Inc.
Faulkner Boulevard
Chicago, IL   00000

June 22. 198—

Miss Michelle Hawkins
Box 345
Kendall College
Kendall, CA 00000

Dear Ms. Hawkins:

I am pleased to hear of your interest in our junior executive
training program. I hope you will apply for membership in the
Faulkner family.

Yes, we do recruit graduates of two-year colleges who have
majored in retail management or business administration.
Grades, appearance, and sales experience are all factors in
the selection process.

A data sheet, official transcript, and three letters from in-
structors or employers should be sent to me before arranging
an interview at our Chicago office.

Trainees spend two months at our Milwaukee headquarters and
then are sent to branch offices for the next six months. They
are then offered several choices of permanent locations in an
entry-level position.

Please let me know if I can help you further.

Yours truly,

Barbara W. Leggeman

Barbara W. Leggeman
Coordinator, Trainee Program

EXAMPLE 4–11 Letter Giving Instructions

Community College of Rhode Island
400 East Avenue
Warwick, Rhode Island   00000

February 10, 198–

Professor Doris Merriam
Community College of South Dakota
495 Michigan Boulevard
Centerville, SD 00000

Dear Professor Merriam:

The following directions should make your trip from Logan airport to the Community College of Rhode Island a pleasant and simple one of about one hour.

1. Follow the <u>Boston</u> signs out of the airport. They will lead you through the <u>Callahan Tunnel</u>. (Have $.30 ready for the toll here.)

2. When you emerge from the tunnel, take a sharp right.

3. Then take the first left. The sign will say <u>Southeast Expressway, South</u>.

4. Continue on the Southeast Expressway for about ten miles. You will pass downtown Boston and several suburbs.

5. Look for the signs to Route 128. Take the right-hand exit to <u>Route 128, South</u>.

6. Follow Route 128 for about 8 miles, past a large shopping mall on the left.

7. Just after Boston Envelope Company on the right, take the exit that says <u>95, South, Providence</u>.

8. Follow Route 95 for about 35 miles past the cities of Providence and Cranston. You will also pass two Warwick exit signs.

EXAMPLE 4–11 *(continued)*

Professor Doris Merriam   2   February 10, 198–

    9. Just after you pass the large Apex store on the left, turn off at <u>Route 113 West</u>.

  10. Look for the entrance to the college on the left, about ½ mile beyond the turnoff.

  11. Drive up the road and park in the first lot on the left.

I look forward to hearing you speak at our annual conference. Please let me know if I can help in any other way with your arrangements.

           Sincerely,

           Walter Brown

           Walter Brown
           Chairman, CEC

im

EXAMPLE 4–12   Letter Giving Instructions

Handicrafts, Incorporated
3 Melton Street
Laws, SC   00000

July, 26, 198–

Mrs. Lucille Watson
4 Merrymount Drive
Wickford, NH 00000

Dear Mrs. Watson:

The following directions should help you to get maximum satisfaction from your Drum Tight embroidery hoop.

First, put the inner hoop flat on a table with the rounded
lip up. Place your fabric on top of this. Next, loosen the
silver adjustment nut on the outer hoop and place the hoop
over the fabric. Be sure that the fabric is smooth.

Now secure the outer hoop under the lip on the inner hoop.
Tighten the adjustment nut until the fabric is taut. You're
all set to start embroidering.

I know you'll get many hours of enjoyment while working with
this rust–proof comfortable sewing aid. Please let me know if
you have any questions about this or any of our other deluxe
handicrafters' accessories.

Cordially,

Melissa Grant

Mrs. Melissa Grant
Service Department

MG/rls

EXAMPLE 4–13   Letter Not Satisfying the Request

Magic Motors Cars and Trucks
400 Magic Plaza
Detroit, MI 00000

June 15, 198–

Mr. Peter Danford
8234 Prime Avenue
Dulles, GA 00000

Dear Mr. Danford:

Thank you for your interest in next year's model of our Fire
Flyte sports car. We have been assured by our engineers that
it will be even faster and more attractive than the present
X–2100.

Because of labor problems in our Detroit plant, production
has been delayed until February. Therefore, your request for
price and specifications cannot be met at this time. However,
we do hope to have a brochure and other data available by October 1.

We shall send you all the pertinent information the day we
receive it. If you have any further questions, we shall be
happy to help in any way that we can.

Sincerely,

Jay Duhamel

Jay Duhamel
Sports Car Sales

efr

EXAMPLE 4–14　 Letter Not Satisfying the Request

Royalton Office Products
14 Western Drive
Royalton, MO 00000

December 19, 198–

Mr. Philip Brian
Insurance Associates
400 Brick Place
Royalton, MO 00000

Dear Mr. Brian:

Thank you for your interest in the various pension
plans to which our employees contribute through
payroll deductions. We are happy to encourage retirement savings this way.

Because this is voluntary, we have agreed that the
records of these transactions be available only to
the employee or, upon death, to a designated bene-
ficiary. Therefore, specific information about individuals cannot be disclosed. However, I can tell
you that 53 percent of our employees contributed an
average of $872 yearly during the past twelve
months to eight different companies.

I hope that these facts have been of help to you.
If I can offer assistance in some other way, please
write again.

Truly yours,

Stephen B. Donaldson

Stephen B. Donaldson

you say, but you *can* make this person like you. Review the section on communicating bad news in Chapter 1. If you apply the principles discussed there, you will use subordination and the passive voice in your letter.

Follow this format:

1. An opening paragraph that acts as a buffer. Do not say *no* here, but also don't mislead the reader. Perhaps you can mention the request without implying that you are answering it, or thank the reader for interest in your product or firm.
2. Tell why you cannot answer the request.
3. Make the refusal, tactfully and clearly. Try to couch it in the passive voice in the middle of the second or third paragraph.
4. Tell what you can do.
5. Close with a paragraph worded in a positive, cordial manner — try to suggest an alternative or offer future help.

Note how Examples 4–13 and 4–14 follow the above suggestions.

Review Chapter 4 and then, using the following Checklists, apply what you have learned to the exercises which follow.

CHECKLISTS

Letters of Inquiry

- Be courteous.
- Be brief.
- Be specific.
- Emphasize reader benefit where possible.
- Provide for ease of reply where possible.
- Express appreciation.

Replies to Inquiries

- Respond promptly.
- Be gracious.
- Answer questions completely or explain courteously why you are unable to do so.
- Offer further assistance.

EXERCISES

1. How could the following letters be improved? Rewrite them according to the ideas presented in this chapter.

a. Dear Mr. Salesman:

I would like to buy a new living room rug. Please
send me all the details about the rugs you sell.

b. Gentlemen and Ladies

Please send me the booklet you advertised recently.
Thank you.

c. Dear Mr. Robins:

We hope our booklet, <u>Making</u> <u>Money</u> <u>with</u> <u>a</u> <u>Franchise</u>,
is helpful.

d. Dear Dr. Flint

I am writing a paper on new drugs for acne for my
hygiene class. I need a lot of information immediately. Thank you for helping me.

e. Dear Ms. Fuller:

We can't give you the answers to your questions
about our employees' overtime pay because it is none
of your business. How do we know that you won't tell
the wrong people?

f. Dear Mrs. Ronson

We are sending you our booklet that will answer all
your questions. It should arrive soon.

g. Dear Professor Shaver:

The answers to your questions are: Yes, Yes, No, and
$50 a week. We hope that this is helpful.

h. Dear Ms. Lally:

To get to our office building, just get on Highway
22 and then take Routes 16 and 2. If you get off
Route 2 at the correct exit, you should have no
trouble.

i. Dear Mr. Webb:

Company policy forbids us to give out lists of our
stockholders' names.
We are sure that you understand.

j. Dear Dr. Beetle

We haven't the foggiest notion what the price of our
new under-counter refrigerator will be. Write again.

2. Write appropriate letters for the following situations.

    a. An advertisement by the Apex Curtain Rod Company, 400 Las Brisas Avenue, Medway, CA 00000, in *Ladies' Choice* magazine, offers a free booklet, *How to Decorate with Draperies.* Write a letter of inquiry asking for the booklet. You also want to know where in your city Apex rods can be purchased.

    b. Write a reply to the above inquiry.

    c. You are planning a ski vacation this winter. Write to the Chamber of Commerce, 135 White Street, Soloway, NH 00000 asking about available accommodations, equipment rental fees, and restaurants.

    d. Reply to Letter c.

    e. Assume that you need more information to adequately answer the letter required by Problem c. Write an ease-of-reply inquiry letter asking for the additional facts you consider necessary. (*Hint:* ask about the planned dates for this vacation, as prices vary according to peak and non-peak times; also, ask about the desired price range for accommodations.)

    f. You are planning to take courses at your local community college next fall. Write to the registrar asking what steps you must take in order to be accepted as a student.

    g. Use your college catalogue or student handbook to answer Problem f.

    h. You are the sales manager of the Stockton Company, 17 Niagara Street, Falls City, NY 00000. You have just received a letter from Mr. Ralph Roman of the Jensen Company, 429 Roundtree Boulevard, Salisbury, PA 00000. He understands that you have a very successful incentive bonus program for paying your salespeople and thereby increasing sales. He would like to know how your program operates. You do not wish to share this knowledge because (1) you have confidential individual contracts with each salesperson and (2) you have heard that the Jensen Company is contemplating expanding into your area selling competitive merchandise. Write a tactful refusal letter.

5

Orders and Replies to Orders

The Order Letter

A good order letter is clear, concise, and complete. It contains all the information about the product being bought as well as where the buyer learned about it. Ask yourself, "Could I, on the basis of what this letter says, fill this order promptly and to the customer's satisfaction? Does this letter tell me everything I need to know?"

Sources of Information

In addition to sales catalogues, other media such as radio, television, magazines, newspapers, and special flyers are rich sources of products available by mail order.

Mentioning where you learned about the product you are ordering not only lets the seller know that his advertising is reaching out to prospective customers, but it can also help the seller pinpoint the item wanted in case the order letter is not as clear as it should be.

Details

Not only must the order letter be clear, concise, and complete, but its physical form should be easy to read. Wide margins, several spaces between entries, and columns for each item all create a good appearance as well as make it easy for the seller to know exactly what you want. Including all the following information in your letter should guarantee you prompt and efficient service.

1. Your name, address, phone number, and account number, if you have one.
2. A detailed description of the items wanted.
   a. Code number, if available.
   b. Size.
   c. Color.
   d. Name of article.
   e. Quantity.
   f. Unit price.
   g. Total cost if ordering more than one of the same item.
   h. Subtotal of all goods ordered.
   i. Taxes and shipping charges, if any.
3. Special requests, if any, such as sending to another address, including a gift card, or shipping to arrive by specific date.
4. Methods of payment — open account, budget account, charge card, C.O.D., check, or money order. Be specific.
5. Methods of shipment — Parcel Post, UPS, freight, airmail, special handling, and shipping charges (whether included or C.O.D.).

Look over Examples 5–1 and 5–2. Notice the paragraphing and spacing for clarity and the brief yet complete information they present to the reader. The person filling each order knows exactly what the customer wants and, as a result, will be able to process the order without delay.

The Order Form

Most catalogues and a large percentage of advertising flyers and brochures include some kind of order blank. Some companies also include such a form with each shipment to make future ordering easy for the customer. But as simple as the ordering process is, many order forms are returned because the sender has forgotten to give all the information requested. While order forms may vary greatly in design and detail from company to company, the information asked for varies only slightly.

Examples 5–3 and 5–4 illustrate some of those differences and similarities. Whatever the shape and design of the order form, the important thing to remember is to give all the information necessary to be sure of prompt and accurate service. Example 5–5 is another type of order form that has become popular. Usually a printed card, the order form combines the sales pitch, the contract, and the order. All the buyer has to do is sign the card and perhaps mark an X in a square.

EXAMPLE 5–1 An Order Letter

2269 Forsythe Boulevard
Thompsonville, RI 00000
1 September 198—

The Mulberry Tree
592 Hollywood Avenue
Kansas City, KS 00000

Gentlemen:

Please send me via Parcel Post the following items as advertised on p. 98 in the August 198— issue of <u>Popular</u> <u>Mechanics</u>
magazine.

1 set cold steel chisels	#749–X	@ $65.00	$65.00
1 Carpenter's folding rule	#2253	@ 15.00	15.00
3 V–Blocks and clamps ½x2	#425A	@ 10.00	<u>30.00</u>
		Subtotal	$110.00
		Shipping	<u>5.95</u>
		Total	$115.95

My check for $115.95 is enclosed.

Very truly yours,

Jonathan K. Quanto

Jonathan K. Quanto

Enc. 1

EXAMPLE 5-2   An Order Letter

4 Pilsner Street
Orms, MA 00000
9 June 198—

Customer Shopping Service
Jenson's Department Store
Fairchild Mall
Osteria, MA 00000

Gentlemen:

Please send the following items as advertised in the <u>Sunday
Star</u>, 6 June 198— to:

> Mrs. Geoffrey R. Zoltec
> 324 South Memphis Drive
> East Orono, IL 00000

One (1) Ivory tablecloth	#19A24	70x104 in.		$40.00
One (1) dozen ivory napkins	#19N24	14x14	@ 2.00	<u>24.00</u>
			Subtotal	$64.00
			5% SST	3.20
			Shipping	<u>4.25</u>
			Total	$71.45

Please gift wrap and include a card with the following message:

> Happy Birthday with love,
> Carol and Ted

Ship via parcel post and charge to my account number
260 495 621 1.

Very truly yours,

Theodore van Smythe

Theodore van Smythe

EXAMPLE 5–3 An Order Form

JEROME, SMITH & JOHNSON
972 Magnolia Boulevard
West Sussex, Indiana 00000

Telephone: 796-331-0007   **Cable: JESON, West Sussex**

AMERICA'S LARGEST MANUFACTURER OF SMALL TOOLS

Name_____

Address_____

Phone_____

Catalog No.	Quantity	Model No.	Color Code	Size	Description	Unit Cost	Total Cost	Office Use Only

Method of Payment   Subtotal _____

_____ Check or Money Order   Sales Tax _____

_____ Open Account No.   Ind. 5% _____

_____ C.O.D.   Handling _____

All shipments prepaid UPS   Insurance _____

                                                          Total _____

EXAMPLE 5–4   An Order Form

FOR 50 YEARS
THE WORLD'S FINEST CHEESES, SMOKED MEATS, AND OTHER DELICACIES

SPICERS
Dairyville, WI 00000

NAME _____   Fast Service No._____

ADDRESS _____   Date_____

        _____   Enclose Gift Card_____

        _____

PHONE_____   Signed _____
Ship to another address

    Name _____

    Address _____

    _____

    _____ ZIP_____

Page No.	Catalog	How Many	Name	Description	Price	Total	

    Subtotal _____

    Postage   _____

    TOTAL   _____

Method of Payment   See Chart page 41 for postal charges.
                                     For quick service charge orders call
_____Monthly Installment Plan   1-800-761-5790 toll free.

_____Check or Money Order

_____Master Card   _____Visa

Account No._____ Bank No._____

Expiration Date_____   Minimum Card Order – $20.00

EXAMPLE 5–5   A Combination Order Form

GHOSTLY PUBLISHERS, LTD.

A Special Offer for Brave Readers Who Love a Good Scare!

YES! YES! YES! Rush the next issue of GHOULS AND GHOSTS free of charge. If I like what I read, I will send you $6.95 for the next 12 issues. If I decide not to subscribe, I'll check the NO box on the return reservation card. In any case, the free issue is mine to keep.

NAME _____
                                Please Print Clearly

ADDRESS _____

CITY _____

STATE_____   ZIP_____

SIGNATURE _____
In Canada add $1.00 to the subscription price.   X-571-F

Replies to Orders

When an Order Can Be Filled Completely and Promptly

When an order can be filled completely and promptly, many businesses do not bother to acknowledge an order before shipping, especially when the buyer is a regular customer. Some companies do, however, send out a printed card on which the seller indicates the receipt of the order, the amount, and approximate date and method of shipment.

When a Reply Is Necessary

There are a number of situations in which orders should always be acknowledged, ranging from simple good will to the inability or even refusal to do business for one reason or another. In the interest of good will, particularly if a new customer is sending in a first order, a business will use a form letter or even what appears to be a personal letter thanking the buyer for the order, welcoming the buyer as a new customer, and including brochures advertising some of the company's other products.

When an Order Is to Be Shipped in Several Parts

While some companies, especially seed companies, simply stamp on the invoice enclosed with the shipment, "The rest of your order will arrive later," or "Your order is being shipped in several parts," in the interest of good public relations, an acknowledgment that includes the date of shipment should be sent upon receipt of the order. This information prepares the buyer and also gives him or her an opportunity to go elsewhere if the intended shipping date will be too late for his or her needs.

When an Order Can Be Partially Filled or Is Delayed

When an order can only be partially filled, the letter tells the buyer why — the merchandise is on back order, the product is temporarily out of stock, or the item has been discontinued. The letter also tells the buyer when to expect shipment if at all and offers alternatives if there are any.

When there will be a delay, the letter should explain the reason; and if the delay is to be a long one, the writer sometimes will include a card for the buyer to return if he or she does not choose to wait. Sometimes the seller may even suggest another source of supply if the delay will be too great an inconvenience for the purchaser.

When an Order Cannot Be Filled

When an order cannot be filled at all, a reply is mandatory. A few of the reasons an order cannot be filled may be that the writer has supplied incomplete information, the product is out of stock or discontinued, the order was missent, or the company deals only in wholesale services. The acknowledgment letter should explain the reason, should offer suggestions about where to look for the product, and/or should mention other items the company carries that might interest the buyer. In all cases the tone should be pleasant though regretful, the "You" attitude should be emphasized, and the buyer should be thanked for his or her interest in the company's products. If more information is needed, the exact nature of that information must be specified.

Telephone Orders

Orders given over the telephone generally require a written acknowledgment in order to avoid errors and to keep accurate and permanent records. Such acknowledgment has become increasingly important in recent years because of the complicated and rigid tax regulations governing businesses.

Study Examples 5–6 through 5–13. Are they good letters? Are they the kinds of letters you would like to receive under the various conditions? Do any of them bother you? Is the tone of the letters pleasant, yet businesslike? Are they explicit? Are they brief yet complete, or do they run on? Are you left with any questions about what the customer wants? If you were in business, would you want to continue with the companies that sent out the letters? How would you change the letters if you feel they are lacking in any way?

Requests for Exchanges

Every once in a while, there is a need to exchange merchandise for one reason or another. The size or color may be wrong, or the merchandise may be flawed or damaged. Whatever the reason, the letter asking for the exchange should be as clear, concise, and complete as the order letter itself. Occasionally, mail order companies include a form and a mailing label with the shipment in case you need to return merchandise. More often, however, this is not the case, and you will have to write a letter explaining what is wrong and what you want done. Such letters are usually attached to the outside of the package and carry

EXAMPLE 5–6   Card Acknowledgment of Order

THE MULBERRY TREE   *592 Hollywood Ave., Kansas City, KS 00000*

Dear Customer:

　　Your order of _____ received. Shipment will be made on _____ . Thank you.

Kenneth Hudson

Kenneth Hudson

Sales Manager

EXAMPLE 5–7   Acknowledgment Letter

THE MULBERRY TREE   *592 Hollywood Ave.*
Kansas City, KS 00000

3 September 198—

Mr. Jonathan K. Quanto
2269 Forsythe Blvd.
Thompsonville, RI   00000

Dear Mr. Quanto:

Thank you for your order dated 1 September 198— in the amount
of $115.95. It will be filled today and shipped to you on
September 5 by insured Parcel Post.

You have made wise selections as our carpenter's tools are
among the finest made. We are sending you our latest catalogue, which should arrive about the same time as your order.
You will find it very helpful the next time you need tools.
Notice the complete stock of all carpenter's tools and the
reasonable prices for the highest quality found anywhere.

All Mulberry Tree tools are guaranteed or your money will be
cheerfully refunded.

Sincerely,

Kenneth Hudson
Sales Manager

EXAMPLE 5–8   Order to Be Shipped in Several Parts

FARBER'S GIFTS

Fine Linens and Imported China

Prescot Corners   Fairbanks MO   00000

May 10, 198—

Mrs. Joseph J. Wilberston
70 Quaker Lane
San Fillipe, AZ 00000

Dear Mrs. Wilberston:

Thank you for your order of May 6, 198—, which will be sent
to you in two shipments. The sheets, pillowcases, and the
bedspread are being prepared for shipment today from the
Prescot Corners store, while the tablecloth and napkins will
be sent from the Hanover store.

You may expect delivery of both packages by the end of the
week.

When they arrive, be sure to take a few minutes to look over
the colorful brochures included in each package. They describe more of our lovely linens for the discriminating buyer
at very reasonable prices for such outstanding quality and
beauty.

Sincerely,

Kimberly F. Courtney

Kimberly F. Courtney
Vice President

KFC:i

EXAMPLE 5–9   Order Can Be Partially Filled or Is Delayed

THE MULBERRY TREE   *592 Hollywood Ave.*
Kansas City, KS 00000

3 September 198—

Mr. Jonathan K. Quanto
2269 Forsythe Blvd.
Thompsonville, RI 00000

Dear Mr. Quanto:

Thank you for your order of 9/1/8— for $115.95. The cold
steel chisels and the carpenter's folding rule will be sent
out on September 5 by insured Parcel Post, and you should
have them to use in just a few days.

Unfortunately, there will be a slight delay in sending the V—
blocks and clamps, as we are awaiting shipment of a new supply from the manufacturer. As soon as they arrive, we will
rush them to you. We are sorry for the delay and hope you
will not be too inconvenienced.

For your future use, we are sending you today our latest
catalogue. Please take a few minutes to look it over. You
will be pleasantly surprised at the low cost of quality tools
guaranteed to perform or your money refunded. Shopping by
mail is not only fast but economical by saving the cost of
gasoline, the wear and tear on your car, and the sales tax
levied in Rhode Island, not to mention your time.

The next time you need tools, think MULBERRY TREE! Those who
know quality do.

Sincerely,

Kenneth Hudson

Kenneth Hudson
Sales Manager

EXAMPLE 5–10   Order Cannot Be Filled

JENSON'S DEPARTMENT STORE

Fairchild Mall   **Osteria, MA 00000**

11 June 198—

Mr. Theodore van Smythe   Account #260–495–4211
4 Pilsner Street
Orms, MA 00000

Dear Mr. van Smythe:

Thank you for your order for one (1) ivory tablecloth and one
(1) dozen ivory napkins, to be sent gift wrapped with a card
to Mrs. Geoffrey Zoltec in East Orono, IL.

We would like to help you, but the items you have ordered
were a special sales promotion and were limited in number.
Unfortunately, they were sold out by the time your order
reached us.

However, if you will look at the enclosed brochure, you may
find another set you like equally well. Since we know how
very important it is to have birthday gifts arrive on time,
if you find another tablecloth and matching napkin set you
would like, just call our toll-free number 800–717–8000 and
ask for Miss Jones, your personal shopper. She will take your
order, charge your account, and see that your gift is
wrapped, the card enclosed, and the package mailed immediately. We promise you it will arrive by July 2 as you have
requested.

We are sorry for any inconvenience this may have caused and
look forward to serving you again.

Sincerely,

Janet Fromer

Janet Fromer
Customer Service Representative

JF/s

Enc. 1

EXAMPLE 5–11 Order Cannot Be Filled — More Information Is Required

---

Simco Fire Arms Co.
654 Powder Lane
Santa Fe, NM 00000

The Best in Rifles and Shotguns for the Hunter

October 3, 198—

Mr. Jeff Comstock, Treasurer
Allies Rod and Gun Club
41 Wolf Rock Road
West Coventry, CA 00000

Dear Mr. Comstock:

Thank you for your order for six (6) Repeating Winchester 22
rifles.

We know you are anxious to get them and we are eager to fill
your order. But we need some more information in order to
make sure you get just the rifles you want. If you will just
fill in the blanks below, tear on the dotted line, and return
that part of the letter in the enclosed postage—paid, addressed envelope, you will have your rifles within a week to
use and enjoy.

Sincerely,

John P. Jones

John P. Jones
Catalogue Sales Director

Catalogue Number _____
Stock finish: Hand rubbed _____
               Machine finish _____
Stock color: Mahogany _____
               Walnut _____

EXAMPLE 5–12   Order Was Mis-sent

Simco Fire Arms Co.
654 Powder Lane
Santa Fe, NM 00000

October 3, 198—

Mr. Jeff Comstock, Treasurer
Allies Rod and Gun Club
41 Wolf Rock Road
West Coventry, CA 00000

Dear Mr. Comstock:

You must be wondering why you haven't received the six (6)
Repeating Winchester rifles you ordered on September 7. The
order was sent to our old address in Oaklawn, CA, and had to
be forwarded to us here in Santa Fe. You may be sure that we
are now rushing the rifles to you, and they will probably arrive about the time you are reading this letter. To make certain that your next order will receive prompt attention, we
are sending along our new catalogue with our new address on
the order forms.

Take a few minutes to look through the catalogue when it
comes. You will see that we offer a complete line of guns for
the sportsman as well as top-quality hunting clothes for
every activity from duck hunting in the cold marshes to deer
hunting in the Maine woods, all at very reasonable prices.

Sincerely,

John P. Jones

John P. Jones
Catalogue Sales Director

EXAMPLE 5–13   Confirmation of a Telephone Order

Jones Tool and Die Wholesalers
Brighton Industrial Complex
Atlantis, NJ 00000

Telephone 405-771-6000
THE BEST SUPPLIES for the BEST PRICES
Keep your home handyman happy with Jones tools

7 July 198—

Mr. James B. Case, Purchasing Agent
CASE & SMITH HARDWARE, INC.
941 Main Street
Kalamazoo, MI 00000

Dear Mr. Case:

Your telephone order of 5 July 198— has been processed. You
can expect delivery on or about 15 July in plenty of time for
your planned sale-a-thon on 30 July. Here is confirmation of
that order for your records. We have charged your account
#10032 as you requested.

12	Ball peen hammers	H–41–B	@ $3.00	$ 36.00
12	Cold steel chisels	CC–973	2.50	30.00
12	Folding rules – 6 ft.	R–7396	4.75	57.00
12	Chalk lines	L–57	.25	3.00
12	Pkgs. chalk dust	D–9x	.10	1.20
			TOTAL	$127.20

Very truly yours,

JONES TOOL AND DIE WHOLESALERS

Mary C. Smithson

Mary C. Smithson, Sales Manager

MCS/im

first class postage. If you put them inside the package, you should note that on the outside.

The letter should state:

1. The reason for the return.
2. Whether you want a refund, a credit to your account, or an exchange.
3. What you want if an exchange.

It should also include any invoices that came with the shipment. Sometimes service can be speeded by noting on the outside such phrases as "Customer Service," "Merchandise Return," or words to that effect in the lower left corner of the package. Every company will have its own procedure for handling returns and exchanges, but the general rule of thumb is the same as it is when writing the original order letter. Ask yourself, "If I received this letter, would I know exactly what the writer wants?"

Look at Examples 5–14, 5–15, and 5–16. Are they good letters? Do they contain all the information necessary for the reader to know just what the writers want? Are they clear, concise, and complete? Are they too brief? Are they too wordy? What changes would you make, if any?

Replies to Exchange Requests

Occasionally, a customer will write asking for directions on returning merchandise for exchange. Naturally such a request requires an answer. The letter should be concise and explicit. A mailing label specifically designed for return and exchange is usually included along with instructions for wrapping, shipping, and insuring the package.

When the exchange request accompanies the product being returned, a reply should be sent stating the date the shipment arrived, whether the exchange can be made as the customer has requested, and if it cannot stating the reason and offering an alternative that might satisfy the buyer's needs. If credit is to be given, the amount should be stated. The letter also expresses the hope that the customer will be satisfied and that the seller looks forward to continuing serving the buyer in the future.

Mail order companies selling primarily to the householder do not usually acknowledge the receipt of a product if the exchange can be made promptly. Only if there is a problem does correspondence follow the return.

Study Examples 5–17, 5–18, and 5–19. Are they clear? Do they stress the "You" attitude? Would you make any changes in them? If you would, what are they?

You may never have to write some of the letters discussed in this chapter. However, they all illustrate typical situations that may arise occasionally in your private life and are a regular part of many businesses. Familiarity with

EXAMPLE 5–14   Request for Exchange

Case & Smith Hardware, Inc.
941 Main Street
Kalamazoo, Michigan 00000

Small Tools   Plumbing Supplies   Housewares   Wallpaper   Paints
Everything for the home handyman

24 April 198—

Jones Tool and Die Wholesalers
Brighton Industrial Complex
Atlantis, NJ 00000

Gentlemen:

On 22 April we received 6 gross of Round Head Machine screws
— steel, zinc chromatic finish #500-M608 W199 (½x8) at
$25.00 per gross. We did not order these.

If you will refer to the attached invoice and the copy of our
original order, you will note that both the invoice and the
order are for:

    6 gross Pan Head Sheet Metal screws #500-P608 W249
    (¾x6) at $22.00 per gross.

We are returning the Round Head screws by UPS insured. Please
send us the Pan Head screws as originally ordered as soon as
possible by UPS, and adjust our account #10032 accordingly.

Very truly yours,

Case & Smith Hardware, Inc.

James B. Case
Purchasing Agent

JBC/im

Enc. 2

EXAMPLE 5–15   Request for Exchange

10 Red Chimney Drive
East Hissop, ID 00000
March 9, 198—

Bartlett's Clothing Mart
75–A Hurd's Shopping Plaza
Kimberly, ND 00000

Gentlemen:

The blazer I am returning by insured Parcel Post
appears to be mismarked. While the label reads size
10, the blazer is obviously a much larger size and
is too big.

Please exchange it for a correct size 10 in the
same color and style. The shipping invoice is inside the package.

Sincerely,

Jane Zitmar

(Mrs. Seymour X. Zitmar)

EXAMPLE 5–16   Request for Directions on Returning Merchandise

10 Red Chimney Drive
East Hissop, ID 00000
6 September 198—

Bartlett's Clothing Mart
75–A Hurd's Shopping Plaza
Kimberly, ND 00000

Gentlemen:

The cashmere coat I ordered from Bartlett's came
today. Imagine my dismay and disappointment when I
opened the package to find a large black spot on
the right front just below the middle button. I was
particularly upset as I had planned to wear the
coat to an affair this evening.

Please RUSH me directions for returning the coat
for exchange.

Sincerely,

Jane Zitmar

(Mrs. Seymour X. Zitmar)

EXAMPLE 5–17　Reply to Request for Exchange, Items Received

Jones Tool and Die Wholesalers
Brighton Industrial Complex
Atlantis, NJ 00000

Telephone 405-771-6000

THE BEST SUPPLIES for the BEST PRICES
Keep your home handyman happy with Jones tools

28 April 198—

Mr. James B. Case, Purchasing Agent
CASE & SMITH HARDWARE, INC.
941 Main Street
Kalamazoo, MI 00000

Dear Mr. Case:

The UPS shipment of Round Head Machine screws you returned to
us for exchange arrived on 27 April, and your account #10032
has been credited accordingly.

Your order of 6 gross Pan Head Sheet Metal screws #500—P609
W249 (¾x6) at $22.00/gross is on its way today and should
arrive at Case & Smith Hardware by the end of the week.

As you know from the many years you have been ordering from
Jones Tool and Die, we make every effort to fill orders
promptly and carefully. But every once in a while something
goes awry and a shipment is not what the customer wants.

We are sorry for any inconvenience you may have undergone,
and we look forward to serving you again soon.

Sincerely,

JONES TOOL AND DIE WHOLESALERS

Henry Q. Fixit

Henry Q. Fixit
Customer Service Manager

HF: im

EXAMPLE 5–18   Reply to Request for Exchange, Merchandise Received

Bartlett's Clothing Mart
75-A Hurd's Shopping Plaza
Kimberly, ND 00000

15 March 198—

Mrs. Seymour X. Zitmar
10 Red Chimney Drive
East Hissop, ID 00000

Dear Mrs. Zitmar:

The blazer you returned for exchange reached us on 14 March.
A correctly sized blazer is being rushed to you via UPS, and
you should have it within four days.

Unfortunately, mismarking of sizes does happen on occasion,
especially with clothing made outside the country. And although we make every effort to check each shipment, once in a
while an item gets by our quality control inspectors.

We sincerely regret that a good customer like you had to be
inconvenienced. We hope, however, that the pleasure you will
get from wearing the blazer with its smart styling and quality material will make up for that inconvenience.

We look forward to serving you again in the near future.

Sincerely,

Myra P. Wellson

Myra P. Wellson
Customer Service Representative

EXAMPLE 5–19   Directions for Returning Merchandise

Bartlett's Clothing Mart
75-A Hurd's Shopping Plaza
Kimberly, ND 00000

September 198—

Mrs. Seymour X. Zitmar
10 Red Chimney Drive
East Hissop, ID 00000

Dear Mrs. Zitmar:

Returning your coat for exchange is easy.

  1. Wrap the coat securely, using the original box if
     possible.

  2. Fill in the enclosed REQUEST FOR EXCHANGE FORM.

  3. Put the form in the accompanying addressed postage—
     free envelope and attach the envelope to the outside
     of the package.

  4. Insure the package for the value of the coat and re-
     turn by first class mail. Your account will be cred-
     ited for the amount of the shipping charges.

You can be sure a new coat will be sent to you as soon as we
receive your package. As careful as we try to be in filling
orders, occasionally a problem arises. We deeply regret any
inconvenience and disappointment you have experienced. Wear
your new coat with pride and pleasure, and as an old saying
goes, "in good health."

Sincerely,

BARTLETT'S CLOTHING MART

Myra P. Wellson

Myra P. Wellson
Customer Service Representative

Enc. 1

the various types of problems and the letters they require for solution will give you added confidence in your ability to deal with such situations wherever and whenever they may occur.

CHECKLISTS

Orders

- Include your name, address, telephone number, and account number if you have one.
- Be clear, concise, and complete.
- Mention source of information.
- Give all details about items wanted.
- State methods of payment and shipment.

Replies to Orders

- Thank customer for order.
- State date of shipment when order can be filled.
- Describe existing problems, if any, and offer solution.
- Resell products.

Exchanges

- Customer's request.
    a. State reason for exchange.
    b. State what you want done — refund, credit, or exchange.
    c. Include any invoices you may have.
- Answers to exchange requests.
    a. Thank customer.
    b. Repeat details of order or request.
    c. Explain what can be done when customer's request cannot be satisfied.
    d. Resell products.

EXERCISES

1. The Book Mart, 321 Mendon Park, San Francisco, CA 00000, has been a steady customer of the Publishers Clearing Post, Box 784, Muncie, IN 00000, for many years. Mrs. Marthe Watkins, the Book Mart's purchasing agent, has ordered 425 copies of *Grimm's Fairy Tales* on open account #753. You can fill the order immediately. The books sell for $10.25 each. Acknowledge the order (a) by printed card, (b) by letter on company letterhead.

2. Jeremy X. Gasrow, manager of the book department in Bergen's Department Store, 650 Water Street, Tuscaloosa, ND 00000, orders twenty copies of *The Life of an*

American Indian by Chief White Feather. It is published by McMurray and Company. Your company, Histories & Biographies, Ltd., 75 Big Bear Lane, Navaho, CA 00000 can fill only half of this order, but you know that a shipment of these books is due any day as you have already received the shipping invoice. Mr. Gasrow has sent a check for $80.00 for the order to be shipped via UPS C.O.D. Write to Mr. Gasrow in your capacity as sales manager, explain the situation, and offer suggestions on what can be done.

3. You are the purchasing agent for L.T. Smithers Co., Inc. of Jefferson Plaza, Hobnail, Mississippi 00000, and are making out an order to Bowie Knife Company, 1056 Wilkinson Parkway, Sissal Falls, Alabama 00000. The order is taken from their 198- catalogue and consists of three dozen two-blade pocket knives at $2.95 per knife, stock number 756; five dozen Swiss Army knives at $130.00 per dozen, catalogue number SA-10; six steel boning knives at $7.25 each, catalogue number 54; six 12-inch French butcher knives at $11.49 each, catalogue number FB-7c. You want the order insured and sent via UPS with the order plus the shipping charges added to your account #337541.

   a. Design an order form for Bowie Knife Company and fill in your order.
   b. Write an order letter to K. Z. Schultz, Sales Manager, from whom you have bought regularly for several years. You need the knives for a special sale to take place in four weeks. Whatever part of the order you cannot get in time, you do not want.

4. You are now Mr. Schultz, sales manager of Bowie Knife Company.

   a. Acknowledge the order with a standard card acknowledgment. The order can be filled promptly.
   b. Acknowledge the order by letter. It will be filled completely and sent out as requested within twenty-four hours and should arrive within five days.
   c. Answer the order request explaining that the two-blade knives, the Swiss Army knives, and the French butcher knives are in stock and can be shipped immediately. The boning knives are on back order and you cannot guarantee shipment in time for the sale.
   d. Write a letter explaining that you can ship the two-blade pocket knives and the Swiss Army knives within the week; but because the boning knives and the French butcher knives come from a branch factory, the order will be sent in two parts with the branch shipment arriving a week later but in plenty of time for the sale.

5. Write a letter ordering an item you saw advertised in your favorite magazine.

6. Write a letter asking for an exchange of something you have ordered but for some reason do not want as it is.

7. Write a letter ordering four items to be individually gift wrapped and sent to another address. A suitably inscribed card is to be included. Your check including shipping and handling charges is enclosed.

8. You are assistant to Marylin Rosswell (Mrs. Alexander) who is the buyer for Shalimar Style-Setter Salon in Fashion Mall, Fenton Boulevard, Ryener, NY 00000. She has asked you to write a letter for her signature to the Almond Boutique Wholesale Co., 76 Sinclair Ave., Jersey, PA 00000. The Style-Setter Salon has an open account #3197 with Almond Boutique and has been buying from them for a number of years with an excellent credit rating. The order is for the following:

a. 6 embroidered white peasant blouses, stock #9E4; there are to be 2 each in sizes 10, 12, and 14 at $4.00 each.

b. 12 turtleneck sweaters, stock #5366; 4 pink, size 10; 4 green, size 12; 4 lavender and blue floral, size 14 at $5.00 each.

c. 12 pair jeans, stock #J53662 at $6.00 each. The jeans are to be matched in colors and sizes with the sweaters as they will be sold as coordinates.

The order is to be rushed and charged to Style-Setter's account. Shipment is to be made via Holly's Overland Express, C.O.D. The letter is to be called to the attention of Mr. Carlos Santini, Manager of Almond Boutique Wholesale Co., who has always handled Style-Setter's orders.

9. The order in problem 8 arrives on October 16 with a letter explaining that Almond Boutique Wholesale Co. is out of stock #9E4 and will not have any more for at least three months. Knowing you are in a hurry and knowing the type of merchandise you usually buy from him, Mr. Santini has substituted peasant blouses stock #9A4. Mrs. Rosswell does not like the substitutes and asks you to write a letter for her signature to Almond Boutique Wholesale Co., attention Mr. Santini. She wants you to tell him that the blouses are being returned because they are unsatisfactory, thank him for his thoughtfulness, and request the necessary adjustment to Shalimar Style-Setter's account. She is satisfied with the rest of the order. A copy of this letter is to go to Mr. J. P. Hazzard, president of Shalimar Style-Setter Salon.

10. Decide what is wrong with the following letters, then rewrite each one to improve it.

a. You dunderhead! Don't you recognize colors? Can't you tell blue from green or are you color blind and your add was just another one of those comeons we read so much about? Here is that ugly green coat you sent me instead of the blue one I wanted. Get on the ball and fill my order right or take the coat and give me my money back pronto!

b. Please send me one of those electric pencil sharpeners you had on display at the office equipment show in Fancy Mall last week/ I think it cost about $21.00 but I'm not quite sure and it was sort of yellow in color with three different colored lights that went on to tell the pencil was ready. When I get it, if it is the right one I'll send you a check.

c. If you expect us to fill your order, you need to give us the facts. We have hundreds of men's sports jackets in all sizes, styles and colors as well as in five different fabrics. Your request for "the jacket at the bottom of page 90 in Sunday's paper is not enough to go by as there were twelve jackets pictured at the bottom of the page.

d. You don't really expect us to send you a $70.00 saw for you to pay for if you like it when we have never heard of you before? What if you don't like it? Do you keep it and forget to pay us or do you send it

back? Anyway we don't sell to individuals only to
retail merchants. Go to your local dealer and have
him order it for you if he doesn't have it in stock.
After all, he has to make a living too.

11. You own a car dealership that handles the very exclusive and costly Hi-Fly sportscar
as well as less expensive family cars. Prices on the Hi-Fly range from $27,000 to
$40,000 for the super-deluxe model. You have just sold the last of the twelve cars
you had on the lot when you get an urgent phone call from the manufacturer's
troubleshooter, Harvey C. Wyman. He tells you that a flaw in the fuel-injection
system of the Hi-Fly Model XZ has just been discovered. The flaw is a very
dangerous one as the slightest impact could make the car explode and burn, trapping
those inside. You have sold six of the Model XZ within the past three months. Mr.
Wyman wants you to recall the cars for replacement of the fuel-injection system
discreetly, with as little publicity as possible and without alarming the owners and
potential buyers. You feel it is the manufacturer's responsibility to notify the buyers.
You have also just mailed an order for ten more of the Model XZ Hi-Fly sportscars
that morning.

   a. Write a letter (the body only) to the manufacturer's troubleshooter telling him
   that you feel it is his job to notify the buyers, giving him the six names
   and addresses, and notifying him that you will do nothing until you get his
   answer.

   b. Write the body only of a letter to the sales manager of the company cancelling
   your order and telling him that you will order no more Model XZs until the
   problem has been resolved.

   c. Write the body of a form letter to be sent to each of the people who bought
   the XZ model from you telling them about the recall.

12. Write an answer to the following letter using the facts listed at the end of the
problem in any order you think suitable. Explain carefully and try to keep your
customer, as the machine shop is a good steady customer buying several thousand
dollars worth of parts about every three months.

Gentlemen:

Our order A 8806 for six number ten spur gears,
catalogue number A 3496, and eighteen worm gears,
catalogue number B 891, was sent from here on 12 November, over two months ago.

Since we have had neither an acknowledgment of the
order nor the gears themselves, we wonder whether
the order may have gone astray.

We shall want the gears for use in an order for
drill presses, which we have promised to our customer on 15 February. We can still meet our delivery
date if we have the gears by 28 January.

Can you ship them in time?

Sincerely,

Facts: a. You will ship the gears by air freight so the customer will have them on time.

b. You think that a letter of explanation had been sent out.

c. A fire in a portion of your plant has delayed all of your operations and destroyed some of the company's records. All this was explained in the letter you thought had gone out, but in the confusion it is quite possible that the form letter was not sent to the customer.

d. Assure the customer that you will be able to give normal service on the next order.

6

Adjustment Letters

"A soft answer turneth away wrath" is an old, well-known proverb whose truth cannot be denied when it comes to creating good will and getting the adjustments you seek. It does not matter whether you are a customer with a problem or a business responding to customer complaints about poor service, requests for repairs, adjustments or refunds — a pleasant tone or soft answer is essential. The only letters that should be written in anger are those destined for the shredder or the wastebasket. That particular action clears the mind and emotions, leaving you ready for a calm, realistic approach to writing the letter either asking for or responding to a request for adjustment. Sarcasm, anger, and blame serve only to antagonize and will hinder rather than help the writer get what he wants.

The consumer today is protected by laws such as the Consumer Safety Act and the Truth-in-Lending Act. Federal laws also protect the public from mail fraud. Consumer advisory protection agencies, while not law enforcement agencies, can help the consumer with information about a company's reputation for honesty and fair dealing. The most well-known of these is the Better Business Bureau. The popular Action Line has many resources for helping people get fair treatment and just restitution.

Businesses are very image conscious. A disgruntled customer who passes the word on to friends and business associates that XYZ Company is dishonest or engages in unfair practices can, in a relatively short time, render worthless thousands of dollars spent on advertising and public relations.

Requests for Adjustments

The claims letter should be courteous, as brief as possible, and complete. It should explain the problem, present the pertinent facts, describe the inconvenience suffered, and suggest a possible solution. It should speak to the seller's pride, self-interest, and sense of fair play.

If the problem concerns an order, the letter should include the order number, date of order, any stock numbers, and other facts necessary for the supplier to know exactly what is wrong. Explain what the problem is, how you may have been affected by it, and finally, offer a possible solution. A firm, positive but neutral, and civil tone is the key, even when you feel you are being cheated.

Today, the most difficult and frustrating problem for consumers comes from computerized billing services, particularly when the credit office is at a different address from the ordering and shipping departments. This arrangement is all too often a case of the right hand not knowing what the left hand is doing. Once an error has been programmed into the computer, it takes time and costs money to correct it. Letter after letter can be written to convince the powers sending out the collection letters that the bill was paid on time five months earlier and that you have the cancelled check to prove it.

Sheer frustration has prompted many customers into tearing the offending notice in half and returning it — to no avail, for the following month another notice arrives. Other irate consumers, when several claims letters have elicited no response, have resorted to tearing the notice in half, stapling the pieces to a card with two or three staples, then attaching the card to the claims letter with a safety pin. Since computers and scanners do balk at metal, eventually a human being ends up with the information and something is done. Writing on such notices has no effect unless the writing appears in the space marked, "Do not write here" or "For office use only." Keep in mind, however, that such drastic measures are employed when all else fails to get the desired action.

Study Examples 6–1 through 6–7, letters covering a variety of requests for adjustments. As you read them, ask yourself the following questions and be prepared to discuss them in class.

1. Is the tone pleasant or offensive?
2. Is each claim fair? If not, why not?
3. If I were to receive each of these letters, would I know what each writer wanted?
4. Does each writer present all the facts necessary to permit a prompt investigation of the problem?
5. Would I be inclined to respond favorably or unfavorably if company policy permits?

EXAMPLE 6–1   Exchange

Jelson's Kitchenwares, Inc.
49 Watts Avenue
Omaha, NE 00000

June 30, 198–

Brookman's Electrical Supply House
Woodbine Plaza Store 7–A
Orely, CA 00000

Gentlemen:

Please refer to the attached copy of my order #790 dated May
30. In it I ordered 6 duplex toaster ovens #T–5 and 6 broilers #B–5.

When my order arrived, it contained 12 duplex toaster ovens.

I am returning 6 of these toaster ovens by insured Parcel
Post. Please replace them with the six broilers I ordered
originally.

As there are customers waiting for the broilers, I would appreciate shipment as soon as possible.

Sincerely,

JELSON'S KITCHENWARES, INC.

Jerry Jelson

Jerry Jelson
Manager

im

Enc: 1

EXAMPLE 6–2   Overcharges

Goodson's Auto Shop
10 Main Street
Macon, GA 00000

October 16, 198–

Quality Car Accessories Wholesalers
9764 Fiberglass Lane
Austin, TX   00000

Gentlemen:

On September 5, I ordered and charged to my account #79541:

10	Alloy lug nut sockets	@ 11.95	$119.50
12	Magnetic drain plugs #356	@ 5.95	71.40
10	Front shock absorbers #1976	@ 52.50	525.00
10	Rear shock absorbers #1976R	@ 47.95	479.50

The prices shown were taken from your latest catalogue dated
September 198–.

When I received my bill, the price listed for the front
shocks was $55.50 each, and the price for the rear shocks was
$50.95 each.

Unless there has been a change in price since I received your
latest catalogue, I believe I have been overcharged. Please
check to determine which is the correct price. My check for
$1195.40, the cost as indicated by your catalogue, is en-
closed. Should the bill be accurate, please add the difference to my account to be shown on my November billing.

Sincerely,

Jack Goodson

Jack Goodson

i

Enc: Check

EXAMPLE 6–3 Order Incorrectly Filled

Strawberry Field Road
Succotash, RI 00000
November 2, 198—

Leathercrafters Delight
Ranchhand Drive
Tulsa, OK 00000

Gentlemen:

On October 3, I ordered one 12 x 5 x 12 genuine leather tote
bag #C 3391 at $28.75 and one pair of size 8 pigskin gloves #
C 3392 at $14.95.

When my order arrived, instead of the 12 x 5 x 12 bag, I received a 15 x 6 x 16 size bag and size 9 gloves.

Because I cannot use the larger bag nor the gloves, which are
too big, I am returning them by UPS. As soon as possible,
please send me the 12 x 5 x 12 leather tote bag and the size
8 pigskin gloves as originally ordered.

As I had counted on taking both the bag and gloves with me, I
would be most appreciative if they could arrive before December 6 when I leave for Europe.

Sincerely,

Marybelle Flutter

(Mrs. John Flutter)

EXAMPLE 6–4   Order Incompletely Filled

The Candy Corner Shop
Cranberry Mall
Salisbury, GA 00000

October 29, 198–

Jorgenson, Partridge and Sons
296 Walnut Boulevard
Orlando, FL 00000

Gentlemen:

Our October shipment of candy was incomplete. If you will
check the attached copy of our order #612 dated 9/10/8– you
will find that in addition to our standing monthly order for
50 pounds each of jelly eggs, gumdrops, and Mexican hats, we
had also ordered 20 pounds of dark chocolate-covered caramels, 25 pounds of cashew nut clusters, and 15 pounds of caramel corn balls.

The jelly eggs, gumdrops, and Mexican hats came October 20,
but we have not as yet received the rest of the order. As
Jorgenson's is so prompt and accurate in filling our orders,
we wonder if perhaps the shipment was lost in transit. Please
investigate for us. We are planning a big promotional event
around the addition of the caramels, nut clusters, and corn
balls to our regular line and would like to have them as soon
as possible.

Very truly yours,

THE CANDY CORNER SHOP

Corliss Archer

Corliss Archer
Manager

ik

Enc: 1

EXAMPLE 6–5   Damaged Merchandise

**Paulsing Department Store
95 Chinaberry Lane
Santa Fe, NM 00000**

10 April 198—

Account #107049

Fine China Distributors, Inc.
Export Lane
San Remo, CA 00000

Gentlemen:

On March 4, we sent in our order #6025 (copy attached) for 6
sets of service for 12 of Moray Bone China dinnerware Zenabia
pattern #25.

When we unpacked the shipment, in one crate three of the dinner plates were cracked, the handles were broken off three of
the teacups, and four saucers were shattered. The other six
crates were sound.

Please rush replacements. This situation could mean a considerable loss of business for us as May is the beginning of the
bridal shower season, and we already have registered six
brides for the Zenabia pattern of Moray Bone China.

We are returning via Parcel Post the damaged pieces in the
original carton for your inspection.

Sincerely,

annette C. Mirasal

Annette C. Mirasal
Buyer, China Department

mi

Enc: 1

EXAMPLE 6–6   Order Delayed or Unfilled

2403 Rockledge Road
Graniteville, VT 00000
June 12, 198—

Magazine Subscription Service
P.O. Box 71
Selma, AL 00000

Gentlemen:

On March 1, I sent my check #4001 for $15.95 drawn
on Graniteville Trust Company and a subscription
order for twelve issues of <u>Garden</u> <u>Joy</u> magazine. The
first issue was to arrive within six weeks. Eleven
weeks have passed and I still have no magazine, but
I do have my cancelled check.

Please look into the problem. I really want the
magazine and will appreciate anything you can do to
speed delivery.

Sincerely,

Helga Swenson

Helga Swenson

EXAMPLE 6–7   Other Types of Dissatisfaction

High Hawk Trail
Petaquanscutt, OH 00000
September 20, 198–

Jeffries Department Store
Copeland Highway
Stanford, OH 00000

Attention: Personnel Manager

Gentlemen:

Knowing that Jeffries Department Store has always prided itself on its courtesy to customers, I feel you would want to
know about the very rude and discourteous treatment I received on September 18 in the shoe department.

The clerk, whose name tag read "Marcy," asked if she could
help me. When I asked to see a certain shoe in size 10AAAA/
AAAAA, she looked me up and down, snapped her chewing gum,
and said, "Egads Woman! How could anyone as little as you are
have such clodhoppers for feet! What you really need are the
shoe boxes." She went on to say that Jeffries never carried
that size and probably never would, all the while snapping
gum and scratching her head. That statement I know to be un-
true as I have been buying my shoes for twenty-five years in
Jeffries' shoe department.

Needless to say I was shocked and embarrassed not only by
what she said, but by the way she said it. Her voice was so
loud that everyone in the shoe section turned to look. I was
so offended and upset I left the store.

In my twenty-five years of shopping at Jeffries I have experienced only warm consideration and, above all, courtesy. I
sincerely hope that what happened is just an isolated incident. I certainly do not want to be subjected to such discom-
fiture ever again.

Sincerely,

Harriet Crawford

(Mrs. Horace M. Crawford)

Answering Adjustment Requests

Answering claims can be easy when you are able to do what the writer wants. Most people are honest, and their claims are justified — if not for full restitution at least for a compromise satisfactory to both parties.

The attitude of businesses toward requests for adjustments varies from that of *caveat emptor* (let the buyer beware) to *caveat venditor* (the customer is always right). Most businesses fall somewhere in between in attitude.

The way adjustment letters are written, and their tone in particular, can create or destroy good will. Businesses usually welcome sincere, well-written letters from dissatisfied customers as a means of checking on the quality of their products, the care used when packing shipments, and the attitude of their employees. Customers with legitimate complaints may actually be doing a company a favor by writing about their dissatisfaction. Some companies keep a permanent file of such letters as a regular part of their quality-control operations.

A study of the adjustment requests collected over a period of time can help the investigator locate and eliminate the trouble spots within a business. If, for example, a great number of claims concern faulty packaging, obviously someone in the shipping department is not doing a proper packing job. If a large percentage of letters are asking where orders are and your efforts at tracing them are fruitless, you might suspect the problem to be with the department printing the shipping labels or with the delivery service. If you manufacture fine glazed china and you suddenly receive a rash of letters complaining about the glaze cracking, you would investigate the glazing department and the baking process.

Many of the recalls of unsafe or faulty products have been prompted by consumer complaints as well as by government inspections. Everyone is familiar with automobile recalls, and the news media regularly warn the public about certain contaminated canned goods or dangerous electrical appliances and children's toys. All of these recalls, in addition to maintaining quality control and protecting the manufacturing company from expensive lawsuits, are also earning consumer respect and creating good will. They show the consumer that the business is sincere about putting out a good product. Other companies, to show confidence in their products, offer free trials or guarantee money back if the consumer is not satisfied.

There are two schools of thought about whether or not the adjustor should apologize for the problem. Some say yes, while others say no, that one should simply take a positive approach. Whichever technique is used, certain key phrases recur. A few of those phrases follow:

1. You are right in expecting only the best in quality from us.
2. We appreciate learning of your dissatisfaction.
3. Thank you for calling our attention to . . .
4. Despite the best of intentions, occasionally . . .

5. As carefully as we inspect each article, once in a while . . .
6. Whenever a good customer like yourself has a problem, we want to hear about it.

The implication in all of these statements is that the customer is honest, has a reasonable claim, and you are glad to be told about the problem so you can do something about it.

Review the letters asking for adjustments, Examples 6–1 through 6–7, then study the answers to each of those letters, Examples 6–8 through 6–14, in which the adjustor responds favorably by granting the request, solving the problem, or correcting a bad situation.

How do you react to the answers? If you received any one of them, would you be satisfied? Do any of the letters imply a reluctance on the part of the writer to honor the request? Do any of the letters imply that the claim may not be legitimate? Does the tone of the various letters indicate regret over the problem and a sincere desire to remedy the situation?

When the Request Must Be Refused

A soft answer is really important when a request must be refused. The writer must say no in such a way that the customer is not offended. This situation involves an explanation and, whenever possible, a compromise satisfactory to both parties. Tact is indeed the watchword. Put yourself in the reader's place. How would you feel if you had the same problem and received the same answer? Would you say to yourself, "Why that no-good so and so! Who does (s)he think (s)he is to treat me that way! I'll never buy another thing there!" Or would you feel that the reason for refusing you was a fair one, even though you did not like it? If a compromise was offered, was it presented in such a way that you would accept it and feel the writer was offering the best possible solution? If you can answer yes to these questions, then you have written a good letter.

There are a few techniques and precautions to which the writer should pay heed when denying a request. The most important precaution is not to scold. Avoid all signs of anger, sarcasm, and blame. If at all possible, try to find some way to agree with the claimant. Explain from an adjustor's point of view. Sandwich the refusal in the middle of the letter, then refer to something positive so that the letter ends on an upbeat note, reselling your business. Remember, you want to keep the customers coming back. Therefore, you must convince them you are treating them fairly, just as you treat all your customers. You must restore their confidence in your product, company, or service. You want to retain their good will and try to make them feel that they understand your decision was the only one you could make. One customer's bad experience can have far-reaching effects.

Mr. A and Mr. B both own their own businesses. Mr. A's request for an adjustment on some damaged merchandise ordered from S Company was met

EXAMPLE 6–8 Exchange

Brookman's Electrical Supply House
Woodbine Plaza Store 7-A   **Orley, CA 00000**

5 July 198—

Mr. Jerry Jelson, Manager
Jelson's Kitchenware, Inc.
49 Watts Avenue
Omaha, NE 00000

Dear Mr. Jelson:

You are right. According to your order copy we did send too
many toaster ovens. As careful as we try to be, sometimes,
when we are training new shipping clerks as we were the last
week in June, orders are not always filled properly.

Your 6 broilers were shipped this morning by UPS, and you
should have them within three days. We regret any inconvenience this may have caused you and your customers, but we are
certain they will be so pleased with the broilers that the
extra wait will have been worthwhile.

The enclosed pamphlet describes the new automatic coffee
maker we have just added to our line of quality products. You
may want to consider it in your next order.

Sincerely,

BROOKMAN'S ELECTRICAL SUPPLY HOUSE

Oscar Olson

Oscar Olson
Sales Manager

co

Enc: 1

EXAMPLE 6–9   Overcharges

Quality Car Accessories Wholesalers
9764 Fiberglass Lane
Austin, TX 00000

October 26, 198—

Mr. Jack Goodson
Goodson's Auto Shop
10 Main Street
Macon, GA 00000

Dear Mr. Goodson:

Thank you for calling the overcharge in your bill to our attention. I believe I can explain how that happened. As you
know prices have been steadily rising, and the prices listed
in your bill are the new ones that went into effect on October 16. The change in price was programmed on your billing
date and was therefore reflected in your October statement.

Please disregard the increase. Your order was processed before the increase became effective, and your check for
$1195.40 covers the transaction completely for, as you know,
we prepay all shipping charges.

I am also taking this opportunity to thank you for the fine
way you have always handled your account. We value good customers like you.

Sincerely,

Sydney Carson

Sydney Carson
Credit Manager

ikm

EXAMPLE 6–10 Order Incorrectly Filled

Leathercrafters Delight
Ranchhand Drive
Tulsa, OK 00000

November 7, 198–

Mrs. Marybelle Flutter
Strawberry Field Road
Succotash, RI 00000

Dear Mrs. Flutter:

As carefully as we check each order before it is sent out,
occasionally something happens and what the customer receives
is not what she ordered.

The right size bag and gloves have already been mailed to you
by special delivery so you will be sure to have them in
plenty of time for that European trip in December. We sincerely regret the disappointment you must have felt and hope
that the enjoyment you get from the Leathercrafters Tote Bag
and pigskin gloves will more than make up for it. Bon Voyage!

Sincerely,

Leathercrafters Delight

Sara Handy
Sara Handy
Shopping Service Manager

co

EXAMPLE 6–11   Order Incompletely Filled

Jorgenson, Partridge and Sons
296 Walnut Boulevard
Orlando, Florida 00000

November 4, 198—

Ms. Corliss Archer
The Candy Corner Shop
Cranberry Mall
Salisbury, GA 00000

Dear Ms. Archer:

When a faithful customer like the Candy Corner Shop suddenly
has a problem like yours we certainly want to hear about it
so we can do something about it immediately.

First, so you may continue with your promotional plan on
schedule, I have instructed the shipping department to process a new order for you today. You should receive it within
three days.

Second, I have put a tracer on the shipment. Should the last
order by any chance eventually find its way to you, simply
refuse to accept it and the shipment will be returned to us
at our expense.

Have a most successful sale. Remember you are selling the
best-tasting, purest candy made.

Sincerely,

Hancock Hayes

Hancock Hayes
Service Representative

cj

EXAMPLE 6–12   Damaged Merchandise

Fine China Distributors, Inc.
Export Lane
San Remo, CA 00000

Phone 000 000-0000
Cable ETLAN
Dining on Fine China Is Dining in Style

15 April 198—

Ms. Annette C. Mirasal, Buyer
Paulsing Department Store
95 Chinaberry Lane
Santa Fe, NM 00000   Account #107049

Dear Ms. Mirasal:

Look for your replacement pieces on Thursday, April 16, as they were shipped this morning by Air Freight with a ground delivery by special messenger. Because the Zenabia pattern #25 is open stock, there is no problem in replacing the damaged pieces.

We know how important those bridal registrations are. When they run smoothly, both Paulsing and Fine China benefit. Customers return to Paulsing's, and Paulsing returns to Fine China.

Thank you for returning the damaged pieces and especially for the original packing. You may be sure we will examine them carefully to try to discover what went awry between the time they left here and arrived at Paulsing's.

Sincerely,

Joel Darcy

Joel Darcy
Customer Service

km

EXAMPLE 6–13   Order Delayed or Unfilled

Magazine Subscription Service
P.O. Box 71
Selma, AL 00000

June 24, 198—

Ms. Helga Swenson
2403 Rockledge Road
Graniteville, VT 00000

Dear Ms. Swenson:

We have checked on your subscription order and discovered
that the delay was caused by a fire in our mailroom. While
damage to the building was slight, the fire did destroy one
mailing list for new subscriptions and we had no way of letting new subscribers know directly. We did advertise in several major papers explaining the problem and asking all new
subscribers who had not received their first issue to so inform us.

The current <u>Garden Joy</u> magazine will be coming to you very
soon, along with the back issues you have missed. By way of
apology for the delay, we are extending your subscription by
four extra issues at no charge to you.

You will enjoy each issue of <u>Garden Joy</u> magazine with its
timely articles on plant care and the beautiful colored pictures of actual gardens. The question and answer section is
also very helpful, even for experienced gardeners.

Cordially yours,

Abraham Pilsner

Abraham Pilsner
Circulation Manager

km

EXAMPLE 6–14   Other Types of Dissatisfaction

Jeffries Department Store
Copeland Highway
Stanford, OH 00000

Everything for the home and family for over 30 years
Courtesy is our watchword

March 25, 198—

Mrs. Harriet Crawford
High Hawk Trail
Petaquanscutt, OH 00000

Dear Mrs. Crawford:

Thank you for calling to our attention the thoughtless discourtesy with which you were treated by one of our shoe department clerks. We apologize on behalf of the whole Jeffries
family for the needless discomfort you must have felt.

We will do everything we can to prevent such an incident from
happening again. In fact all sales personnel are now undergoing refresher training in Jeffries' concept of behavior and
courtesy toward the customer expected of all Jeffries' employees.

The young woman involved has been dismissed. Such behavior
after the intensive training program all new employees
undergo is unforgivable, and that kind of person is not welcome as a member of Jeffries Department Store personnel.

Please do come in again soon. We have just received a new
shipment of beautiful shoes for spring and summer in your
size. We have a $10 gift certificate toward a new pair of
shoes waiting for you.

Sincerely,

Caesar Colefax

Caesar Colefax
Personnel Manager

cm

with a very rude letter refusing the adjustment and hinting that Mr. A's claim was not really honest. Mr. A is furious and thinks at first about pursuing the matter further. He finally decides it would be a waste of time and energy as he won't get anywhere. He will simply not buy anything from S Company and will spread the word to all his associates. Mr. A calls the Better Business Bureau, which tells him there have been other similar complaints about S Company. Mr. A then tells his story to Mr. B, who spreads the word to his business friends at the golf club. Eventually S Company loses several customers and has no idea why. If you keep in mind that the customer is honest, but mistaken or misinformed, you will more easily develop the right tone.

Just as there are key phrases used in answering requests for adjustments positively, so are there key phrases used when requests must be denied or a compromise offered. Of course, some of the phrases used in granting a request may also be appropriate in a refusal letter. The following are a few commonly used:

1. Only by open and frank discussion can we . . .
2. We appreciate your giving us the opportunity to explain why we cannot . . .
3. We strive to treat all customers fairly.
4. In fairness to all our other customers . . .
5. We sympathize with your dilemma, but . . .

The letters in Examples 6–15 through 6–21 either refuse the requests made in Examples 6–1 through 6–7 or offer a compromise. The same questions asked before still apply about the tone and attitude of the writer. How will the reader react?

Practicing tact and courtesy in all instances of asking for or handling adjustments will always help you get the desired results. As a customer requesting adjustments, you must restrain your annoyance and not reveal it in your letters. As the adjustor, you must act tactfully in granting an adjustment, especially when you believe the request is unjustified. It is even more important to do so when you must refuse a request as you may want to keep the customer. Remember, tact and courtesy are never out of style and go far in establishing good business relations.

EXAMPLE 6–15 Exchange

Brookman's Electrical Supply House
Woodbine Plaza Store 7-A   **Orley, CA 00000**

July 5, 198–

Mr. Jerry Jelson, Manager
Jelson's Kitchenware, Inc.
49 Watts Avenue
Omaha, NE 00000

Dear Mr. Jelson:

Your order did specify 6 broilers and 6 toaster ovens. However, because the broilers were recently discontinued, we
sent 6 extra toaster ovens as a substitute. A letter explaining the shipment was supposed to have been enclosed. I am
sorry it was not.

However, all is not lost.

Did you know that broiling can also be done in the toaster
oven? In fact, the oven is a much better buy for your customers than the broiler as the oven can bake, toast, and broil
at the turn of a switch, whereas the broiler can only broil.

Should you decide you do want the extra 6 toaster ovens, just
call our toll-free number 1–800–000–0000 and ask for Marion,
who will be glad to handle your order. We will credit your
account for the ovens should you decide to return them.

Sincerely,

Oscar Olson

Oscar Olson
Sales Manager

co

EXAMPLE 6–16   Overcharges

Quality Car Accessories Wholesalers
9764 Fiberglass Lane
Austin, TX 00000

October 26, 198–

Mr. Jack Goodson
Goodson's Auto Shop
10 Main Street
Macon, GA 00000

Dear Mr. Goodson:

Thank you for allowing us the opportunity to explain the difference between the prices listed in our catalogue and those
found on your latest bill.

Between the time our catalogue was printed and you placed
your order a price increase went into effect at the manufacturing plant. This increase in our cost was reflected in your
bill. If you look at the bottom of the first page of this
catalogue, you will notice in fairly large letters the words
"Prices subject to change without notice." We have to do this
because of the time it takes to develop, print, and mail a
new price listing. One is now being sent out to all our regular customers, and you should have yours within 5 days.

The additional $60 will be included in your bill for Novem-
ber, as you have requested.

Very truly yours,

Sydney Carson

Sydney Carson
Credit Manager

ikm

EXAMPLE 6–17   Order Incorrectly Filled

Leathercrafters Delight
Ranchhand Drive
Tulsa, OK 00000

November 7, 198—

Mrs. Marybelle Flutter
Strawberry Field Road
Succotash, RI 00000

Dear Mrs. Flutter:

Thank you for telling us about your problem with the tote bag
and gloves in time for us to do something about it prior to
your trip.

We cannot send you the same bag and gloves in the smaller
sizes that you need because we received a limited number from
our supplier with the notice that there would be no more
forthcoming. However, we do have a bag and gloves in the same
color but a slightly different style in the sizes you want.
We have enclosed a picture of them and a sample patch of the
leather for your examination. The quality and price of this
set is the same as the set you originally ordered.

We will rush this bag and the gloves to you if you will call
our toll-free number 1-800-000-0000 and ask for Mary Krane,
our telephone shopper. Tell her you want bag #C3393 and glove
size 8 #63394. You will have them in plenty of time for that
December 6 departure.

Sincerely,

Sara Handy

Sara Handy
Shopping Service Manager

co

Enc: 1

EXAMPLE 6–18   Order Incompletely Filled

> *Jorgenson, Partridge and Sons*
> *296 Walnut Boulevard*
> *Orlando, Florida 00000*

November 4, 198—

Ms. Corliss Archer
The Candy Corner Shop
Cranberry Mall
Salisbury, GA 00000

Dear Ms. Archer:

We are actively trying to find your lost shipment of candy
but with little success. Unfortunately, we cannot even replace that shipment as we are completely sold out.

There is a bright side to the situation, however. We have
just received a shipment of specialty chocolate candies for
Thanksgiving and Christmas. They come in various shapes and
sizes: some wrapped in colored foils, others loose and varying from large turkeys and Santas to tiny toy and animal
shapes. All are of top-quality light or dark chocolate. Some
are filled with chopped nuts, others with caramel.

To help ease your disappointment, we will let you have these
candies at the same price per pound you paid for the chocolate-covered caramels, even though the regular price is five
cents more per pound.

Just check the appropriate box on the enclosed postage-paid
addressed card, drop it in the mail, and within a week you
will have your new line of exciting chocolate holiday candy.

Sincerely,

Hancock Hayes

Hancock Hayes
Service Representative

cj

Enc: 1

EXAMPLE 6–19 Damaged Merchandise

Fine China Distributors, Inc.
Export Lane
San Remo, CA 00000

Phone 000 000-0000
Cable ETLAN
Dining on Fine China Is Dining in Style

15 April, 198—   Account #107049

Ms. Annette C. Mirasal, Buyer
Paulsing Department Store
95 Chinaberry Lane
Santa Fe, NM 00000

Dear Ms. Mirasal:

When your shipment of china left our packing room, it was in
perfect condition. Somewhere in transit it was damaged. Such
things do happen occasionally and we have filed an insurance
claim.

However, as the Zenabia pattern #25 is not open stock, we are
unable to replace the individual pieces. The minimum order is
for a full place setting. As you know, Fine China Distributors takes pride in its fairness to customers, and we cannot
make exceptions to this policy. We will, of course, credit
your account for the amount of the damaged china.

To reorder the number of place settings you will need, simply
fill in the enclosed order form and send it back to us in the
addressed postage-paid envelope. Your order will be sent out
as soon as it is received.

Sincerely,

Joel Darcy

Joel Darcy
Customer Service

km

Encl: 1

EXAMPLE 6–20 Order Delayed or Unfilled

**Magazine Subscription Service
P.O. Box 71
Selma, AL 00000**

June 24, 198–

Ms. Helga Swenson
2403 Rockledge Road
Graniteville, VT 00000

Dear Ms. Swenson:

We have investigated the status of your subscription to <u>Garden Joy</u> magazine and learned to our dismay that the company publishing the magazine has filed for bankruptcy.

What this means to you and all other subscribers who have ordered subscriptions but did not receive any issues is that you will have to file a claim with the receiver, Hightown Citizens Trust, Hightown, AL 00000 for the subscription amount. Then it is a matter of waiting until the publisher's assets have been realized and apportioned to its creditors.

Such occurrences, while infrequent, are of course beyond the control of a subscription service such as ours and are events about which we are powerless to do anything. We are sorry this had to happen, and if we can help you with any other subscriptions, just fill out the enclosed order form and we will take care of it for you.

Sincerely,

Abraham Pilsner

Abraham Pilsner
Circulation Manager

km

Enc: 1

EXAMPLE 6–21   Other Types of Dissatisfaction

Jeffries Department Store
Copeland Highway
Stanford, OH 00000

Everything for the home and family for over 30 years
Courtesy is our watchword

March 25, 198–

Mrs. Harriet Crawford
High Hawk Trail
Petaquanscutt, OH 00000

Dear Mrs. Crawford:

We appreciate your bringing the discourtesy of one of our
shoe clerks to our attention. She has been reprimanded and
has written you a letter of apology.

We did not dismiss her, as good clerks — i.e., those who
really know how to fit shoes — are hard to find and not
everyone can be trained to do so. Miss Y is good at her job.
We hope you can look at her actions as the tactless high
spirits and utter frankness of today's younger generation.
While we do not excuse her behavior, we deal with so many
young people that we are, perhaps, more used to their habit
of speaking first and thinking afterward.

We have included with this letter a brochure showing the new
shipment of shoes for spring and summer. Won't you come in to
look at them and let Miss Y apologize in person? She is anxious to make amends for her thoughtlessness.

Sincerely,

Caesar Colefax

Caesar Colefax
Personnel Manager

cm

Enc: 1

CHECKLIST

Adjustment Letters

- Customer's letter requesting adjustment.
    a. Be courteous, brief, and complete.
    b. Explain problem.
    c. Present all pertinent facts.
    d. Describe inconvenience.
    e. Suggest solution.
    f. Speak to seller's pride, self-interest, and sense of fair play.
- Seller's reply to adjustment requests.
    a. Be courteous.
    b. Agree with customer's proposal or offer alternatives.
    c. Give reasons if nothing can be done.
    d. Resell products/service.

EXERCISES

1. You have had your new Racer CVX for two months. You like everything about it except the leak around the right side of the windshield. When it rains, the water comes down the side and drips onto your left foot. You have had the car back to the dealer three times, but he still hasn't fixed it. You don't know whether he really can't or if he is just giving you the runaround. Write a letter to the car manufacturer explaining the problem and asking for a company representative to come and check it out.

2. Answer your letter in problem 1 granting the request.

3. Answer your letter in problem 1 denying the request.

4. Write a letter asking your bank to hold back the final payment to the contractor building your new house until he has fixed a leaking faucet, two doors that won't shut properly, and a lock that won't work.

5. Write a letter to the contractor telling him what you have done and asking him to do the repairs as soon as possible.

6. Revise the following sentences.
    a. After much thought we have decided to send you a new sofa to replace the damaged one even though it is against our established policy.
    b. It was the fault of a new bookkeeper who did not know about the discount or much else about our business.
    c. Because we cannot allow you an adjustment on the toaster, we will give you a 3 percent discount to keep you happy.
    d. We have shipped the part and you can expect it in the near future. Hurry up and let us know what you intend doing about this matter immediately.
    e. We want to say again that we regret exceedingly the great inconvenience we have caused you by shipping a faulty lawnmower.

    f. In reply to yours of Oct. 29, 198–, we are sorry to tell you that we have to refuse your claim for a refund on the damaged books. Whatever could we do with them if you can't sell them?

    g. I regret to inform you that the glasses arrived in a damaged state, all smashed up because of the lousy job your shipping department did in packing them.

    h. Your complaint received and duly considered for all the good it will do you.

    i. We hope that this explanation will suffice and you will stop bugging us with letter after letter of complaint.

    j. Unless we receive a favorable adjustment soon, I will send our orders elsewhere and tell all our associates what a bad company you are to deal with.

    k. Upon investigation we find you are wrong regarding the charge for labor; the amount stated on the invoice is right. Why are you trying to cheat me?

    l. Your letter of the twenty-eighth inst., in which you claim that you returned the folder on the accident, is at hand.

    m. We are sorry to have to refuse an adjustment on the second hand car you bought here but our policy compels us to as whatever you buy from us you buy as is.

    n. We are surprised that the bookcase did not arrive in good condition. Are you sure you didn't dent it when you unpacked?

7. Use the following information to write Letters A.–H.

The Customer:

Andrews Ball Bearings, Inc., 4312 East Sycamore Street, New Athens, Wisconsin, 00000. Mr. Raymond C. Pendergast, Purchasing Agent.

The Seller:

Standard Office Equipment Company, 19 West Main Street, Glandale, Ohio, 00000. Mrs. Howard P. Carpenter (Alison M.), Assistant Sales Manager.

Standard Office Equipment makes a four-drawer filing cabinet that is heavily insulated and called fire-resistant. It would be used for storage of valuable papers such as contracts, policies, bank documents, leases, and other such papers. A four-drawer file large enough to hold $8\frac{1}{2} \times 11$ correspondence is Catalog Number A-8. A similar file large enough to hold 9×14 sheets is Catalog Number A-9L.

Andrews Ball Bearings has bought model A-8 from a dealer, New Athens Stationery Company. Shortly after the file cabinet was delivered to Andrews, Stuart K. Linson, the owner and manager of the stationery company, was killed in an airplane crash.

A combination of the death of the owner-manager, the fact that a fairly large sum of money had been borrowed to finance the expansion of the business, and the fact that Mr. Linson died without having made a will, caused the banks and courts to close the business temporarily.

The file purchased by Andrews was intended for use in new office facilities under construction, and the file was left in its crate until it could be set up in a new building. When it was set up, the keys sent with the file proved to be the wrong ones.

The file was not locked when crated, and the keys were inside one of the open drawers. As soon as the file was in place, it was opened and the key given to Mr. Pendergast's secretary. Important papers, including contracts, were immediately put in the file, and the file locked by pushing in the latch, or knob or plunger, that is part of the lock mechanism.

The next morning, Mr. Pendergast's secretary tried to use the keys and found that although the key could be inserted, it could not be turned. Careful examination showed a very small number, M696, stamped on the outer surface of the plunger. The number stamped on the key was N (blurred) 696.

a. *Letter A:* Andrews to Standard. The problem, and New Athens Stationery can't help. Can you?

b. *Letter B:* Standard to Andrews. No key M696 available. They will check with the supplier of locks and will go over their own records. If necessary, Andrews to hire a locksmith; Standard will pay.

c. *Letter C:* Andrews to Standard. No immediate need for locksmith. Not all papers transferred. Hope they will be successful in search for key.

d. *Letter D:* Standard to Andrews. Lock company says Standard had locks and keys numbered M696 and N696. Standard has found that a file similar to Andrews' was sold and is now in transit to Canada. Their records show lock number N696. They have written to the customer to ask him to check the key and lock numbers and to send the keys numbered M696 to Andrews if they show up. Would Andrews be willing to airmail N696 if this is the way to solve the problem?

e. *Letter E:* Andrews to Standard. Appreciate the possibility of a solution to the problem. Of course, will send the keys as soon as they know to whom.

f. *Letter F:* Standard to Andrews. Key M696 has been found. Please send N696 to Victoria Junior College, 1100 College Drive, Victoria, British Columbia, Canada. VJC is sending M696 to Andrews. Sorry, and thanks for patience.

g. *Letter G:* Andrews to Standard. Key is here, everything is fine. We like the file, now that we can use it. Does New Athens Stationery have a Catalog Number 9L? Is there another supplier near, or will New Athens be in business again?

h. *Letter H:* Standard to Andrews. New Athens will reopen. They do have a 9L in stock.

8. Rewrite the body of this letter.

Jones Auto Supply Company

All Parts Guaranteed or Your Money Refunded

28 January 198–

Mr. Henry Wilder
976 Hawthorne Drive
Collingwood, Connecticut 00000

Sir,

Just who do you think you are, complaining like that in your letter about a product as good as ours. We have been in business in that town of yours for over thirty years and never in all those years has anyone ever complained. Why do you suppose we guarantee our products! Are you sure you installed it right? Did you read the directions? Are you sure you have the right one for your model car? Our products are so

carefully inspected that I find it hard to believe
that a part could be faulty. Maybe you just are not
mechanically good. Why not take your car to a good
garage.

But since we do guarantee all our products, and
since you claim the part was faulty when you took it
out of the package, I guess that in line with company policy of <u>Caveat</u> <u>Venditor</u> we'll have to send
you a new one. To get a replacement, send us the
faulty one so we can check it, and we will send the
new one out as soon as we can. But we are pretty
busy now and it may take some time to get around to
it.

Hoping to do more business with you in the future, I
remain

respectivelly yours,

Jones Auto Supply Company

John H. Dillman

Manager

JHD/oc

9. Rewrite the following letters answering claims. Keep in mind consideration of the
   reader, a positive tone, a courteous attitude, and a convincing letter. Correct all
   grammar, misspelling, and incorrect punctuation.

   a. We are awful sorry to hear that your having trouble
      with your're Ames vacuum cleaner. You must have let
      it get to full or something, or did some other thing
      wrong, because most women use them successfully. We
      sure dont get many gripes like your's. It is a defi-
      nate convenience if it is used properly and reasona-
      bly, but they wont take all the dirt from your
      floors over a long period of time without being emp-
      tied.

      We have referred your inquiry of September 28 rela-
      tive to a new plastic pully to the manufacturer with
      the request that they contact you directly.

      This in view of the fact that we do not stock parts.
      Well known people say that Ames cleaners give com-
      plete satisfaction for a lifetime if people are
      smart enough to take care of them. We hope you are
      so you dont get no more problems with a good product
      like ours.

   b. We cannot dig your fault finding with our Fruit Loz-
      enges you claim you bought recently. Our products
      are always fresh and demand for them is so great

that they cannot possibly get stale. Are you sure
you didnt buy it ages ago, stick it back on the
shelf and forget it until the other day?

Anyway even though it is against company policy we
are sending you two free boxes of Fruit Lozenges to
pacify you. After all what do you expect for a lousy
20 cents a box.

c. We are sorry to have your complaint about the poor
performance of our Super 8 batteries. You claim your
radio was damaged. Under separate cover we are sending you a new radio which we hope is not inferior to
the one you submitted to us under our guarantee.
Super 8 batteries are included. They were tested be-
forehand for any obvious defects.

Less than ½ percent of our total production is unsatisfactory, and we are usually inclined to feel
that the user of the radio is at fault, not the batteries. Since it is possible for some defective batteries to slip by our rigid inspection process, we
follow the practice of replacing any damaged flash-
lights that are called to our attention.

It is unfortunate that you have had this inconvenience. We trust you will experience no further difficulties with our product.

10. Use the following information to write Letters A.–F. on claims and adjustments.

On August 6, 198–, you sent in an order card, account number 773 X 540-9, to the James C. Herter Co., Inc., 693 West Tenth Street, St. Louis, Missouri 00000, ordering a set of antique Colonial candlesticks made of solid brass. The terms of the agreement were as follows. Examine for ten days. If satisfied, send $3.98 per month for 6 months, or pay the full amount of $25.90 plus $3.98 for postage and handling.

The shipment arrived on 20 August, and you find upon opening the box that it contains a brass Revere bowl. Since you have to buy a wedding gift for a close friend, you decide to keep the bowl, but you still want the candlesticks for yourself. There is no invoice with the bowl, so you have no idea of its cost.

a. *Letter A:* On August 22, you write to the company explaining the error, and you tell them that you want to keep the bowl. You request a bill and stress the fact that you still want the candlesticks.

b. *Letter B:* On August 23 (the day after you mail your letter), you receive a letter from a Mr. George Leavens, District Manager of the James C. Herter Co., Inc., 741 North Billingsly Road, St. Louis, Missouri, stating that an error may have been made in your order. He tells you that if there is an error, to let him know in the enclosed, postage paid, return-addressed envelope immediately, and he will send instructions on how to return the merchandise. It is obvious that he has not read your letter of 22 August.

c. *Letter C:* On August 25, you write to Mr. Leavens at the address given in his letter to you, telling him the same things that you said in the letter to the company sent to the West Tenth St. address and asking him please to check on the matter for you.

While waiting for an answer from Mr. Leavens, you receive on August 30 a bill for the candlesticks, which you have never received. On September 1, you get a package from the Herter Co. containing another brass bowl and again no bill for it. You did not open the package because it states the contents on the outside of the box. Exasperated and disgusted, you make two copies of every piece of correspondence, including a reminder that arrived on September 5 of an overdue payment for the candlesticks. You write two cover letters: one to Mr. Leavens and one to the company at the West Tenth St. address and attach to each a complete file of all the correspondence, making a total of four enclosures of past correspondence. A carbon copy of Mr. Leavens' letter goes to the West Tenth St. address, and a carbon copy of the letter to that address goes to Mr. Leavens, making a total of five enclosures for each letter.

d. *Letter D:* September 9. This letter to Mr. Leavens explains that you have enclosed copies of all the correspondence with him and with the shipping plant. You explain about the payment reminder for merchandise not received, the receipt of the second unwanted bowl, and reiterate the following statements: (1) You will keep the first bowl. (2) You want a bill for the first bowl. (3) You do not want the second bowl. (4) You still want the candlesticks. You ask him please to straighten out the whole bloody mess!

e. *Letter E:* This letter goes to the West Tenth St. address, to which the original order was sent. You tell them that they have not received payment for the candlesticks because you have not received them. You state that the attached correspondence will explain the problem. You ask them to contact the district manager, Mr. Leavens, to solve the problem.

f. *Letter F:* On September 18, you finally get a letter from Mr. Leavens, written September 15. He has received your letter of September 9 and is sorry about the mix-up. Enclosed is a shipping label for the package to be returned and a postcard already addressed to be mailed separately when the package is shipped. On the card is a place for the date of shipment, the town from which shipment is made, and the insurance number, if any. There is also a check for $1.23 to pay for postage. He also says that he has placed a rush order for the candlesticks, which you should receive within fifteen days.

Design the shipping label and the return card to be attached to the letters you write.

7

The Credit Process

Credit today has become as indispensible to our lives as salt and pepper are to our eating habits. Instead of cash, we use plastic cards. We finance cars, mortgage homes, and use revolving charge plans in department stores or in ordering by mail. Businesses receive and extend credit. In fact, one could say that the whole economy of the United States runs on credit. Even the Soviet Union honors some major credit cards in stores reserved for foreigners. Young children soon learn to say "charge it."

What Is Credit?

Exactly what is credit? Why do we need it? How do we get it? How do we keep it? Who determines who gets it and how much they get?

The word *credit* comes from the Latin word *credo,* meaning "I believe." Thus, when an individual is granted credit, he or she accepts a privilege with obligations. The grantor is saying in effect, "I believe in you — your honesty and integrity, your ability to pay, and your intent to fulfill your obligations." When a business is granted credit, the supplier is indicating a belief in the management and the solvency of the business. In this way businesses can maintain their inventory. They in turn extend credit to the consumer.

For the consumer, credit has many uses. It is the only way most people can buy cars, homes, or other large purchases, or finance their children's education. Credit helps in an emergency when one is short of ready cash, and it can allow the home manager to take advantage of special sales without having to keep large amounts of cash on hand. Travelers, in particular, do not like to flash large amounts of money and, therefore, rely heavily on charge cards for everything from telephone calls to hotel bills. Business people rely on the detailed records from charges for tax purposes as well as reimbursement for expenses. Banks profit by charging interest on loans and credit card accounts.

Asking for Credit

There are two ways of asking for credit. One is a simple letter requesting credit; the other, and more common, is the credit application.

To speed the process of getting the credit desired, the writer must supply certain information. Failure to do so can mean time lost in unnecessary extra correspondence. The most important information in the letter for a business asking for credit is contained in the list of references. This list should include a bank, at least two firms with whom the applicant has done business long enough to establish a rating, and any listings in the National Trade Reporting Services such as Dun & Bradstreet, Moody's and Nestor Service, and Standard and Poor's Corporation. The applicant may include any other pertinent information needed to determine credit worthiness that may not be in a financial statement.

Example 7–1 is a typical credit application for the individual consumer. Notice the questions asked. Although the applicant can check one of the blocks for Mr., Miss, etc., such information is not required under the law. Note also that the application asks for the number of dependents, not whether the dependents are children or a spouse. Creditors can no longer ask about child-raising intentions, marital status, or sex. They can no longer ignore as income court-ordered alimony or child support, nor can they end credit because of a change in marital status.

Example 7–2 is a sample letter from an individual consumer wanting to open a department store account. Note that the references here include other department stores and also the name of the bank with which the family has accounts. Example 7–3 is from a store requesting credit without including an order. Example 7–4 is a similar letter, which includes an order and a financial statement. Example 7–5 is a letter asking for a raise in the credit limit.

Credit Ratings

Not too many years ago consumers were kept in the dark about their credit ratings. The only way they knew whether their rating was good or bad was if their application for credit had been approved or rejected. Today, the laws protecting the consumer are quite specific. Businesses, however, are not quite as well protected and can be refused credit more easily than the individual. Consumer displeasure with the secrecy of credit information collection agencies did much to prompt the passage of laws now in existence.

Until the Fair Credit Reporting Act of 1970, it was nearly impossible for an individual to determine why he was refused credit, or who gave the poor or incorrect rating, because the records were confidential. The FCRA gives con-

EXAMPLE 7–1 Consumer Application

CHARGE APPLICATION

JASPER'S 7960 CUMQUAT STREET RASONOLLA, IL 00000
Request subject to Jasper's credit approval
Allow 3 weeks for processing

Mr. ☐   Mrs. ☐

Miss ☐   Ms. ☐   Name_____ Home phone_____

Address_____ City_____ State_____ Zip_____

How long at this address_____ Own ☐   Rent ☐   Board ☐   Other ☐ _____

Previous address if less than 2 years_____

How long _____

Age_____ Number of Dependents_____

Employer_____ How long_____

Address_____ Business phone _____

Occupation_____ Salary_____ Weekly ☐   Monthly ☐   Yearly ☐

Previous employer if less than 1 year_____ How long_____

Other income_____ Weekly ☐   Monthly ☐   Yearly ☐   Source_____

Bank name_____ Bank address_____

Kind of account: Savings ☐   Checking ☐   Mortgage ☐   Loan ☐

Credit references – Bank cards, stores, finance companies, etc.:

Name_____ Account No._____ Address_____

Name_____ Account No._____ Address_____

Name_____ Account No._____ Address_____

Nearest relative not at present address_____

Relationship _____

Name_____ Address_____

I understand that my orders for products will be subject to the terms specified in the current catalogue. I also understand you may order a consumer report on me and will, at my request, tell me if such a request was made and the names of the reporting agency.

Applicant signature_____ Date_____
Social Security number _____

EXAMPLE 7–2   Consumer Letter Asking for Credit

10 Pierpoint Circle
Hancock, AL 00000
September 2, 198—

Handles Department Store
76—A Citation Mall
Hancock, AL 00000

Gentlemen:

With my family, I have recently moved to Hancock and would
like to open a charge account at Handles Department Store.
Prior to the move I had accounts with Hollands, Acct. #79—
64312; Monson's, Acct. #8940; and Hobart's, Acct. #116935 —
all department stores in Hollandia, AL. If you check with
them, you will find I had active accounts and a fine credit
rating.

Here in Hancock we are banking at Hancock National Bank and
have both a savings account and a checking account. We also
own our own home.

Please send me an application form at your earliest convenience.

Very truly yours,

Alma Homestar

Alma Homestar
(Mrs. Axel Homestar)

EXAMPLE 7–3   Store Requesting Credit without an Order

Junior Boutique
9 Foxfire Circle
Santa Fe, NM 00000

August 10, 198—

The Mulberry Bush, Ltd.
Stratford
England

Gentlemen:

Smythe—Colton of London with whom we have been doing business
on open account for ten years has recommended The Mulberry
Bush as a source of fine kilts made from 100 percent wool in
authentic tartans.

We would like to open an account with you according to your
regular terms. We expect our first order to be about $1,500,
with regular monthly orders of $750 to $1,000.

In addition to Smythe—Colton, we refer you to:

        Supernational Bank
        Main Avenue
        Santa Fe, NM 00000
        U.S.A.

        Giovanni's
        Via Paloma
        Rome, Italy

As soon as we hear from you, we will place our first order,
which we are now putting together.

Very truly yours,

Junior Boutique

T. Jacques Fox

T. Jacques Fox
Purchasing Agent

mk

EXAMPLE 7–4   Store Requesting Credit with an Order

Junior Boutique
9 Foxfire Circle
Santa Fe, NM   00000

August 10, 198–

Holiday Wholesale House
Blacksmith Plaza
Dawson, NM   00000

Gentlemen:

Attached you will find our order No. 0534. We would appreciate your sending the order on open account according to your
regular terms of 2/10 net 30.

Because this is our first order with you, we refer you to the
following companies with whom we have been buying on open account for five years and our bank for credit references.

     Delta Clothing Manufacturers
     Smelters Depot
     Acton, NM   00000

     Petite Originals, Inc.
     Sunspot Road
     Clearwater, FL   00000

We have also included a recent financial statement. Information as to when we might expect shipment will be greatly appreciated.

Sincerely,

Junior Boutique

T. Jacques Fox

T. Jacques Fox
Purchasing Agent

mk

Enc: 2

EXAMPLE 7–5 Request for Raise of Credit Limit

Junior Boutique
9 Foxfire Circle
Santa Fe, NM 00000

August 10, 198–

Marchant and Manning
Wilkinson Parkway So.
Fortune, TN 00000

Attention: Credit Manager

Gentlemen:

For the past five years, Junior Boutique has been ordering
from Marchant and Manning on a monthly basis. We have always
paid our bills in time to take advantage of your 2 percent
discount.

We would now like to have our credit line raised from $1,000
to $3,000. This would allow us to increase our inventory oc-
casionally for special sales promotions.

Look at our most recent financial statement, which is attached, and you will see that Junior Boutique is sound and
steadily increasing its assets.

We would appreciate a quick answer.

Sincerely,

Junior Boutique

T. Jacques Fox

T. Jacques Fox
Purchasing Agent

mk

Encl. 1

sumers the right to see all the information compiled and the names of those contributing that information. Consumers can demand the names of all who have received such reports. They can correct faulty reports and have the corrections sent to all who have made the inquiries, and they can have all outdated and/or inaccurate information removed.

The Fair Credit Reporting Act was followed in 1974 by the "Credit Billing" amendment to the Truth-in-Lending Act, the 1975 Privacy Act, and the 1975 Equal Credit Opportunity Act. The ECOA prohibits discrimination because of sex or marital status. Until this law went into effect, a single, widowed, or divorced woman usually could not get credit in her own name for major purchases such as a car or house. Even today some car salespeople will not discuss the purchase of a car with a married woman if her husband is not present, even when it is the woman who is buying the car and will be the one to drive it. Such people have to be reminded that their attitude is illegal. Until recently, a man's credit rating died with him. Today, credit cards and charge accounts are usually listed in both the husband's and wife's names and each has his or her own card. Single women with adequate income no longer have a problem in obtaining credit. The laws are strict and the penalties severe for violation. Unfortunately, the more red tape involving businesses and the laws, the greater the business expense, which is in turn passed on to the consumer.

Who Gets Credit?

Most businesses issuing credit have a credit department with its own manager and personnel. Its functions are to maintain and promote credit accounts; the credit department determines who gets how much under what terms. While the department must collect overdue bills, it may also help a financially troubled customer plan payments to fit changed circumstances by revising an original agreement. Because businesses want to stay in business by keeping customers, it is to their advantage to collect in full over a longer period rather than not to collect at all, or to go to collection agencies or court.

Four criteria are universally used to determine who gets credit. An applicant must meet at least three of them and give indication that the remaining one will be met at a later date.

Character.   Character in this context is the individual's or management's attitude toward responsibilities involved in credit and other areas. A sense of ethics, fairness, and honesty are far more important than most people realize. Character is evaluated by looking at the reputation and past actions of the applicant. Ability and money cannot overcome a reputation for cheating, dishonesty, and refusing to pay debts.

Capacity.   Having the ability to run a business and thereby having the ability to pay one's bills is important. Can the individual make good decisions? How well does he or she know the business? Can the individual work well with colleagues and employees? Can he or she manage personnel? Does he or she know how to judge the market? Will he or she overstock and be forced to sell at a loss or be realistic in buying and sell profitably? Does the individual advertise effectively? Can he or she keep accurate records? Does he or she have an awareness of tax responsibilities? These and numerous other points are considered when evaluating the capacity of a credit applicant.

Capital.   An old adage describes succinctly the need for capital or backing. "Them as has, gits!" To get credit, income or capital must be greater than expenditures. Cash-in-hand plus convertible assets, stock already on hand, and ownership of property all add up to backing or capital and as indications of potential success exert great influence in the decision to grant credit.

Conditions.   The current state of the economy is considered carefully. When unemployment is high, money is scarce, and consumers do not spend as they would when there is a steady income. Questions that would be asked might be: Is the product a luxury or a necessity? Does the applicant have unfilled orders? Is there really a demand for the product or service?

Location is another consideration. Is the business in an area subject to periodic flooding, which could mean severe loss of stock and business? Is there adequate insurance coverage? Is the business in an area subject to vandalism or riots?

Based on evaluation in terms of these four criteria, credit applicants fall into three categories.

1. The *good risk* meets all the criteria to a considerable degree, has a good reputation, and enjoys a good credit rating by paying bills promptly.
2. The *fair risk* meets at least three of the criteria to varying degrees, but although he or she pays regularly, it is slowly. While the fair risk generally can get credit, it is often for less than the amount desired.
3. The *bad risk* may meet one or two of the criteria to some degree. This person has a reputation for paying bills erratically, is almost always late in remitting, and sometimes does not pay at all. Some of his or her business dealings may have been questionable and this individual may not be noted for honesty and fair dealing with customers.

Types of Credit Available to Consumers

For the consumer four types of credit are available: the thirty-day account, the ninety-day account, the revolving account, and the long-term installment plan.

The thirty-day account.   The most well known and perhaps the oldest is the thirty-day account. The customer charges purchases, receives a monthly bill on a specific date to be paid in full within 10–30 days from the billing date. A finance charge may be added on any balance after the due date, the maximum percentage determined by law. There is usually a notation at the bottom or back of the bill reading like the following:

A Finance Charge at the periodic rate of 1.50 percent up to $500 and a periodic rate of 1 percent of the excess over $500 which will be applied to the previous balance after deducting payments and credits which is the net amount outstanding 30 days or more after billing date including unpaid finance charges. To avoid additional finance charges, please pay amount due within thirty days of the above billing date.

The ninety-day account. The ninety-day account is one in which the payments are made in three equal payments with no interest charges unless payment is late. This kind of agreement is used quite often for larger purchases such as televisions, washers, or refrigerators.

The revolving account. The revolving account has become more and more popular. Mail order houses in particular promote this type of account as do many large department stores. The seller sets a credit line for each charge customer — the maximum a customer may owe — and sets a scale of monthly payments depending on the amount owed. A monthly finance charge is levied against the unpaid average daily balance; the percentage is determined by law and varies according to the size of the balance due. The account holder may pay in full at any time to avoid the finance charges or may pay any amount over the minimum due to lower the charges assessed. The consumer can continue to make purchases up to the amount of the credit line.

Good credit risks who clear their accounts at regular intervals or who consistently pay more than the minimum due may eventually have their credit line raised. The minimum payments vary from business to business, but the average is about 10 percent of the total amount due. Some businesses also state on their bills that in the event of a late payment they can call in the whole amount due.

Examples 7–6 and 7–7 are sample tables of payments for this type of account, including the finance charges and how the average daily balance can be computed. Note the different payments and finance charges in Examples 7–6 and 7–7.

In all types of accounts, the consumer has the right to dispute what he or she believes to be an error. For the laws governing the right to dispute, refer to Chapter 8, "Payments and the Collection Process."

The long-term installment plan. The long-term installment plan is a contract between buyer and seller for a particular item with a specified number of payments and a set finance charge included in those payments. The term of the contract may run from six to thirty-six or forty-eight months. Six to twelve months is the usual time for appliances, while thirty-six to forty-eight months is the usual time for cars.

EXAMPLE 7–6 Sample Table of Payment for a Revolving Account

When the Highest New Balance Reaches:	The New Minimum Monthly Payment Will Be:
$ .01 to $ 10.00	Balance
10.01 to 160.00	$10.00
160.01 to 180.00	11.00
180.01 to 200.00	12.00
200.01 to 220.00	13.00
220.01 to 240.00	14.00
240.01 to 260.00	15.00
260.01 to 290.00	16.00
291.01 to 340.00	17.00
340.01 to 380.00	18.00
380.01 to 410.00	19.00
410.01 to 440.00	20.00
440.01 to 470.00	21.00
470.01 to 500.00	22.00

You may always pay more than the required minimum monthly payment. The minimum payment will change only if charges to the account increase the balance to a new high. The minimum payment will not decrease until the New Balance is paid in full.

Over $500.00 – 1/23rd of Highest Account Balance rounded to next higher whole dollar amount.

Finance Charge. If the entire New Balance is not paid within *30* days (*28* days for February statements) of the monthly billing date, a FINANCE CHARGE will be added to the account for the current monthly billing period. The FINANCE CHARGE will be either a minimum *50¢*, if the Average Daily Balance is $28.50 or less, or a periodic rate of *1.75%* per month (ANNUAL PERCENTAGE RATE of *21%*) on the Average Daily Balance.

How to Determine the Average Daily Balance. Jackson's will determine each day's outstanding balance in the monthly billing period and divide the total of these daily balances by the number of days in the monthly billing period. The result is the Average Daily Balance. Jackson's will include the current month's charges but will not include unpaid Finance or Insurance Charge(s), if any, when determining a daily balance. All payments and other credits will be subtracted from the previous day's balance.

EXAMPLE 7–7   Sample Table of Payment for a Revolving Account

Hobart Credit Terms

Minimum Monthly Payment	$ 20	25	30	35	40	45
Buys Up To	$ 300	600	750	900	1,050	1,200
Minimum Monthly Payment	$ 50	55	60	65	70	75
Buys Up To	$1,350	1,500	1,650	1,800	1,950	2,100

On accounts with maximum balances higher than $2,100, the minimum payment increases $5.00 for every additional $150.00 maximum account balance or part thereof. All credit orders are subject to credit approval.

FINANCE CHARGES

FINANCE CHARGES on the monthly payment plan are computed by the Average Daily Balance method, which is the sum of the actual daily balances each day during the billing cycle divided by the number of days in that cycle, calculated at a periodic rate of 1.995% monthly (or a minimum of 50¢ monthly on balances under $25.06), which is an ANNUAL PERCENTAGE RATE of 23.94% (except for residents of states listed below). Hobart reserves the right to change the terms of this agreement upon advance written notice to you as required by law. Any change in items will be applied to your existing balance and future purchases. Payments are credited on the day of receipt, early payments or payments in excess of minimum payment due result in smaller FINANCE CHARGES. There is no FINANCE CHARGE if the first statement is paid in full within 25 days of the statement date. If on any subsequent statement your NEW BALANCE is paid in full within 25 days of the statement date, there will be no further FINANCE CHARGE.

Residents of Ala., Alaska, Calif., Colo., Conn., Ind., Iowa, Kans., Maine, Md., Mass., Mich., N.C., Okla., Pa., S.C., S.Dak., Wash., W.Va., Wis. and Wyo. write to us at the following address for credit terms in your state. Hobart, P.O. Box 22222, Forest Heights, TX 00000.

Credit for Businesses

For businesses there are three general types of accounts. The most common for the business with a good rating is the *open account*. This account is quite similar to the consumer thirty-day account. Charges are made regularly with the terms thirty days net. Some suppliers may offer a 2 percent discount if the bill is paid within ten days and is noted on the bill as 2/10 net 30. If an open account customer fails to pay, the creditor cannot repossess the products but must rely on other methods to collect. For details on these methods refer to Chapter 8 on collection letters.

In a *secured credit agreement* the applicant signs a contract of some kind such as a conditional sales agreement or a chattel mortgage. Should this applicant fail to pay, the creditor can repossess. This type of credit contract is like that the car buyer signs. Failure to pay the installments can result in repossession of the car by the dealer.

A *partial credit grant* is a limited line of credit often extended to a new business on a wait-and-see attitude. It is much like the credit line set for a consumer revolving account except that the business must pay in full every month. Once the new business has established a good reputation, the creditor may increase the amount of credit allowed or even offer an open account instead.

Answering Requests for Credit

Granting Credit

When a request for credit can be granted immediately, the answer is usually easy to write. The letter often begins with a welcoming statement and continues with an explanation of the company's terms and a reselling of the products or services. If an order was included with the request for credit, the letter would tell when and how it would be shipped. Examples 7–8 and 7–9 are positive answers to credit requests, and Examples 7–10 and 7–11 are compromises.

When granting credit is delayed because of insufficient information or because a credit check has to be made, the letter opens with a welcome and then explains the delay (see Example 7–12). The writer may include an application to be filled in, ask for references, or stress the routineness of the credit check. If an order was included, the writer offers alternatives to charging by suggesting COD for the first shipment. If the order was an unusually large one, the writer may suggest a smaller order COD immediately, holding the rest of the order until either the necessary information is received or the credit check is completed.

EXAMPLE 7–8 Consumer Request for Credit Granted

Handel's Department Store
76-A Citation Mall
Hancock, AL 00000

Everything for the Home and Family

September 10, 198—

Mrs. Axel Homestar
10 Pierpont Circle
Hancock, AL 00000

Dear Mrs. Homestar:

Welcome to Hancock and to the growing Handel family. We are happy to include in this letter your Handel charge card. Your account is ready for your use, and we look forward to the pleasure of serving you soon.

Our terms are simple. You will be billed on the tenth of each month with payment due in 30 days. Should you need to spread your payments over an extended period, the minimum amount due each month is 10 percent of the total due. A small finance charge would be added based on the average daily balance. All transactions will be noted in detail on each statement.

Come in and take advantage of our pre—season sale on winter coats and suits and boots for the whole family. For those cold winter nights, there is nothing nicer than our fleecy electric blankets. Visit all our departments and simply say "Charge it" when you see something you would like to have.

Cordially yours,

Sally Trigger

Sally Trigger
Credit Manager

cjm

Enc: 1

EXAMPLE 7–9   Store Request for Credit Granted

The Mulberry Bush, Ltd.
Stratford, England
Cable — Bush

September 1, 198—

Mr. T. Jacques Fox, Purchasing Agent
Junior Boutique
9 Foxfire Circle
Santa Fe, NM 00000

Dear Mr. Fox:

We are pleased to open an account for you at The Mulberry
Bush. The delay in answering your letter was partly due to
the postal service and the time it takes to do the routine
credit check procedures we follow for all new customers.
Smythe—Colton of London spoke very highly of the way you handle your account with them, as did your other references.

Our terms are the usual 2/10 net 30. Shipping charges are
added to your monthly statement, as they must be prepaid.
Your import taxes will be paid in the United States and will
not be reflected in your open account #US79646B.

Your order will be processed the day it arrives. Air freight
is the quickest means of delivery to the states with UPS from
the airport to your store. Ground shipment is slow but less
expensive. Please include your preference in your order.

Thank you for including us as one of your overseas suppliers.
You will be pleased with the quality and beauty of our kilts.
You may also want to try our matching lamb's wool sweaters.

We are airmailing our latest catalogue and fabric samplers.

Sincerely,

Fenwick C. Winterbottom

Fenwick C. Winterbottom
Credit Manager, The Mulberry Bush

dlh

EXAMPLE 7–10   Compromise on Credit Request

The Mulberry Bush, Ltd.
Stratford, England
Cable — Bush

August 25, 198–

Mr. T. Jacques Fox, Purchasing Agent
Junior Boutique
9 Foxfire Circle
Santa Fe, NM 00000

Dear Mr. Fox:

Thank you for your interest in an account with The Mulberry Bush. It is pleasant to know we have such a good reputation for authenticity and quality in our tartans and woolens.

During the thirty years we have been in business, we have limited our open accounts to the British Isles only, except for what we call our modified thirty-day account offered to overseas businesses with impeccable reputations and ratings. Because Smythe-Colton of London as well as your other references gave you such fine recommendations, we are pleased to offer you our modified account. The terms are simple: one-third of the total amount to accompany the order, the balance due in thirty days. Shipment can be made by sea or air with shipping charges added to the balance due. A finance charge of 20 percent will be levied on any overdue balance.

Your modified account is ready for your use and your order will be processed as soon as your accompanying check is cleared. We look forward to serving you in the immediate future. If for any reason you are dissatisfied with any items, you can, of course, return them at our expense.

Sincerely,

Fenwick C. Winterbottom

Fenwick C. Winterbottom
Credit Manager, The Mulberry Bush

dlh

EXAMPLE 7–11   Compromise on Request for Raise of Credit Line

---

Marchant and Manning
Wilkinson Parkway So.
Fortune, TN 00000

The Best in Girls' and Women's Attire for All Occasions

August 21, 198—

Mr. T. Jacques Fox
Purchasing Agent
Junior Boutique
9 Foxfire Circle
Santa Fe, NM 00000

Dear Mr. Fox:

We have been considering your request for raising your credit
line from $1,000 to $3,000. While your business is certainly
sound according to your financial statement, we feel that a
$2,000 increase at this time is rather high. We believe a
safer increase would be $1,000, raising your credit line to
$2,000. Should the coming year prove to be as successful as
your records indicate it will, we will then be prepared to
consider favorably another increase.

We hope the suggested compromise will serve your purposes. We
value your continued patronage and feel that our decision is
in your best interests.

Sincerely,

Henry J. Manning

Henry J. Manning
Financial Vice-President
Marchant and Manning

EXAMPLE 7–12 Delay of Credit Acceptance

Brook Supply Depot
Railroad Street
Caboose, NY 00000

Lamps — Fixtures — Wiring
for Home and Business

January 26, 198–

Mr. Anthony Giselle
Giselle Hardware Co.
South Main Avenue
Coleson, NY 00000

Dear Mr. Giselle:

Thank you for your interest in an account with Brook Supply
Depot. While we welcome new customers, it is our usual practice to ask for credit references. As you did not list any in
your letter, would you take the time to do so now by simply
filling in the enclosed application.

If you are in a hurry for the lamps and fixtures you ordered,
may we send them C.O.D.? If you agree, just call 000–0000 and
ask for Mary. She will set the process in motion, and your
order should be at your store within three days.

Should we not hear from you, we will assume you prefer to
wait for your account to be activated.

Sincerely,

Sigmund Brook

Sigmund Brook

km

Enc.

Refusing Credit

When refusing credit, the writer must be very careful not to violate the laws governing the credit process. The content of the refusal letter will vary according to the reasons for the denial. These reasons may range from the applicant's being a deadbeat to an applicant's having temporary financial difficulties. The writer must keep in mind that the applicant may one day be solvent and be the kind of person or business the company may want as a charge customer. In the interim the company would like to get the applicant as a cash customer. The writer must then convince the applicant that there are good reasons for cash buying, such as keeping inventory up to date, especially in the rapidly changing world of fashion or seasonable items. Smaller orders mean smaller inventory, which in turn means greater turnover and thus more shelf space for new items. Cash buying can then lead to a sound financial basis for the business, resulting in the development of a good rating upon which credit can be established.

The refusal letter usually takes a middle-of-the-road approach. While it may express appreciation for the request, it in no way implies that credit will be granted. An order if included is acknowledged. When getting into the refusal itself, the writer should not use a lecturing tone, should try to avoid the negative, and without being condescending indicate concern about the applicant's company. The letter ends by making alternative suggestions such as layaway for consumers or COD for business and consumers alike.

If the refusal is based on information from sources other than the applicant, such as a credit reporting agency, the writer must supply the name and address of that agency. If the informant is a third party that is not a credit reporting agency, then the business refusing credit must tell the applicant that he or she has sixty days in which to learn the type of information on which the decision was based.

Any business or individual who gives second-hand information or who makes a subjective judgment becomes under the law a credit reporting agency. Therefore, the writer of the refusal letter must stick to the facts and use extremely careful language. For example, assume you own a retail store and you get a request from retail store X for a credit check on Mr. Someone who wants to open a charge account at store X. Mr. Someone is a poor payer and sometimes lets his bills run two or three months overdue. You have to send him dunning letters quite regularly and once had to take him to small claims court. You cannot tell store X that Mr. Someone is in your opinion a deadbeat, but you can say that Mr. Someone did not pay his January bill of $50.75 until April 16 after you had sent him a reminder on February 1, March 1, and April 1. The facts speak for themselves and no judgment is necessary.

When evaluating information supplied by consumers whose incomes are not sufficient to warrant the kind of credit they want, the writer can be more candid and say that at the present time their income is just barely sufficient to meet their current expenses and obligations, and you would not want to add to their financial burdens (see Example 7–13). In this way, the writer is dealing with facts and is not making any value judgments or casting reflections on character. While the applicants may not like the refusal, they know the decision was made objectively. They might still become cash customers until their financial conditions allow for credit.

Getting Credit Information about Potential Customers

Much has been said about getting credit information about a potential customer. How does a business go about it? The process is fairly simple. Some firms have a request card as in Example 7–14, or a request letter such as in Example 7–15.

While fairness is important when giving information about a business or individual customer, careful wording is even more important. Give in writing only facts and such information as you know firsthand. What is said or implied in conversation is another matter, as it is one person's word against another's. But care must still be exercised to avoid accusations. The following example is a typical factual response.

```
Dear Mr. Pender:

     1. Junior Boutique has paid its bills promptly and
only once, in October of this year, failed to take advan-
tage of our 2 percent discount if payment is made within
10 days of billing.
     2. Orders were consistent in size and regularity:
were placed usually on a monthly basis, occasionally twice
a month.
     3. We have never actually imposed a credit line, as
the orders never ran more than $2,500 at any time.
     4. We have been supplying Junior Boutique for 7
years.
```

Occasionally, when giving a bad report, the writer will avoid using the subject's name, as in the following example of a factual response.

```
     Here is an example of the subject's payment habits
taken from our files.

     1. May 1 bill paid July 10. Reminders sent June 1 and
July 1. July bill paid on November 1. Reminders sent Au-
gust 1, September 1, October 1. October 10 account turned
over to collection agency.
     2. Orders varied in amounts and were spasmodic in
coming. Orders sent in on April 20, July 10 of this year.
     3. Credit limit $600.00.
```

EXAMPLE 7–13   Request for Credit Denied

Hereford and Sons
Hardwood Plaza
Mapleville, NH 00000

Cabinet Makers Par Excellence

July 19, 198–

Mr. Marvin Salmon
Salmon's Furniture Mart
Price Alley
Havenhurst, NH 00000

Dear Mr. Salmon:

Thank you for your recent request for an account with us. We have consulted the references you have given us as well as the Jones Credit Information Agency.

The information we received leads us to believe that it is in your best interests that we do not offer you an open account at this time. It appears that you are having difficulty meeting your current obligations and to add another account would only create undue hardship for you.

We would suggest smaller cash orders at regular intervals until things are easier for you financially. In this way you will be able to determine what sells best for you with a minimum outlay. You will also have fresh stock regularly, eliminating the need for storage and the breakage that goes along with it. With a cash purchase we offer a 2 percent discount, so you see, Mr Salmon, you will save all the way along.

Let us know your decision.

Sincerely,

Sanford Singleberry

Sanford Singleberry
Credit Manager

sc

EXAMPLE 7–14   Request Card for Credit Information

Gentlemen:

_____ Company has given your name as a reference in their credit application.

We would appreciate your answering the following questions. Your reply will be kept confidential.

1. How long has the company been buying from you?_____

2. What type of account?_____

3. Terms_____

4. Usual size of the account_____

5. Amount now due_____

6. Maximum credit extended _____

7. Comments _____

_____

_____

Signature_____

Date_____

```
        4. We were subject's supplier for two years until Oc-
    tober 10 when we closed the account.

        We hope this confidential information answers all
    your questions.
```

The next example, a form letter to a bank, asks for information about a company's financial standing:

```
    Gentlemen:

        We are extending credit to _____ of _____ using
    accounts receivable as collateral. We would appreciate any
    information you can give us about the company's ability to
    meet their trade obligations. We are especially interested
    in the company's financial responsibility, borrowing expe-
    rience, and recent checking account.
        All information will be treated confidentially.
```

EXAMPLE 7–15   Request Letter for Credit Information

Holiday Wholesale House
Blacksmith Plaza
Dawson, NM 00000

June 5, 198–

Credit Department
Marchant and Manning
Wilkinson Parkway So.
Fortune, TN 00000

Gentlemen:

Junior Boutique of Santa Fe, NM has given your name as a reference in their credit application to us. We are considering
raising their credit line by 2 to $3,000.

We would appreciate any information you may give us about the
company. Of particular interest is the way they have handled
their account.

    1. Were bills paid promptly?

    2. Were orders sent in regularly?

    3. What were the maximum credit limits for
       their account?

    4. How many years have you been their supplier?

Any information you give us will be treated confidentially,
and if we can reciprocate at any time please let us know.

Sincerely,

Harry Pender

Harry Pender
Credit Manager

st

The answer to such a request is also a form letter:

```
    A regular checking account in (company name) has been
active since (date). Balances are currently averaging
about (general amount, i.e., 6 figures, etc.). The account
has been handled according to the rules governing that
type of account and has never been overdrawn.
    (Company name) has borrowed money and always repaid
loans before the due date.
    We are pleased to send you this confidential informa-
tion.
```

Note that the balance reported by the bank is not actually in dollars but in the number of figures indicating overall volume of business in rounded thousands of dollars. The credit limit granted to the customer will be based on those figures. For instance, if the bank states that Halliwell Products account averages 6 to 7 figures yearly, the inquirer knows that Halliwell is doing business in the one hundred thousand to one million dollar bracket on a regular basis. Since the letter also states that Halliwell has repaid loans ahead of time, the inquirer knows that the company has a top credit rating. Halliwell would, therefore, be extended a higher credit limit in open accounts than would a company whose account was in the 4-figure bracket with a top credit rating.

Honesty is important in all business transactions, but never more so than when asking for, granting, or denying credit. While the laws protect both the seller and the consumer from legal violations with severe penalties of fines and/ or jail sentences, there is little to protect the consumer from ethical violations such as misrepresentation of a product. But a bad reputation or a poor rating with the Better Business Bureau and credit rating companies can be disastrous to a business. Thus in all credit transactions, honesty is still the best policy.

CHECKLIST

The Credit Process

- Asking for credit.
  - a. State name, address, business.
  - b. State type of credit desired.
  - c. Include financial statement when possible and references.
  - d. Add any other pertinent information available to establish credit worthiness.
  - e. Know your rights under the Fair Credit Reporting Act.
- Refusing credit.
  - a. Be courteous — emphasize the "You" attitude.
  - b. Keep in mind you may want applicant as a credit customer later.

   c. Stick to facts but be tactful.

   d. Tell applicant of his right to learn substance and sources of information collected by a Consumer Reporting Agency.

   e. Offer alternatives to credit if situation warrants.

- Reporting credit rating.

   a. Stick to facts.

   b. Give no opinions.

   c. Know the Fair Credit Reporting Act.

EXERCISES

1. Rewrite the following phrases, adding or deleting words as needed to achieve the proper tone.

   a. Our informants tell us you are a deadbeat.

   b. You are a poor risk.

   c. Your reputation is such that we don't want you for a customer.

   d. With your record, the only way we can do business is cash and carry.

   e. How do you expect us to give you, a total stranger, credit when you haven't given us any references?

   f. You must be kidding asking for a charge account at a high-class store like this on your income. Your salary is so low you can hardly pay your rent.

2. Rewrite this letter.

```
Dear Sirs;

     Acknowledging your esteemed favor of March 31st
in which you, per our request, forwarded copies of
your financial statements for the past three years,
we also greatly appreciate the co-operation of your
references who, in due course of time, spoke very
favorably of you.
     A study of your balance sheet, however, calls
for us to kindly advise you of certain points. Per-
mit us to state that the ratio of your current as-
sets to your current liabilities is very low. Upon
investigation we also found the high ratio of ac-
counts receivable to sales very disturbing.
     With a sincere desire to help you we beg to
state that to help you strengthen the financial
structure of your business you should secure $2,000
to $3,000 additional capital. The writer wishes to
state that you should also tighten up on your credit
and collection policies.
     Please be assured that while you are effecting
these changes we will be willing to serve you on a
C.O.D. basis. Why not avail yourself of the opportu-
nity of the cash discounts.
     Hoping to hear from you soon, we remain

                              Regretfully yours,
```

3. You are the manager of a department store. You receive an inquiry from a store in another city asking for information about the credit status of a Mr. Talbot Nunes who wants to open a charge account. Mr. Nunes has been a customer at your store for the past fifteen years. When you check his account, you find that he has been fairly regular in his payments until early this year when he received two reminders of an overdue account. The amount was small, only $10.95, but it took three months to get it. You learn that he had been seriously ill at the time and in the hospital. Since then Mr. Nunes has used his account twice and each time paid promptly. Write an appropriate letter to the other store.

4. You own a wholesale supply house dealing in office furniture. A new store, which has recently opened in your city, has written asking for an open account. The writer lists no references but does include an order for $2,000. Write asking for references and suggesting an alternative plan of purchase.

5. Assume the writer in problem 4 has included references as well as the order.
   a. Write a letter explaining your policy of credit checking, stating your terms, and granting the account on the basis of information received from the references.
   b. Write a letter denying credit on the basis of information received from the sources.

6. You are the credit manager of a company that makes spin-off tops, which look and sound like the movie version of a space ship. The toy has really caught on and you are swamped with orders. One of your regular customers, a small mom-and-pop variety store, has placed an unusually large order for spin-offs. You know that while they have always paid their account on time, it has often been a real hardship for them. You also know that the store's clientele cannot afford expensive toys. In short, you believe the store has overextended itself. Write a letter recommending a smaller first order in line with the amount the store usually spends each month and suggesting a wait-and-see attitude about reorders later on.

7. You receive a letter from the credit manager of a department store in a state across the country asking for information about John Doe, who wants to open a revolving charge account with a credit line of $1,500. Your experience with Mr. Doe has been a bad one. He not only ignored payments but also skipped town still owing $1,000 and leaving no forwarding address. You are angry and appalled that he would dare to use your store as a reference. Write a letter to the other store giving them the facts as you know them. You also want his address so you can try to collect some of what he owes.

8. You receive a letter from one of your customers, the owner of a moderate-sized hardware store, asking for an increase in their credit limit from $1,000 to $2,500. Your check reveals that the store is very sound and has done an unsually large volume of business for a town its size, indicating that many of its customers come from out of town to shop there. The store has been buying from you for the past five years with a good record of payment.
   a. Write a letter granting the increase.
   b. Assume the store's record of payment is only fair. Bills were always paid eventually but sometimes slowly. Each time, however, the owner would always ask for an extension of time so you know he would eventually pay in full.

Write a letter suggesting a compromise of $1,500 for now with the suggestion of reconsidering an additional increase later after seeing how things go.

9. You are new in town and want to open an account at a local department store. Back in the town you left, you had numerous charge accounts and a bank account that you have transferred to a branch of the same bank in the new town. Write a letter to the store asking for an account and giving references.

10. Answer the letter in problem 9 granting the account. Then answer the letter in problem 9 refusing the account.

8

Payments and the Collection Process

Business in the United States is built primarily on credit. According to a United States Department of Commerce survey, between 80 and 95 percent of all purchases are charged. Credit cards, or "plastic money," have become a way of life for the large majority of consumers in this country. Few profit-and-sales–oriented businesses or professions can afford to maintain a "strictly for cash" policy. They rely instead on the elaborate credit research procedures described in Chapter 7 to guarantee that they will be paid.

However, even with the most careful selection of credit customers, collection problems do arise. Perhaps fewer of these problems would occur if more purchasers took the advice of one couple who avoid impulse buying by keeping their credit cards inside a large block of ice in their freezer. While their cards are thawing, these people are forced to take the time to be sure that they really want and can afford a contemplated expenditure.

Consumer Letters and Replies

A customer who fails to meet a payment because of financial problems or discontent should write an explanatory letter *before* his or her obligation is overdue. This letter should be honest and courteous. Not only should this letter account for nonpayment, but it should also offer a proposal for financing or specify what problems need to be solved before payment will be forthcoming. Creditors are generally flexible if the circumstances are adequately explained.

Example 8–1 shows a letter explaining a change in financial condition that necessitates amending the payment agreement. Example 8–2 is a letter

EXAMPLE 8–1   Explanation of Change in Financial Condition

15 Medberry Avenue
Median, NJ 00000
May 14, 198–

Rock's Appliances
25 Weybosset Street
Median, NJ 00000

Gentlemen:

   I have just received the bill for the General Goods refrigerator, Model 832, which I purchased from you on May 8. I
gave a $75 deposit and agreed to pay $100 monthly for eight
months.

   Yesterday I learned that I will be put on part–time work
for the summer because of poor conditions in the jewelry in-
dustry. As my paycheck will be cut in half, I can afford to
send you only $50 monthly during June, July, and August.
Hopefully, I will be working full time by September and will
then start to pay $100 monthly.

   I am enclosing my check for $50 and hope that this new
payment plan will be satisfactory.

                          Sincerely yours,

                          Maisie B. Sudbery

                          Mrs. William Sudbery

Enclosure

EXAMPLE 8–2 Payment Withheld Due to Dissatisfaction

5 East Street
Ocala, WY 00000
June 26, 198—

The China World
600 Broadway
Marston, WY 00000

Gentlemen:

On May 15, I purchased a Belleek jar at your store for
$37.50. When I got home, I discovered that there was a large
crack in the cover.

I mailed the jar back to you and asked that I be sent one in
perfect condition; it has not yet arrived.

I have your bill, which is due in five days, for $37.50. How—
ever, I do not feel that I am obligated to pay until the re—
placement is delivered.

If you cannot send the identical piece or if there is going
to be a delay of more than three weeks, please cancel both my
order and the charges and notify me.

Yours truly,

Roland F. Lacrosse

Roland F. Lacrosse

written when payment is withheld because of dissatisfaction. Examples 8–3 and 8–4 are replies to the above letters. Notice how tactfully each of the situations is handled.

The Collection Process

Sending the Bill

The first step in the collection process is sending a bill, which usually contains an itemized list of the charges for goods or services as well as the date on which payment is due. According to the Fair Credit Billing Act of 1975, any creditor who extends open-end credit of more than four installments or charges interest on an unpaid balance must inform customers of certain rights. Generally these rights, which apply to billing errors and actual interest rates, are printed on the bill or on an accompanying sheet. The creditor must, when the customer is given a time period in which to pay a bill without finance charge, mail or deliver the bill within fourteen days before the end of the period.

However, sometimes the process is not concluded because debtors, for various reasons, do not settle. The reasons for nonsettlement fall into four categories.

1. *Neglect* — Some debtors are careless about paying their bills.
2. *Inability* — Some debtors become financially unable to meet their obligations.
3. *Dissatisfaction* — Some debtors are displeased with either the merchandise or services or they believe that the charges are unjust.
4. *Dishonesty* — Some debtors have no intention of paying.

When a bill becomes overdue, the collection letter writer begins the attempt to collect. Because the first assumption is that the debtor is merely forgetful, the writer's goal is twofold: (1) to retain the customer's good will and (2) to obtain the payment as soon as possible.

Collection Letters

All good collection letters are written with a tactful "You" attitude. The sender should constantly demonstrate how the receiver will benefit by paying promptly. From the first appeal to common human nature (e.g., "We all forget sometimes") to the final appeal through fear (e.g., "Turning your account over to our attorney will affect your fine credit rating"), the emphasis must be on the reader's interests. The Fair Debt Collection Practices Act of 1978 prohibits abusive debt collection practices such as threatening harm to the debtor, his property, or reputation; harassing by telephone, mail, or in person; unreasonably publicizing debt information; or making false statements about what can be done to the debtor or about the amount owed.

EXAMPLE 8–3   Reply to Explanation of Change in Financial Condition

---

Rock's Appliances
25 Weybosset Street
Median, NJ 00000

May 20, 198–

Mrs. William Sudbery
15 Medberry Avenue
Median, NJ 00000

Dear Mrs. Sudbery

We appreciate your frank letter concerning the payment plan
for your May 8 purchase and are pleased to grant your request.

Because of your circumstances, we shall expect $50 monthly
for the next two months, $100 monthly from September through
February, and a final $50 payment in March.

Your new General Goods Food Master with its frostless freezer
and automatic ice maker will, we know, provide you with many
years of care-free pleasure. Congratulations on this wise investment.

Sincerely

John P. Doakes

John P. Doakes
Manager
Rock's Appliances

JD/pih

EXAMPLE 8–4   Reply to Payment Withheld Due to Dissatisfaction

The China World
600 Broadway
Marston, WY 00000

July 1, 198–

Mr. Roland F. Lacrosse
5 East Street
Ocala, WY 00000

Dear Mr. Lacrosse:

We have placed a rush order for your Belleek jar, and it should arrive at our warehouse within ten days. We will send it to you immediately.

Please disregard our May 31 statement as we will cancel those charges and enclose your new bill with the jar.

We hope that these plans are satisfactory. Please call our Customer Service Department (1–800–000–0000) if you have any questions.

Sincerely yours,

Malcolm Reeves

Malcolm Reeves
Customer Service Representative

wrk

An in-depth study of credit and collection legislation is not within the scope of this book; however, copies of the Fair Credit Billing Act, the Fair Debt Collection Practices Act, and other pertinent updated information can be obtained by writing to: The Federal Trade Commission, Washington, DC 20580.

Although increasing forcefulness is used in this series of letters to one party, never should the letter employ accusations or offensive wording. Avoid such expressions as:

We must conclude that you are dishonest.
You are a deadbeat.
You didn't deserve our trust in you.
You have ignored our requests for money.
We cannot understand your failure to pay.

Each collection letter should contain:

1. Specific details about what the debt is for: date(s) and exact items or services.
2. The exact amount owed: specifying the original charge, noting any payments already made, and also giving details of any interest or late payment charges.
3. Mention of the terms of the payment agreement.
4. Reference to previous contacts, especially if there have been more than one.
5. Request for payment.
6. Ease of reply: a stamped or prepaid addressed envelope (eliminates the weak excuses "I didn't have postage" or "I couldn't find an envelope").

The Collection Series

The collection series varies from business to business and also from situation to situation. Good credit or collection managers handle each case individually. Thus, a long-time customer who has usually paid promptly would receive several first-stage letters before more pressure would be applied; whereas a newer customer, especially one with poorer financial credentials, would be handled in a more urgent manner. Large organizations often have a prewritten series of letters of gradually increasing forcefulness; the individual chance of loss determines how rapidly and in what succession these letters are sent. Although prompt and systematic contact is always desirable, there should also be adaptation according to the quality of the risk as well as flexibility based on the individual circumstances.

Regardless of how many letters are sent, the collection series breaks down into five stages: (1) simple notification, (2) reminder with a push, (3) inquiry, (4) pressure, and (5) ultimatum.

The Simple Notification

The simple notification may be a letter, a short note, or a sticker attached to a copy of the bill. Usually it is sent when a payment is a few days overdue. Its appeal is based on the common human nature theme or the suggestion that perhaps the statement failed to arrive. A typical sticker might say, "Did they cross in the mail?" or "Just a friendly reminder." A letter conveys the message that the customer will gladly pay when he recalls the obligation. Examples 8–5 and 8–6 are samples of typical first-stage, simple notification letters.

The Reminder with a Push

This letter is sent when one or more first-stage contacts have not elicited a payment or response. It assumes that the patron is aware of the past-due payment, appeals to the patron's sense of fair play, and adds a push to the earlier message. Sometimes this second stage is omitted, especially in the case of a poorer risk. Then the writer may move from the first stage to the third. The reminder with a push is a more direct request than the simple notification. Note how Examples 8–7 and 8–8 ask courteously but rather firmly for payment.

The Inquiry

The inquiry letter is the turning point of a collection series. The earlier letters have attributed nonpayment to oversight or nonreceipt of a bill. The inquiry letter assumes that there is a reason, such as financial difficulty or dissatisfaction, for the lack of payment. It asks the debtor to either pay or explain; it may also offer to cooperate in solving any problems that are preventing settlement. Even though consumers should write before the expiration of the credit date if a payment problem exists (see Examples 8–1 and 8–2), many do not do so until they receive a straightforward request. Often this letter is written on the top half of the stationery, leaving the bottom half for the return message; a memo page may also be inserted to facilitate replying. This third-stage letter is decisive because, if ignored, the writer infers that there is not a legitimate reason for the delinquency. Stage-three letters appeal to the patron's sense of honor and his or her obligation to settle or justify nonpayment. Examples 8–9 and 8–10 are inquiry-stage collection letters.

EXAMPLE 8–5   Stage One: Simple Notification

**Hilton's
5 Oahu Way
Hila, HI 00000**

April 28, 198—

Mr. John Swift
65 Lei Court
Hila, HI 00000

Dear Mr. Swift:

Slipped your mind?

Just a friendly reminder that the April 1 payment
of $50 on your Ilikon watch is past due.

Your check in the enclosed envelope will be received with a hearty "thank you."

Sincerely yours,

Marjorie Newhart

Marjorie Newhart
Credit Manager

Enc.

EXAMPLE 8–6   Stage One: Simple Notification

Leila's Fine Clothing
724 Main Street
Harbrace, UT 00000

December 28, 198–

Mrs. Enid Wood
54 Newbold Street
Harbrace, UT   00000

Dear Mrs. Wood

Did the mailman let us down? Perhaps he never delivered the original of the enclosed invoice for
the suit you purchased on November 5. Or perhaps
your payment is still in his hands. If so, just
disregard this notice and accept our thanks.

We look forward to your continued patronage in "The
Store That Fashion Built."

Yours truly

John J. Hart
Accounts Department

JJH:tej

enclosures: invoice
            stamped, prepaid envelope

EXAMPLE 8–7   Stage Two: Reminder with a Push

Fred's Fine Appliances
890 Elmwood Street
Pocono, OK 00000

September 4, 198–

Ms. Collette Weldon
32 Webb Avenue
Pocono, OK 00000

Dear Ms. Weldon:

As we reminded you on August 5, your payment for the air conditioner purchased on June 1 is now past due. The amount now owed is $443 ($430 plus 1½ percent interest charge for two months).

You enjoyed our extra discount on major appliances offered with 30-day settlement terms. Therefore, we ask that you send your check for $443 as soon as possible.

A stamped, addressed envelope is enclosed for your convenience.

Sincerely,

Glenn Palmer

Enclosure

EXAMPLE 8–8   Stage Two: Reminder with a Push

Santa's Workshops
Reindeer Way
Sparkle, AK 00000

December 1, 198—

Mr. Burton Martin
Martin's Gifts
653 Bryant Avenue
Mizzola, DE 00000

Dear Mr. Martin:

Thank you again for your September 15 order for 100 sets of our Glow and Sparkle Christmas lights at $4.32 per set. We are sure that they have made your shop's cash register ring with profit.

On November 20 we wrote reminding you that your check for $432 was due by November 15 according to our agreement.

Please take a moment to send your payment in the enclosed prepaid envelope.

Sincerely,

Sanford S. Mott

Sanford S. Mott
Credit Department

SSM:rfh

Enclosure

EXAMPLE 8–9   Stage Three: Inquiry with Space Left for Response

---

Shea's Furniture Store
365 Broad Street
Flint KY 00000

June 30, 198—

Miss Maude Volker
Simms Street
Flint KY 00000

Dear Miss Volker:

Is there a problem?

On May 1, June 1, and June 15 we wrote you concerning your
bill for $325 for the Lightsleeper boxspring and mattress
that you purchased on April 13.

As you have always had a fine payment record with Shea's Furniture Store, we wonder if there is a reason why we haven't
heard from you.

We'll feel a lot better when we know, because "Satisfaction
Is Our Guarantee."

So please use the bottom of this paper for your message and
tell us if we can help. Or, if there is no problem, just mail
your check in the enclosed envelope.

Yours truly,

Robert L. Shea

Robert L. Shea

Enc.

FOR YOUR ANSWER:

EXAMPLE 8–10   Stage Three: Inquiry

Artistic Florists
5 Hibiscus Way
Floria, PR 00000

September 1, 198–

Mr. Lionel Meyers
69 Southwood Apartments
Natura, PR 00000

Dear Mr. Meyers

TALK TO ME!

Silence may be golden to some, but not to the Artistic Florists. Just as talking to plants helps their growth, so does communication enhance a business relationship.

And we have not heard from you although we've written twice about your $324 past-due payment for the patio plants installed on June 12.

If there is a reason for your nonpayment, please come in and talk about it with us. We'll do our best to help.

If not, let your check do the talking in the enclosed postpaid envelope.

Sincerely

Samuel Floss

Samuel Floss
Manager

SF/jik

Enc. Postpaid envelope

The Pressure Letter

When no reply to the inquiry letter is forthcoming, the collector assumes that the debtor does not have a legitimate reason for the failure to pay. It is now time to appeal tactfully to the sense of self-interest by politely pointing out the advantages of meeting financial obligations. The desire to maintain good credit rating or to be eligible for future merchandise or service may create the necessary motivation. This fourth-stage letter is still a fair-play appeal; the urgency of abiding by the credit agreement is stressed.

Notice how the "You" attitude, the readers' benefits, are stressed in the following stage-four letters, Examples 8–11 and 8–12.

The Ultimatum

If nothing else has brought the desired remittance, a final appeal to the sense of fear must be made. The tone of this letter will be courteous, but firm; clear, but not offensive. Here, the writer describes exactly what action will be taken if payment is not received by a definite date, usually about ten days later. The writer proposes a legally acceptable alternative, such as turning the account over to a lawyer or a collection agency or repossessing unpaid-for items. Never does the collector intimate libel or violence. Also, the collector must be prepared to carry through the action — never should he or she make idle threats. Often this fifth-stage letter is sent Registered Mail, Return Receipt Requested. With their emphasis on embarrassment and additional costs, these letters are usually effective in producing payment. Notice how firmly, but still pleasantly, Examples 8–13 and 8–14 ask for immediate payment.

Review the letters presented in this chapter. First, note the obligation of the consumer to write promptly if he or she will not meet a payment because of financial problems or dissatisfaction with a product or service. The wise customer who explains a problem often can both preserve a good credit rating and eliminate the need for the writing of a collection letter.

When collection letters must be written, always remember their twofold purpose: (1) to retain good will, and (2) to collect the money. Although the collection series gradually becomes more forceful, these letters should always be tactfully couched in the "You" attitude.

EXAMPLE 8–11 Stage Four: Pressure Letter

The Leib Menagerie
600 Mason Building
Yemana, VA 00000

January 15, 198—

Mr. Milton Taunton
Taunton's Toys
40 Woodmansee Street
Laurel, MN 00000

Dear Mr. Taunton:

With the Easter season coming up, we know you'll soon be
placing your usual order for Leib stuffed animals with us.
They have been big sellers in your store for the past five
years because they're the softest, most cuddly little fellows
on the market.

But this year we'll be unable to meet your needs — that is,
unless your account balance of $3,822.81 for Christmas tree
ornaments is paid in full. On October 20 we mailed an invoice
with your order; payment was expected by November 10. We have
sent three reminders but have received no response.

Please help us to retain you as a customer of our exclusive
lines of toys and decorations. Send your check for $3,822.81
and your Easter order TODAY.

Sincerely,

Joseph Pink
Credit Manager

JP:rto

Enclosure

EXAMPLE 8–12   Stage Four: Pressure Letter

The Haberdashery
Mercury Plaza
Atherton, NM 00000

March 1, 198–

Mr. Cedric Johnson
1536 Bally Court
Atherton, NM 00000

Dear Mr. Johnson:

The word <u>credit</u> comes from the Latin word <u>credo</u>, meaning
<u>I believe</u>. To have good credit standing, to have others be-
lieve in you, is one of your most important assets.

However, you are jeopardizing this valuable possession
by nonpayment of your $72.95 bill for the shirts you pur-
chased on December 15. We have written you four times without
result. As a member of the Rockland Credit Bureau, we are
obliged to report delinquencies of more than three months to
its Retail Accounts Division.

Please be fair to yourself. Send your check today in the
enclosed envelope.

Yours truly,

Lucinda Potts

Lucinda Potts
Credit Department
The Haberdashery

LP/thd

Enc.

EXAMPLE 8–13   Stage Five: Ultimatum

Bill's Garage
42 Mechanic's Road
Carytown, OR 00000

September 1, 198—

Mr. Jimmy Bond
89 Columbia Street
Carytown, OR 00000

Dear Mr. Bond:

On March 1 we rebuilt the engine and made transmission repairs on your Sinclair Sports car. We have corresponded with
you five times during the last five months about your past-
due bill of $789.95 for this work.

Unless payment is received within ten days, we have no alternative but to place this matter in the hands of our attor-
neys, Blythe and Blythe. Not only will court action be costly
for you, but your credit rating will be severely damaged.

Please do not force us to take this unpleasant action. Send
your check for $789.95 immediately.

Sincerely,

Joan P. Milton

Joan P. Milton

Enclosure: stamped, addressed envelope

EXAMPLE 8–14   Stage Five: Ultimatum

Bender's Furniture Store
Blaidell Shopping Mall
Rondelle, AL 00000

January 15, 198–

Mrs. Elizabeth Cuddy
1 Roundtree Street
Marlene, AL 00000

Dear Mrs. Cuddy:

When you purchased your New Era dining room suite on August
15, you signed and retained a copy of our sales agreement.
This contract, in which you promised to pay $50 weekly toward
the $1,123.50 charges, stated that Bender's Department Store
is "absolute owner of said goods until the full purchase
price is paid."

Since October 15 we have received no installments on the balance owed, $673.50, nor have you responded to our five let-
ters and four telephone calls.

If full payment is not made within ten days, we shall be
forced to repossess the furniture. You will not only lose
your investment, but according to our contract, are also liable for cost of removal and any required repairs.

Only your prompt payment in the enclosed envelope can avoid
these unpleasant actions.

Yours truly,

Stanton Evans

Stanton Evans
President

SE:jk

Enc.

CHECKLIST

Collection Letters

- Start to contact overdue accounts promptly.
- Be systematic.
- Use gradually increasing forcefulness.
  a. Simple notification.
  b. Reminder with a push.
  c. Inquiry.
  d. Pressure.
  e. Ultimatum.
- Be tactful.
- Emphasize reader benefit.
- Include specific details about:
  a. Product or service.
  b. Exact amount owed.
  c. Terms of payment agreement.
  d. Previous payment requests.
- Provide for ease of reply — enclose a stamped, addressed envelope.

EXERCISES

1. How might the following letters be improved? Rewrite them according to the ideas presented in this chapter.

   a. Dear Dr. Denson:

   We fail to understand why you have not paid your last month's bill for office supplies.

   Send the money immediately.

   b. Dear Mrs. Eliason:

   We simply cannot tolerate overdue bills. After all, we have to pay our obligations and need your money to do so.

   Send the $89.95 you owe for the dress you bought six weeks ago so that we can satisfy our own creditors.

   c. Gentlemen:

   Please stop sending me dunning bills. I am out of work and certainly can't pay you. After all, you can't get blood from a stone.

   d. Dear Mrs. Elkins:

   You have not paid your bill for $82.95 for the clock

radio you bought two months ago. We sent you a bill, and you ignored it. We only sell excellent merchandise, so we are sure you are not having problems with your purchase.

We must conclude that you are dishonest unless you send your check immediately.

e. Gentlemen:

That desk you sold me is lousy, so I'm not going to pay for it.

I think you cheated me, and I'm going to report you to the Better Business Bureau.

f. Gentlemen:

We're not going to fill the order you just sent because you haven't paid for the last one yet. And from now on we'll only do business with you on a strictly cash basis.

If you don't like this, take your orders and your business elsewhere.

g. Dear Ms. Oldham:

If you look at the two bills we sent you recently, you'll see that you owe us a lot of money.

Pay up or we'll have a sheriff remove all of the merchandise. We'll also send letters to all of your neighbors telling them how dishonest you are.

h. Dear Miss Simms:

I wonder if you'll be happy to know that we have given your name to the Beanville Credit Bureau as a deadbeat.

This is what happens to people who don't pay their bills on time.

i. Dear Mr. Golding:

Your dishonesty has left us no recourse but to turn your account over to our attorney.

You should have realized that this would happen when you didn't pay on time.

j. Dear Miss Frazier:

If we let everybody who lost a job put off paying us, we'd go bankrupt.

We suggest you take out a loan or borrow from a friend. After all, why should we suffer?

2. Write appropriate letters for the following situations.

   a. You owe $532 to Dr. Robert Langham, 352 Angell Street, Marion, VT 00000, for treatment for an eye infection and for glasses. You had told his secretary that you would send $100 monthly toward the bill. After sending one payment, you have had a family problem. Your mother has become too ill to manage her home alone, and you now have to contribute $50 a month toward the cost of a housekeeper. Write to Dr. Langham explaining the circumstances and asking him to accept $50 monthly.

   b. Write a courteous reply to problem a. from either Dr. Langham or his secretary.

   c. In December, Mr. Walter Mottram, 18 Meni Court, Lakeland, AZ 00000 purchased a mink coat in your store for $2,800. As it was a Christmas present for his wife, you did not insist that he put it on layaway until paid for; instead, you let him take it after giving an $800 deposit. He is a new customer who said he had no credit references because he always pays cash. He promised to pay $500 monthly by the fifteenth of each of the next four months. Write an appropriate letter to be sent on January 31 if the first payment was not made.

   d. Refer to problem c. It is now February 18 and still no payment has arrived. Write a second-stage reminder.

   e. It is now March 1 and still you have received no money from Mr. Mottram (see problem c.). Try a third-stage inquiry letter.

   f. It is April 1 and Mr. Mottram (see problem c.) has continued to ignore you. You have decided to skip stage four and write a fifth-stage ultimatum letter. As a worn fur coat has little value, you will turn the matter over to a collection agency if you have no reply after ten days.

   g. Mrs. Nancy Heath, 215 Modena Road, Vistaview, NJ 00000 has been an excellent credit customer for ten years. Two months ago, on May 30, she purchased a raincoat for $69.95. You billed her six weeks ago but have not received payment. Write a simple notification letter to her.

   h. Mrs. Heath (see problem g.) has still not paid by August 30. Write a reminder-with-a-push letter.

   i. It is September 30 and you still have no answer from Mrs. Heath (see problem g.). Because of your past experience with her, you are sure there must be some problem. Write a tactful letter of inquiry.

   j. You have sent first-, second-, and third-stage letters to Mr. Arthur Willing, 695 Bayview, Waterville, SC 00000 regarding his bill for $100 for cuff links and a tie pin bought in your store on February 10. You check his records and see that he has been a slow payer in the past but that he has always paid after three or four months. It is May 15. Send him a stage-four letter, using a bit of pressure.

   k. You manufacture Wear Well dungarees. You have just received a letter from one of your good customers, The Dude Store, 59 Main Street, Malbone, WA 00000. The Dude Store owes you $1,800, which is due on May 1, one week from now. Mr. Flower, the owner, explains that a fire in his store three weeks ago has caused him to close the business for a month for repairs; he plans to reopen on May 4. He asks for a month's extension on the debt. Write a cordial letter granting his request.

9

Sales Letters

Selling by Letter

While every business letter is, in some way, a form of sales letter, direct selling may not necessarily be the main objective. Selling is the main goal of the direct sales letter. Its whole purpose is to create in you, the reader, such an irresistible desire for the particular product or service the letter is promoting that you are transformed from a reader to a buyer.

Why do businesses bother with the time and expense involved in creating sales letters when a great number of potential consumers live within driving distance, and radio and television daily bombard the listener and viewer with commercials? Why would sales letters be of interest to store managers when they can send buyers directly to the source of supply? Many businesses have supplier's catalogues from which they order on a regular basis. Just what are the advantages of selling by letter?

Advantages of Selling by Letter

Selling by letter has several advantages. The number and variety of people the letters can reach may well be the most important one. Sales letters can be targeted to a specific audience such as a limited number of dentists in a given area or to all college seniors in the major universities in the country. On the other hand, the seller may want a mass mailing to the general public in a thousand cities all over the country with the letters addressed simply to "Occupant." The possibilities are endless. Such letters are often of special interest to the housebound who are unable to go out to the stores and who shop primarily by mail orders.

Ease of reply is another advantage. The well-constructed sales letter makes replying easy with enclosures, and it relies heavily on the benefit of "shopping from the comfort of your own living room, free from the hassle of crowds and confusion of busy stores."

A letter can be more personal than a flyer or other media by using the potential buyer's name. Mass-produced letters can be made to look as if each were individually typed, with the customer's name used throughout the body. Letters (by using a question-and-answer format) can create a feeling of one-to-one conversation that is next to impossible in a large, crowded store. They can call the attention of regular customers to a special offer or to a new product introduced after a catalogue was sent out.

Disadvantages of Selling by Letter

As with everything else, sales letters also have some disadvantages. The greatest is that the letter may be discarded unread. The saturation techniques of television, radio, magazines, and newspapers may have turned the recipient against all advertising. The potential reader may have been inundated with what many consider to be junk mail. The recipient may be skeptical of all sales letters because of a prior disappointment with a mail order purchase. As strict as the laws are governing the use of the mails to defraud, occasionally an unscrupulous business does get by with cheating a customer.

Selecting the Potential Customer

If a sales letter is to be effective and stimulate sales, it must reach the right reader. Obviously a manufacturing company that makes surgical equipment and supplies would not send sales letters to an automobile dealer.

Mailing lists of all kinds are quite easily available. There are companies that sell lists of addresses purchased from such groups as professional organizations, mail order companies, and magazine publishers. Sometimes one business may buy another company's list. Some other sources are credit-rating books, city directories, tax books, professional directories, public records, newspapers, yellow pages, any of the *Who's Who* biographies, and alumni offices.

Before writing the sales letter and selecting the mailing list, the seller must know the product or service well, who would use it, why and how it would be used, and the advantages to having and using it. Then the decision on how many letters will be sent must be made. Is a mass mailing practical, or would a test mailing be the wiser choice?

For example, Mary Moler and John Johnstone are working on a sales campaign for a manufacturer of surgical supplies and operating room equipment. The research department has just completed development of a revolutionary new form of tapeless, self-adhering, antibiotic impregnated bandage in all sizes from the one-half-inch bandage to large surgical dressings. They will not irritate the most tender and sensitive skin nor pull the skin when removed. As part of the advertising campaign, Mary and John plan to send out an exciting, attention-grabbing sales letter with samples to hospitals, nursing homes, pharmacies, and supermarket chains all over the country. Creating the letter is no problem. But getting the letter to the right places could be expensive, with no guarantee that the results would be worth the cost. Consequently, John and Mary decide a test mailing would be the wisest course of action. They will send the sales letter with an appropriate sample to three hospitals, three pharmacies, two nursing homes, and two supermarkets in each of three states — one state on the northeast coast, one in the midwest, and one on the southwest coast. Consulting the available mailing lists, they select the individual places to which they will mail the letters. The response to the test mailing and a follow-up visit by a sales representative will determine future action in the campaign.

Writing the Effective Sales Letter

The key to writing an effective sales letter is knowing your product or service, knowing what it will do, and knowing how it will do it. Will the product or service save money? Will it relieve pain? Will it create pleasure or enhance beauty? Will it make the worker more efficient, the job easier? Will it improve health?

The whole purpose of the sales letter is to promote sales, to convince potential buyers that they just cannot exist without the product or service, and then to induce them to buy. Emphasizing the "You" attitude, what the product can do for the buyer rather than what it can do for the seller, is vitally important. But beware of the oversell. The soft sell — the "let us serve you" attitude rather than the high pressure sell — is generally more effective. Nothing is more apt to turn a prospective customer away from a product or service, and sometimes from a company's whole line of products, than the high-pressure sales approach. When the letter makes the product or service so attractive that consumers feel they must have it, sales follow, and the letter has done its job.

Attracting attention.   Unless the sales letter attracts the reader's attention immediately, it is useless. Therefore, the appearance of the letter is important. The color and texture of the paper and the printing and spacing of the content should all be appealing to the senses. The letter should be attractive and easy to read. The texture of the paper should feel pleasant to the touch. Even the scent or lack of scent is important. One well-known flower and seed company impregnates its sales brochures for rose bushes with the actual scent of the roses advertised. The combination of the beautiful flowers and their perfume is quite irresistible to any rose-loving gardener. The sales pitch is limited and is almost unnecessary, as the brochure speaks for itself. Quality in the physical aspects of the letter, as well as good content, implies a quality product just as cheap-looking paper with crowded, poorly worded copy implies a shoddy product.

The appearance of the envelope is also important, as that alone can often determine whether the potential reader opens it or discards it unopened. Often the envelope has an eye-catching logo, a slogan, or even a question to attract attention. Visualize an envelope with a small picture of a hula dancer under a palm tree in the upper left corner. In the lower left corner you read, "Yes! You *can* spend a week in Hawaii!" Wouldn't you take a few minutes to open and read that letter? The envelope address can affect the potential customer's attitude. Envelopes addressed to Occupant are much more likely to be discarded unopened than the one addressed to a specific person, or the one with a handwritten address.

A sales letter can live or die on the strength of the opening sentence or paragraph. The letter must attract the reader's attention or it will go unread. The rest of the opening paragraph must hold that attention and stimulate curiosity so the reader will continue to the end.

Letters can open with a question, an anecdote, a joke, a testimonial, or even a pun. Look at the following examples. Which ones would make you toss the letter in the wastebasket unread? Which would make you want to read on?

1. Are you tired of the sights, sounds, and smells of the city streets in the hot, muggy days of August? Wouldn't you rather get away to clean, clear, fresh air, cool breezes, and swim in sparkling lake water or fish for the fightingest trout you have ever encountered?

2. How does basking in the warm sun by a shimmering pool, tanning to a golden glow under tropical skies, or just plain relaxing with a tall, cool drink served at poolside sound to you as you look out your window at two feet of soot-covered snow and listen to the bitter-cold wind howling around the corner of the building?

3. Create gourmet meals in no time at all? Impossible you say? Well, not anymore! Not when you use our new DO-IT-ALL food processor. Gone are the endless hours of slicing and chopping! Gone are the cut fingers! Say hello to perfectly sliced or chopped food in seconds when you use the DO-IT-ALL.

4. Come to our camp in the mountains if you like to fish. It's clean, comfortable, and so cheap you can bring the whole family for less than it would cost you to go alone to a fancier resort.

5. Do your friends call you a hypochondriac behind your back because you ache all over? Relieve those aches and pains with SOOTHE-IT, a greaseless, circulation-stimulating cream you simply rub on. SOOTHE-IT will help ease away the ache so quickly you will wonder why you suffered so long.

6. Sea and Sun Resort is just the place for you this winter. It's warm enough to swim every day, cool enough to play golf, and sunny enough to get a tan. In addition it is economical and the food is good.

7. Do you want to spend your whole life working? Statistics show that workaholics die young. Live longer by making money at home with little or no effort. Write for our free booklet on how to make life easier by MAKING THAT FIRST MILLION.

8. The late Mae West, in one of her early films, was supposed to have said, "Come up and see me some time." While we cannot introduce you to Mae West, we do want you to come up and see us sometime soon and look at our new line of luscious lingerie. To show our appreciation for your past patronage, we have arranged a gala evening on November first at seven o'clock when we will show our new line for the first time. There will be music, models, and refreshments for your pleasure. Do your Christmas shopping early in comfort and in style by being our guest on the first of November.

Creating desire.   After arousing the reader's interest, the sales letter must create a desire for the product or service. Ask yourself, "Why should Max or Maxine buy my product? Why is it better than any other similar product? How is it unique? How can I induce Max or Maxine to want my product enough to actually buy it?"

The focus of the letter can appeal to any number of feelings such as guilt, pride, loyalty, vanity, or a sense of altruism. It can play on the desire for status, popularity, and peer approval; it can work to create feelings of nostalgia for the "good old days" or appeal to basic needs. What kind of feelings would the following be apt to stimulate?

1. Watch the neighbors stare open-mouthed when you drive down the street in your new custom-built PHANTOM!

2. Wouldn't it be great to have every weekend filled with exciting dates? Come to our SLIM-DOWN PAVILION and shed those few extra pounds and inches that keep the calendar empty.

3. Do you envy the man next door because all your friends comment on his beautiful, green, weed-free lawn? Is yours the only one on the street specializing in crab grass and dandelions? Restore your pride and your lawn with WEEDS DOWN AND GRASS UP lawn fertilizer. In just a few short weeks you will be hearing the compliments about the prettiest lawn in the neighborhood as your friends kick off their shoes to walk barefoot on your soft, green turf.

4. Don't wonder anymore how Sue at the next desk affords (on the same salary as yours!) the smashing outfits she wears. You too can be as smart looking as Sue for very little money when you shop at STYLE WITH ECONOMY BOUTIQUE. Come in and browse. Our sales personnel will be happy to help you plan your new wardrobe or add to your present one. Ask them about our various easy-payment plans designed with the career girl in mind.

5. When you plan that very special dinner, you want to serve the best of everything, especially the wines. Let Henri at the EPICURE SHOP help you select just the right vintage to complement every part of your perfect dinner from the hors d'oeuvres to dessert and coffee.

6. If you are the discriminating reader that our sources say you are, then you will assuredly want to receive our monthly MONEY PAPER on finances.

While the sales letter can be written in glowing terms, the writer must beware of making promises the seller has no intention of keeping or of claiming a product can perform miracles. To do so can be construed as using the mails to defraud, for which the penalties can be severe. Thus in choosing words, the writer must consider carefully their *denotation,* or the dictionary definition, the literal meaning. It is on the *connotation* of words, the images they conjure up, that sales letters depend for effect. The implications, the innuendos, and the feelings that words evoke in the reader are the grist for the sales letter writer's mill.

Look back at the examples of the opening sentences and paragraphs on pages 189 and 190. They make no rash promises, but they do create images in the mind of the reader according to each individual's connotation of the words. For example, to some the snow and cold wind mean winter sports, sliding down a mountainside, or gliding over the ice. To others the snow and cold wind mean the misery of aching joints, skidding cars, falling on the ice, and sky-high oil bills. To some, basking in the sun creates an image of peace and relaxation, of paradise here and now; while to others the same words convey painful sunburn, mosquito bites, and heat stroke.

Enclosures are another means of creating desire. Attractive colored brochures catch the eye. Swatches of material the reader can touch add appeal to colored pictures. Free samples of the product for sale allow the reader to experience firsthand and at no cost what the product can do. Discount slips, coupons for cash refunds, and contest tickets are all effective in creating desire. This is especially so when the enclosure falls out of the envelope as it is opened. Rare, indeed, is the individual who can resist picking up and examining that item. Another insert gaining in popularity is the folded and sealed paper or card labeled, "Open this only if you have decided not to buy." When the reader does open it, as will probably happen regardless of whether a decision has been made, the copy usually begins with a comment like this:

Frankly, I am puzzled why anyone would turn down an offer like this, and why anyone would refuse to try a free FIZIT when there is no obligation involved.

The text then goes on to describe briefly once again the highlights of the product and to urge the reader to change his or her mind.

Sometimes a pin, paperclip, or ribbon is enclosed with a note attached suggesting that the item be worn or attached to a checkbook as a reminder to make out an order, visit a store, or watch for a new catalogue that is on the way.

Testimonials from satisfied consumers are frequently used, especially for patent medicines, cleaning compounds, home appliances, cars, and trucks. A familiar approach is a picture of a handsome man and a beautiful woman standing by a long, sleek, shining, and expensive automobile. The camera angle makes the car look much longer than it really is. The accompanying dialogue goes like this:

> "Oh Sebastian! What a beauty! I simply can't wait to ride in your new Prometheus with those comfortable-looking seats and that absolutely gorgeous maroon leather upholstery."
>
> "You have a real experience ahead of you, Audrey. Not only is my new Prometheus a beauty, but it is as quiet and comfortable as it is powerful with XYZ number of horses under the hood."

The sales letter can also try to justify the reader's desire for the product with practical reasons using facts and statistics in a down-to-earth, logical manner. This technique is often used in letters selling office equipment, trucks, and home appliances. The commentary might emphasize efficiency, time and money saved, ease and economy of operation, and safety features. The letter stresses facts and figures, usually presented with an explanation of how they were determined through actual use or laboratory tests, to convince the reader that the product is the best of its kind.

The following illustrate some of the various kinds of opening sentences used to spark interest and create desire.

1. 5000 successful farmers can't be wrong!
2. Three out of four doctors recommend . . .
3. Statistics show that CLEAN WELL WASHERS outlast and outclean all other brands.
4. Nine out of ten men and women lost ten pounds in ten days with KILL-THE-URGE-TO-EAT tablets.
5. Even your best friend won't tell you! So to be safe use . . .

Getting action.   Ease of reply is a key factor in getting action from the sales letter, especially if the seller is in a mail order business. Great numbers of people do not have easy access to stores or cannot do the walking required to shop in person and must purchase most of what they need by mail, so mail order companies make sure that responding is easy. Postage-paid, addressed envelopes or order cards are enclosed with the sales letter. For larger orders the order forms and envelopes are sent with the catalogue. For fast service and charges, a toll-free telephone is listed. Sometimes a small pencil or pen is attached to make signing the response easier. If the envelope or order card is not postage free, an added inducement is often a stamp for the reader to attach or coins with which to buy a stamp.

The free trial sample is a sure way of getting people to try your product; the idea is "Try it: you'll like it."

1. Use this free sample of FLOOR-BRIGHT on your shop floors. When you see how they shine without being slippery, eliminating the danger of falls and lawsuits, you won't believe your eyes.
2. Keep your name up front with all your customers! Give them NEVER-SKIP pens with your embossed name and product.
3. Make it easy for your customers to remember you all year long! Give them our compact desk calendar with your name and address at the bottom of each page.

The money-back guarantee or the warranty on a product also promotes sales.

1. You must be convinced that our XYZ copier gives you clearer copies on better-quality paper faster and at less cost than any copier you have ever used or INSTANT PRINT will gladly refund your money and remove the copier from your premises without charge.
2. We are so sure your cat will love PUSSYBURGERS that should he turn up his aristocratic nose and refuse to eat after his first sniff, just return the empty can to us, and we will give you double your money back.

Everyone is familiar with the contest or sweepstakes sales letter stating, "no purchase necessary to enter." Many letters explain that a computer has already selected the winning numbers, while others rely on a drawing. Some require only that the reader mark squares on a card, while others have tickets to be returned in either "Yes, I will order" or "No, I will not order now but tell me if I have won" envelopes. Other promotions are more elaborate. The potential buyer receives a card or imitation telegram announcing the imminent arrival of very important documents within a week and advising the recipient to watch the mails for them. The very important documents are contest tickets along with a sales letter describing a product or service. The envelope may have a window through which one sees phrases such as "You may already have won . . ." or "You could be the lucky winner if . . ."

Another scheme involves a sample of the product imprinted with several numbers and a sheet of paper listing more numbers. If the number on the sample matches a number on the list, the reader has won a prize.

One technique practically guaranteeing that the potential consumer will open the envelope and read the contents is the check routine. Two methods are used in this promotion. In one, the envelope looks like those the government uses for its checks. Usually no return address is printed on the front of the envelope and sometimes none is on the back. In the other, the envelope window has what appears to be a check, but the amount is not shown. Whatever the amount, the check is good only as a down payment toward a product.

The free vacation is another popular promotion used to sell real estate, particularly in the Sun Belt or the winter resorts in the north. Once there, the potential customer is subjected to on-site sales promotion.

All of these approaches appeal to the eternal hope for the big break and make the reader feel there is nothing to lose by responding. Each response, in turn, tells the seller that the message has reached out to a potential buyer. The name of the product or service remains with the ticket stubs or the free sample.

For Class Discussion

Zachary Pitt is the personnel manager of Dickson & Farrer Manufacturing Co. One of his duties is the semiannual evaluation of each employee who has been with the company more than six months. These evaluations become a part of the employee's permanent file for as long as each remains with the company. While Mr. Pitt has an executive secretary, Cecily Grange, who types all his confidential papers, her desk and typewriter are just outside Mr. Pitt's office door where anyone going in or out could read the copy from which she is typing. This is not a problem when Ms. Grange is working from shorthand, but more often than not she is typing from Mr. Pitt's handwritten copy done while he was waiting in a hotel or flying to a meeting.

The situation creates a problem with the confidentiality of personnel reports, and the shop union has asked that something be done about it. Moving Ms. Grange's desk to a more private area is out of the question, and the office does not have any sort of dictating and transcribing machinery, which would appear to be the only solution.

How do you think Mr. Pitt and Ms. Grange would react to the letter in Example 9–1 from Corinne Talson, Sales Manager of Casdict Company, Inc.?

Analyze Corinne Talson's letter. Be prepared to answer the following questions in class.

1. Does the writer know her product? On what do you base your answer?
2. Does the letter's content indicate Miss Talson knows the buyer's needs? What are those indications, if any?
3. Does the letter have a central focus? If it does, what is it?
4. Does the letter emphasize the key points? If it does, what are they?
5. Does the letter stress the "You" attitude? How?
6. Is the meaning clear? If not, how would you change the letter to make it clear?
7. Would you call the letter a high-pressure sales approach? If not, why not? If yes, why?
8. If you were Zachary Pitt, would you respond to the letter? Has the letter aroused your interest as a possible solution to the problem? Why?

EXAMPLE 9–1 Sales Letter

Casdict Co., Inc.
70 Soundtrack Highway   **Volumetown, CT 00000**
Quality Recording Equipment for the Office and the Home

17 October 198—

Mr. Zachary Pitt
Personnel Manager
Dickson & Farrer Manufacturing Co.
100 Mainline Avenue
Finchberry, RI 00000

Dear Mr. Pitt:

As the owner of a CASDICT CASSETTE player–recorder, you are
aware of the high quality and fine sound reproduction of your
CASDICT machine and cassette tapes. I am sure you have enjoyed many hours of fine listening since you purchased the
machine last Christmas.

Maintaining the same high standards of quality, CASDICT has
recently developed, just for the busy executive like yourself, a new concept in office dictating systems with advantages for the user not found in any other similar equipment.
The recorder is small, lightweight, and pencil slim. It will
fit in your jacket pocket and is just the thing for dictating
in the privacy of your office, while driving your car, riding
on a train or bus, or even flying in a plane. The built-in
microphone is so powerful that to record a meeting, you only
have to push the button marked <u>Conf</u>.

The tonal reproduction under any circumstances is remarkable
because your CASDICT recorder filters out all extraneous
noise when you push in the button marked <u>Filt</u>. Even more reasonable is the power source—one small round battery like
that found in a fine watch. These are but a few of the many
features and advantages you will find in this CASDICT system.

Your secretary will be delighted with the transcription machine. It is more compact and lighter in weight than any
other models on the market and has all the features found in
the larger, heavier machines. The headset is designed with
the typist's comfort in mind and is easy to put on and take
off. You have the option of hand, knee, or foot controls. The
speed and volume controls are easy to use.

EXAMPLE 9–1   *(continued)*

Mr. Zachary Pitt   2   17 October 198—

On top of all these features, the price is unbelievably reasonable. The cassettes are economical, and, while we naturally recommend CASDICT cassettes because of their high quality, you can in a pinch use any other brand of cassette tape.
The system is just what you need to ensure the confidentiality of reports, correspondence, and evaluations because there
is no written copy visible to the onlooker. All anyone in the
office can see or hear is your secretary working and the
click of the typewriter. Best of all, the money you will save
in secretarial work hours will pay for your CASDICT system in
just one year. You will save time because no longer does your
secretary have to sit and take dictation. There will be more
time to type up that correspondence and those reports while
you are dictating into your CASDICT recorder. No matter where
you are, you can keep up to date without even having to
bother with paper and pen.

          Want a permanent record other than a written one?
          Keep the tape.
          Want to review what happened at that important meeting?
          Listen to the recording you made.
          Or you can just erase the tape and use it over and over.
          CASDICT cassette tapes have an unusually long life.

Jeffery Xavier, our CASDICT demonstrator, will be in Finchberry the last week in October through the first week in
November. Just check the date most convenient for you on the
postage—paid, addressed card and drop it in the mail. Mr.
Xavier will come to your office and at absolutely no charge
or obligation to you will demonstrate the CASDICT dictating
system.

Let us help you make your work easier.

Very truly yours,

Corinne Talson

Corinne Talson
Sales Manager
CASDICT CO., Inc.

Enc.

Telephone Sales

The spoken sales letter, or the telephone sales letter, is another form of sales communication gaining in popularity. Some businesses, after a series of mailings that have brought no response, will have trained personnel call prospective customers and push the product or service. Different approaches may be used, but all have some things in common. The caller, whether male or female, has a very pleasant, cultured voice and a well-memorized sales talk. Some callers recite so rapidly that the listener must either hang up in the middle at the risk of being rude or listen through to the end. Some act as if they are old friends. If the listener has already bought a product from the company at some previous time, the caller may ask if the product was satisfactory. All are very persuasive, polite, and persistent. One such call may sound like this.

> "Hello. Am I speaking to the lady of the house?"
>
> "Yes."
>
> "How-do-you-do. My name is Sheri and I have a free gift for you. I am going to send you 48 issues of HOBBIES FOR THE CLUMSY absolutely free. All you have to do is buy our hobby kit called EVERYTHING FOR EVERY HOBBY at the low, low price of only $75.00. The best part is you don't even have to make out a check. Just give me your ALL-PURPOSE CHARGE CARD number, verify your name and address, and you will get your first free issue along with the hobby kit in six short weeks."

Another approach may go this way.

> "Hello. May I speak to Mrs. Doe please?"
>
> "This is she speaking."
>
> "Mrs. John Doe at 000-000-0000?"
>
> "Yes."
>
> "Mrs. Doe, this is Freddy Smoothie and I'm calling long distance from our office in Georgia. Did you see the latest brochure and write-up we sent you a few weeks ago about GREAT LIZARDS AND OTHER WEIRD CREATURES?"
>
> "I don't recall it."
>
> "Well, we did send it to you. When we did not receive your order, and knowing you to be a regular purchaser of our NATURE SERIES books, we thought perhaps you had been away or just too busy to order. So I decided to call you to remind you that we have a copy right here with your name on it. Believe me, Mrs. Doe, if you enjoyed SPIDERS AND OTHER INSECTS, you will love this new book about lizards. The pictures are marvelous, the printing is easy to read, and the paper is of unusual quality. All you have to do is say yes, and I will personally send out your copy today. Look it over for ten days, and if you don't think it is one of the best books of its kind you have seen in a long time, why,

Mrs. Doe, just send it back to us in the original box. If you like it, as I am sure you will, simply send us your check for $9.95 in the envelope that comes with the invoice attached to the front of the mailing carton."

Although the actual sales promotion is done through a telephone conversation, before this can take place, someone has to write the dialogue for the salesperson to memorize. The writer has to use the same guidelines in writing a sales script for speaking about a product or service as are used in writing sales letters for mailing.

Sales letters can be the most enjoyable kinds of letters you may ever have to write. You can let your imagination and creativity run free playing with words to create vivid mental pictures in the reader's mind. You can play with words, develop innuendo, exaggerate without being dishonest yet not telling the whole truth. Your sales letters plant the germ of an idea creating desire, and the readers take it from there, seeing in the sales pitch whatever they want to see. In order to do this successfully, you the writer must know your product and what it will do. You must visualize clearly the types of people to whom your product will appeal and speak to them in language they will appreciate. As the examples and problems in this chapter show, sales letters can be fun.

CHECKLIST

Sales Letters

- Know your product/service well.
- Select potential customers.
- Attract attention in opening paragraph.
- Create desire for product/service by appeal to senses and emotions.
- Use paper, envelopes, and language compatible with product/service and type of potential customer.
- Make no promises that cannot be kept.
- Avoid oversell.

EXERCISES

1. What images do the words below create in your mind? Write a sentence or two describing that image.
   a. car
   b. jalopy
   c. shower
   d. thunderstorm
   e. designer jeans
   f. cowboy boots

g. cheap

h. economical

i. surf's up

j. moonlight on the lake

2. Study the following examples of sales letters and then answer questions (1) through (5) below.

a. Dear Busy Executive:

You know what you want and so do we! How? Because we know the kind of person you are—a hard-driving, hard-working, successful businessperson well on the way up the corporate ladder. We also know that however busy you are, whatever the pressure to succeed, you have not forgotten the need to keep yourself physically fit and trim.

To make that important part of your life a pleasure instead of a grind, take time to bring this letter in person to the PRESTIGE SWIM & HEALTH CLUB for a tour of the facilities, a swim in the pool, and a healthful lunch as our guest.

Everything is here for your enjoyment from the jogging track to the sauna and health-food bar. As a club member you can enjoy a healthy workout or just relaxing at any time of day from six in the morning 'til eleven o'clock at night seven days a week. Our staff physician will give you that much-needed thorough physical exam and design a fitness program geared to your individual needs.

You have nothing to lose and everything to gain by taking advantage of this free offer on your next lunch hour. Come in and visit, swim in the pool, and let us tell you all about the many advantages a PRESTIGE SWIM & HEALTH CLUB membership holds for you.

I look forward to meeting you soon.

John Jones

JOHN JONES, PRESIDENT
PRESTIGE SWIM & HEALTH CLUB

P.S. We also have family memberships available.

b. Dear Reader:

Are you the kind of person who likes to know what is going on in the world? We mean the TRUTH about what is happening, not some writer's unsupported version of what is transpiring?

If you are, and we are certain you are, then you are just the person who will want to read THE TRUTH IN THE NEWS magazine. Here you will find the truth about politics, crime, medicine, world hunger, and many, many other subjects. THE TRUTH IN THE NEWS tells you the truth and only the truth about all those topics and more.

For only $15.00 a year (that's only $1.50 per issue, a savings of $.20 a copy over what you pay at the newsstand) you will receive the next ten issues of THE TRUTH IN THE NEWS and be the best—informed member of your crowd.

Act now! Sign the enclosed card and mail it to—day. If, after reading the first issue, you are not convinced that THE TRUTH IN THE NEWS is the most in—formative news magazine you have ever read, then keep the first issue as our free gift and mark can—cel on the bill that comes with it. If you are as pleased with the first issue of THE TRUTH IN THE NEWS as we believe you will be, just send us your check in the stamped, addressed envelope and we will see that the next nine fact—filled issues are deliv—ered to your door—one every six weeks. You'll be glad you acted today!

c. Dear Mrs. Smyth van Astor:

As a well—known collector of fine porcelain, you will want to be one of the first to know that WORLD—WIDE IMPORTS has just received six sets of limited—edition bone china plates. Each exquisite plate is hand—crafted and banded in platinum. A world—famous artist created the center design, a spray of wild flowers and ferns in the most delicate colors and of such remarkable beauty that the most discerning eye can find no flaw in their perfection. Truly a set worthy of a discriminating collector like yourself. Each of the six plates in the collec—tion is registered and will become more valuable as time goes by. You can buy them today for only $150.00, just $25.00 a plate.

To be sure of your set, Mrs. Smyth van Astor, you must act now. Simply sign the enclosed card and mail it to us or call our Mr. Stonely in customer service at 800—000—0000. Either way we will deliver your set as soon as we hear from you and bill your account. You must act promptly, though, as our sup—ply is very limited. When our other patrons who are also connoisseurs of fine china hear of our offer, the demand will be considerable. Those who delay are doomed to disappointment.

(1) Do the writers know their products?
(2) Which letter is the most effective? Why?
(3) To what human interests does each letter appeal?
(4) Is the intent of each letter clear?
(5) Would you classify any letter as a hard-sell or high-pressure sales pitch? If so, which one(s)? Why?

3. Study the following letter and list the things you feel are not quite right with it, e.g., vocabulary, tone, etc. Then rewrite the letter (body only) as you think it should be written adding any information you believe is lacking.

    a. ```
I'm tired of city living. Aren't you? The stink! The
noise! The muggings! The slums! They all make me
sick. I'd love to enjoy good country cooking and
soak up the sun, and swim and fish in clean water. I
should guess you would too. Right? If you all agree
with me I know just where you can go. Blue Trout
Lake in Maine on the East River. Theres a great
lodge there thats so cheap you can take the whole
family for peanuts. Why not send me a card at the
address above at the top of the page and i'll send
you a reservation form and a picture of me with a
big trout I caught last year. Oh yeah. It also has a
picture of the lodge in the background. Get with it
man in Maine.
```

4. Write no more than two opening sentences that you feel will create a desire in the reader for the products or services described below.

    a. A gallon jug of Olde Yankee Vermont Maple Syrup.
    b. A Seahorse portable outboard motor.
    c. A series of disco dancing lessons at the Modern Arts Dance Studio.
    d. Summer costume jewelry.
    e. Designer jeans.
    f. A spring vacation for students in Bermuda.
    g. A motorcycle.
    h. An office cleaning service.
    i. A 16-gauge shotgun.
    j. A winter weekend in a ski resort.
    k. A low-calorie soft drink.
    l. A new brand of dog biscuit.
    m. A four-wheel drive jeep.
    n. A surplus school bus that could be converted into a mobile home.
    o. A handyman *How to Do It* magazine.
    p. A twenty-four-hour mail-in film service.
    q. A farm tractor.
    r. Soundproofing ceiling tiles for a business office.
    s. A cast-iron wood stove.
    t. Office furniture.

5. You are preparing to open a store selling office furniture, equipment, and supplies for the business and/or home office. You want to send out flyers announcing your opening through the local newspaper delivery system. You also plan to send to the managers of businesses in the area a sales letter advertising your products and inviting the readers to your grand opening. At that time they will have a chance to meet you and your sales staff, see what you have in stock, and discuss their needs and methods of financing purchases. Refreshments will be served.

    a. Write the copy for the flyer making up your opening date and any other information you think should be included. Incorporate sketches if you wish. Your aim is to get people to come in.
```

    b. Make up a list of the kinds of businesses to whom you want to send your sales letter and list the sources you would consult for the names and addresses.

    c. Write the body of the letter.

6. The Malibar Inn, a luxury hotel with a nine-hole golf course, swimming pool, fully equipped gym, tennis courts, horses, and riding trails on the gulf coast of Florida, will send out a sales letter in November to a list of busy executives in the northern states. The purpose of the letter is to convince the businessmen that they need a vacation in the middle of winter and that the Malibar Inn is the place to take it. A postage-paid, addressed card and a colorful brochure featuring the inn and all its facilities will be included with the letter.

    a. Write the body of the letter.

    b. Design the reservation card.

7. Write a paragraph or two for use in a telephone advertising campaign for each of the following products or services.

    a. A magazine subscription.

    b. A set of cold steel chisels.

    c. Life insurance.

    d. A wet or dry shop vacuum cleaner.

    e. A newspaper delivery service.

    f. A beach club.

    g. An office night cleaning service.

    h. An investment service.

    i. A follow-up call after two sales letters had been sent out for a burglar alarm system for a small store.

8. Briefly describe the type of person to whom each of the phone calls in problem 7 would be made. Include in your description their occupation, age, sex, and financial status. Then reread your paragraphs written for problem 7. Are they really focused on the kinds of people you had in mind? If they are not, why not? What changes need to be made to bring the sales talk into focus?

10

Good-will Letters

Writing Good-will Letters

Good-will letters are those letters you do not have to write. Their purpose is to create in others a feeling of well-being and a feeling of good will toward you, your product, and your business or service. These letters sell indirectly by showing that you care about others. An inexpensive form of advertising, they are an important part of business communications.

Good-will letters can help to bring in new customers or bring back old customers who have stayed away for an unusually long time. They can help to boost morale or soothe a customer's ruffled feelings over some real or imagined offense. With a minimal outlay of time and money, good-will letters create a good feeling about your company that is passed on from one individual or business to another.

At a business lunch, Mr. Jones tells Mr. Smith about the nice letter he received from his supplier thanking him for the recent unusually large order. Mr. Smith tells Mr. Jones about the sympathy note he received from Z Company's president when Mr. Smith's mother died. The men discuss the thought behind the letters and decide that both companies are good to do business with because they care about the individual. Mrs. Haliwell tells Mrs. Jiggs about the lovely letter she received from the Neighborhood Boutique asking her to come in one day soon and see what they have to offer. Mrs. Haliwell dresses well on a limited budget, and Mrs. Jiggs wonders if she could do the same. She might even open a charge there if such a good attitude is typical of the way the store treats its customers. In each instance, the reaction usually is, "What a nice place to do business. Those people must really care about their customers. I'll have to look in one day soon."

Regardless of the occasion prompting the good-will letter, the writer should keep in mind some general guidelines. How well the writer knows the intended reader determines the intimacy of the letter. Naturally, if the recipient is an old and close friend, the letter will be more personal than if the intended reader is a customer or superior whom the writer does not know on a personal basis. Whatever the relationship between the writer and the reader, the letter's tone must be sincere, courteous, and brief. The writer should not talk down, use obvious flattery, or be condescending or obsequious. He or she should also avoid exaggeration, gushiness, and undue familiarity, all of which can have the wrong effect. Instead of thinking, "What a nice thing to do," the reader instinctively backs off, thinking, "What gives? What is this individual after? What's the catch?" In short, the choice of words in the good-will letter is vitally important to ensure the proper tone and to create good feelings in the reader.

Good-will letters are divided into five general categories: (1) thank you, (2) "We've missed you," (3) congratulations, (4) welcome, and (5) sympathy and concern.

Thank You Letters

Thank you letters are probably the most common of good-will letters. Sent for many reasons, none of them really needs to be written. Whether the reason for the letter is to thank someone for a gift, a favor, or a business transaction does not matter. Such letters showing the writer's appreciation are all gestures of good will.

Some businesses make a practice of sending all their regular customers a thank you letter at Christmas, enclosing some inexpensive but useful item such as a calendar, a small ruler, a metric conversion card, or a pen. All the items have the name of the business printed on them in a prominent place.

Other businesses make a practice of writing letters to their old and new customers some time during the year thanking them for the way they have handled their accounts and noting the promptness with which they have paid their bills. Still others will write to regular, long-standing customers who have put in unusually large orders. In these letters, whenever possible, the writer also does a bit of subtle selling.

Study Examples 10–1, 10–2, and 10–3. How would you react to them? What kind of attitude toward the writer would they arouse in you?

"We've Missed You" Letters

The "We've missed you" approach is a version of the good-will letter designed to bring back customers who have not been seen or heard from for a long time. Mail order houses use this type of letter frequently. Department stores often send out such letters to customers who have not used their charge accounts for several months. In addition to making the customer feel important by noting

EXAMPLE 10-1   Thank You Letter for Continued Patronage

Teason's Family Clothing Center

Everything in Clothing for the Whole Family
50 Years of Service

Wayside Avenue   **Seagog, ME 00000**

Christmas 198—

Mr. and Mrs. Aloysius Jiggs
76 Hesperous Circle
Seagog, ME 00000

Dear Mr. and Mrs. Jiggs:

    We at Teason's Family Clothing Center wish you and your
family a very Merry Christmas and a happy, healthy, and pros-
perous New Year. We would also like to take this opportunity
to thank you for your continued patronage. We appreciate your
confidence in us over the years and in our ability to provide
your family with the best in wearing apparel at reasonable
prices.

    Watch for our 198— desk calendar arriving soon. Without
taking a lot of room on your desk, it has enough space to jot
down all those important dates you do not want to miss.

                        Cordially yours,

                        Jason Teason

                        Jason Teason

im

EXAMPLE 10–2   Thank You Letter for Large Order

National Tool Company
40 Sawbuck Avenue
Craftsville, RI 00000

The Best in Small Tools at the Best Prices

23 July 198—

Mr. Roger Rambler
Coldstream Avenue
Springdale, RI 00000

Dear Mr. Rambler:

Thank you for the very large order you sent us on 7
July. We appreciate the orders you have placed regularly every month and the fine way in which you
have handled your account. It is our pleasure to
have you as a customer.

Your special order should have arrived before now,
and we hope you had a very successful sale.

Cordially,

NATIONAL TOOL COMPANY

Charles O'Toole

Charles O'Toole
Credit Manager

im

EXAMPLE 10–3   Thank You Letter for New Account Opened

Produce Cooperative, Inc.
Garden Terrace
Farmersville, SD 00000

April 20, 198—

Ms. Sylvia Sydner, Manager
Sydner's Produce Mart
Gilbert Street
Hannabel, SD 00000

Dear Ms. Sydner:

Thank you for your interest in Produce Cooperative. Your new
account #S–8740 is ready for your use just in time for the
first shipment of delicious California strawberries. You will
certainly want to order some as soon as possible while they
are at their peak.

By now you should have received our produce lists and prices.
All you need to do is call us at 000–0000, place your order,
and it will be ready for pickup by the time you arrive.

We look forward to the pleasure of filling your orders and to
a long and agreeable business relationship.

Sincerely,

Harry Corning

Harry Corning, Manager
PRODUCE COOPERATIVE, INC.

im

his or her absence, the letter may also offer a special inducement to stimulate sales or promote the store's products and services.

Look at Examples 10–4 and 10–5. Why is the first letter better than the second? What is there about the second letter that could be considered annoying? How would you change it?

Congratulations Letters

Congratulatory letters are always good-will letters. The occasion can be a promotion, graduation, retirement, engagement, marriage, birth, or an award. The list is long, and the kinds of letters can range from a simple card to a personal letter, depending upon the writer/reader relationship.

Jewelry stores often watch for engagement announcements in the newspapers and send letters expressing their best wishes to the bride-to-be with an invitation to come in and meet with their bridal consultant. At that time the future bride can register for her silver, china, and crystal. She may even be given a small spoon-shaped silver pin in the pattern she has selected.

Furniture stores send congratulations to engaged couples with colorful brochures picturing lovely rooms filled with their furniture; the couple is invited to come and pick out the furniture for their new home at very reasonable terms.

Sometimes a business agent might clip announcements of promotions, awards, or other articles about regular customers and send them on with a short note of congratulations. Examples 10–6 and 10–7 are two such letters.

Welcome Letters

Welcome letters are probably used more in small towns than in the larger cities, as the merchants in small towns are more apt to know most of their customers personally and be more aware of newcomers moving in. They send out letters of welcome to the new people, inviting them in to open an account or describing an available service. Wherever there is a Welcome Wagon Committee, merchants will supply samples of their products for distribution or give gift certificates to be used toward a larger purchase. Diaper Service companies often give a week's free trial to new parents as an inducement for them to subscribe to their service. The first baby of the new year is generally deluged with free gifts.

New management coming into a business may send a letter or memo to each department explaining a new philosophy or outlining any changes planned for the future and asking for comments and suggestions from the workers. While not exactly a welcome letter, it is a form of greeting designed to create good will among people who could be resentful of change.

Examples 10–8 and 10–9 illustrate a welcome letter and an interoffice memo greeting. Notice the pleasant tone and the "You" attitude of both letters. The appeal to the new parents is to their pride, their desire for the best for their son, and their pocketbook. See how the new manager tries to let the sales

EXAMPLE 10–4 "We've Missed You" Letter

Halberg's Haberdashery
Suffolk Mall
Providence, RI 00000

7 April 198—

Mr. Paul Jenkins
Hoskins Park Road
North Kingstown, RI 00000

Dear Mr. Jenkins:

We've missed you these past six months at Halberg's Haberdashery. But you still have time to take advantage of the
great savings offered in our annual spring clearance sale.
Everything on sale is our regular top-quality, brand-name
men's wear. Shirts, ties, and sweaters are going at half the
regular price; and all slacks and blazers are reduced by 25
percent. We have your size in all your favorite styles and
colors.

Come in and look around. Enjoy the relaxed atmosphere and
pleasant decor. Have a cup of coffee at the hospitality table
and renew acquaintance with your favorite sales clerk.

We look forward to seeing you again.

Sincerely,

Leonard Halberg

Leonard Halberg

co

EXAMPLE 10–5 "We've Missed You" Letter

Philbrook Catalogue Sales
1762 Lakeshore Drive
Chicago, IL 00000

For Quick Service, Call Toll-Free 1-800-000-0000

16 June 198—

Mr. Edmund Clarence
40 Stiles Lane
East Boondock, CN 00000

Dear Mr. Clarence:

It has been over three months since we shipped an order to
the Clarence home in East Boondock. We hope nothing is wrong!
Perhaps you have misplaced your catalogue. Just in case you
did, we are sending you a new one.

Take a few minutes to look over the many colorful pages full
of tempting bargains. Notice all the tools on page 17 and the
new safety equipment on page 30. There is also a whole section on video games to delight the whole family. For the
little woman there are ten pages of kitchen appliances to
make her life easier.

But Mr. Clarence, this is your last opportunity. If you do
not order now, while we regret having to do so, we will just
have to stop sending you our catalogues and remove your name
from our mailing list. We can only assume you are not interested and it will be your loss when you can no longer take
advantage of our sensational bargains.

Cordially yours,

Harriet Champlin

Harriet Champlin
Catalogue Sales

EXAMPLE 10–6   Congratulations Letter

**Kriss Engineering
1439 Jefferson Blvd.
Natick, MA 00000**

3 July 198—

Miss Sandra Curtiss
Forster Computer Manufacturing Co.
1576 Fulton Street
Natick, MA 00000

Dear Sandy:

Congratulations on your promotion! You certainly
deserve it more than anyone I know. Here is a copy
of the article that appeared in yesterday's paper.
I thought you might like to have an extra one to
send to Mary in Texas.

Sincerely,

Terri

Theresa Thornton

im

enc 1

EXAMPLE 10–7   Congratulations Letter

Pro Golf Clubs, Inc.
7 Sycamore Street
Staunton, NH 00000

5 January 198—

Mr. Benjamin Strauss
7 Stilmore Street
Staunton, NH 00000

Dear Ben:

Congratulations on your retirement after 40 years
of dedicated service to our company. Now you will
have all the time you have wished for to enjoy
those rounds of golf and to putter with Grace in
your gardens between those trips you are both so
fond of taking.

Enjoy your three weeks in the islands and remember
to come in and tell us all about them when you
return.

Cordially,

Frederick P. Holmes

Frederick P. Holmes
President

im

EXAMPLE 10–8   Welcome Letter

Comfy Baby Nappies Service
Stork Avenue
Sunglow, Arizona 00000

May 12, 198—

Mr. and Mrs. Sanford
61 Fulton Boulevard
Sunglow, AZ 00000

Dear Mr. and Mrs. Sanford

Congratulations on the birth of your new son. How proud you
both must be. Naturally you want the very best for him in
every way, especially comfort. To introduce you to the best
in diaper service, COMFY BABY NAPPIES is giving you a whole
week of free diaper service.

If you like the service as much as all our other customers
do, and we are sure you will, you need do nothing and delivery will continue at only $10.00 per week. If for any reason
you do not wish to keep on with COMFY BABY NAPPIES just return the enclosed addressed, postage—paid card at the end of
your free week's trial.

Just think, Mrs. Sanford, of the money you save when you do
not have to buy those expensive disposable diapers. Think of
the laundry you will avoid and fuel you will save when you do
not have all that washing in hot water if you use COMFY BABY
NAPPIES SERVICE. We look forward to having you join our ever-
growing family of happy parents and comfy babies.

Very truly yours,

Holly Coverall

Holly Coverall
Sales Manager

im

EXAMPLE 10-9   Interoffice Memo Greeting

```
TO:    All members of the Sales Department
FROM:  Thadeus Paulson, Sales Manager
DATE:  14 May 198—


       As the new sales manager of ORS Company, Inc., I
am taking this opportunity to say hello to those of
you whom I have not yet had the pleasure of meeting. I
look forward to doing so, however, at our next sales
conference on Tuesday, May 19, at two o'clock.

       Let us continue to keep our department on top! At
that meeting I want to hear your ideas and suggestions
for doing so, just as much as I want you to hear mine.

       Until then, let's all start thinking about some
fresh and exciting new plans of action.
```

personnel know he is interested in their ideas and wants to hear them, yet also prepares them for changes he plans to make.

Sympathy and Concern Letters

Letters of condolence and sympathy are for many people the most difficult to write, yet they may very well be among the most important when it comes to generating good will. While numerous beautiful and expressive cards are available on the market, they are not as well received as a letter, however short it may be. The knowledge that an individual cared enough to take time to write personally has great impact. Even a poorly written letter, if sincere, could be better than no letter in this instance.

Regardless of whether the sympathy letter is written to a close friend or to a distant business acquaintance, the main characteristic must be sincerity. Look at the letters in Examples 10-10 through 10-12. Does any one of them seem insincere or lack tact? Would any one of them be upsetting to the reader?

Sincerity and courtesy are the keynotes to effective good-will letters. Put yourself in the reader's place and write what you would like to read were you in the same situation. Ask yourself what you would look for in letters of thanks,

EXAMPLE 10–10   Sympathy Letter

New Fabrics, Inc.
Effram Industrial Center
Hazzard, VT 00000

The Best In Synthetic Fabrics
For Every Use At Home And At Work

12 August 198—

Mr. Solomon Baxter
Senior Vice President ZMC Corp.
Mercantile Square
Fairfield, NJ 00000

Dear Mr. Solomon:

Please accept my deepest sympathy on the loss of
your president. I know you will miss him dreadfully
at ZMC Corporation. Even though he was a hard task-
master in maintaining standards, he built up the
business almost singlehandedly and will be hard to
replace.

Sincerely,

Mary Jordan

Mary Jordan
Design Supervisor

lr

EXAMPLE 10–11   Sympathy Letter

Royce Office Supply Company
670 Main Street
Appanaug, RI 00000

17 May 198—

Miss Jane Worth
16 Sykes Avenue
Seekonk, MA 00000

Dear Jane:

May and I were saddened to hear of the death of
your mother. While we did not have the pleasure of
knowing her personally, we do know how very close
you were. Please accept our sincere sympathy in
your bereavement.

If there is anything at all we can do to help you
through this difficult time, you have only to call
us and we will be there.

Sincerely,

John

John Weiss
Personnel

EXAMPLE 10–12   Concern Letter

Egleberg's Warehouse   **Your Storage and Salvage Depot**
Water Street   **Arlington, SD 00000**

---

30 December 198—

Mr. Joseph M. Sallier, Manager
Kensington Storage Depot
Kensington Plaza
Arlington, SD 00000

Dear Mr. Sallier:

We at Egleberg's Warehouse were very sorry to hear of the
disastrous fire at your Kensington Plaza Storage Depot. We
know that no matter how much insurance a business has, it is
never enough to cover such a loss.

Right now our Salvage Street Warehouse is vacant and will be
for some time. Until your depot is repaired or a new one
built, we would be very happy to have you use it as your main
place of business. Call me and let me know what you want to
do, and if there is any other way in which we can help.

Sincerely,

Walter Sinclair

Walter Sinclair
Plant Manager

co

congratulations, condolences, or farewell, write accordingly, and you cannot go wrong. Your sincerity and concern will be obvious, and your thoughtfulness will be appreciated. The good-will you create will continue for a long time.

CHECKLIST

Good-will Letters

- Be sincere, courteous, and brief.
- Choose words and tone appropriate to purpose of the letter, i.e., sympathy, congratulations.
- Praise when appropriate but don't fawn.
- Sympathize when appropriate but don't overdo.
- Avoid talking down, obsequiousness, and condescension.
- Avoid undue familiarity.

EXERCISES

1. You work for a bank, and it has long been the custom to send a new penny to each local woman whose engagement has been announced in the local paper. The penny was attached to a card with the message, "A penny saved is a penny earned." Your supervisor asks you to compose a form letter to go with the card inviting the young women and their fiancés to come in and discuss savings accounts and all the other services the bank has to offer.

2. You are the credit manager for a large department store. It is the custom each Christmas to send a letter to all charge customers in good standing thanking them for their patronage and the way they have handled their accounts. Write the body of the letter.

3. As executive secretary of the Chamber of Commerce in a small town, it is your job to create a letter to newcomers who have moved into town within the past month. Coupons worth between $5.00 and $10.00 toward merchandise or services have been collected from twenty different businesses and are to be included with each letter. Write the body of the letter.

4. The wife of the president of your company was killed by a hit-and-run driver. It is a small company, and while you have attended many meetings at which the president presided, you are not friends outside the job and are not on a first-name basis on the job. Write a letter of condolence.

5. You own a family clothing store and two of your best customers are retiring and moving south. Mr. and Mrs. Sullen have been buying their clothing from you for fifteen years and you have always served them yourself. You want to thank them for their business over the years and the fine way in which they have always handled their account. You also want to congratulate them on their retirement and wish them good luck in their move to a warmer climate. Write the body of the letter.

6. A close friend who has had business reverses has decided to sell out and salvage what he can before he is forced into bankruptcy. Write him a letter showing your concern over his predicament.

7. You run a wholesale business selling hardware supplies. One of your customers who has placed a moderate-sized order every month for five years has suddenly stopped buying from you. You have heard nothing from him for six months. Rumor has it that he was dissatisfied with his last few orders but no one knows why. You want to know why and if possible to get him back as a steady customer. His orders were steady, and he always paid his bills before the tenth of the month to take advantage of the 2 percent discount you offer. Write the letter.

8. You are the credit manager of a chain of retail department stores. It is the store's policy whenever good charge-account customers move out-of-state to transfer the account to the store nearest the city to which they are moving. Write the body of a letter thanking a customer for past patronage, explaining the action taken, and giving the necessary information about the location of the nearest store in the other state.

9. An old college fraternity brother has received a big promotion resulting in a rather long article in the Alumni newsletter. You want to congratulate him and send him a copy of the article in case he did not see it. Write the body of the letter.

10. A new cashier in your restaurant on an interstate highway gave a transient customer ten dollars too much change. You accept the loss as you certainly don't expect to have the customer return it. Much to your surprise, three days later you receive a letter with a $10 check made out to the restaurant enclosed. The letter explains that the error was not discovered until that evening, when the customer was at home — 300 miles away. As soon as the error was caught, the individual made out the check and wrote the letter.
    a. Write the letter from the customer explaining the check.
    b. Write a letter from the manager thanking the customer for the check and praising his or her honesty.

11. Your biggest competitor is opening a new store in your city. You have been invited to the grand opening, RSVP.
    a. Write a letter accepting the invitation and wishing him good luck.
    b. Write a letter declining the invitation and wishing him good luck.

12. You are the president of a company that manufactures video games. One of your designers has created a new game, the sales of which have exceeded the sale of all your other models. In fact, it is almost impossible to keep up with demand. As a result, the employee has earned a $500 bonus. Write the letter to go with the check congratulating the employee on his or her success and dedication.

13. The store next to your shop had a bad explosion doing many thousands of dollars' worth of damage to stock and furnishings. Only through the heroic efforts of the fire department were neighboring stores kept from being damaged.
    a. Write a letter of condolence to your neighbor.
    b. Write a letter to the fire department thanking them for the fine job they did and enclosing a check for $100 for their Widows and Orphans Fund.

14. You are the owner of a business that sponsors an employees' team in a bowling league made up of teams from your competitors. Your team wins the trophy for

the current season. You had announced at the beginning of the season that if your team won, the business would treat the members to a steak dinner at the best restaurant in the city. Write a letter to the members of the team congratulating them on their victory and announcing the date, time, and place of the victory dinner at which you and your spouse will serve as hosts in order to meet everyone and to congratulate them personally.

11

The Job Process

Finding a Job

Finding a job can be a bewildering and discouraging process. Many professions that only a few years ago were clamoring for people are now closed because of the economy and the lowered birth rate after the World War II baby boom. Take, for example, the teaching profession. In the 1960s there were not enough teachers to go around. Today, teaching jobs are few and far between. Modern technology now demands people trained in computer science and data processing. Secretaries who have prided themselves on their shorthand and typing skills now have to learn how to use word processing machines.

How then does one go about finding a job? The classified ads in newspapers and many professional and trade journals have sections pertaining to job openings. Private employment agencies, for a fee, will help an applicant find a job. Help can also be found in state employment agencies or college placement services. Alumni associations, fraternal organizations, local businesses, business friends of your parents, relatives, civic organizations, banks, and even the members of your church are all potential sources of job information. Mrs. Smith knows Mr. Doe who said that Acme Mattress Company is looking for a new salesperson to replace Mr. Sweeney, who is retiring. Mrs. Hill heard from Mrs. Johnstone that May, the receptionist at the Beautiful Hair Salon, was leaving and the owner was looking for a replacement.

Applicants interested in federal or state jobs should look at the Civil Service Agency. To qualify for a classified position, applicants must take an examination in their particular field. Examinations for all classifications are given periodically. Those who pass an exam in any given area receive a rating appropriate to that particular skill category. Such a rating is necessary before applying for any civil service position. When an opening is available, the top three placers on the exam are notified.

Students attending a college or university usually have available the services of a career planning and placement office. By whatever name it is called, such an office is a good source of information for career and job placement needs. Most placement offices belong to the College Placement Council, Inc., which publishes the College Placement Annual, a treasure-trove of job-related information.

While no two placement offices will function in exactly the same way, the following example illustrates how one might work in bringing together the business world and the potential employee. A typical placement officer is constantly in search of ways to expand job opportunities for the students of the college. In addition to correspondence, personal on-site contact with businesses is vital. The placement officer may travel hundreds of miles throughout a state visiting stores, businesses, banks, and industries in an attempt to open lines of communication between the college, its programs and graduates, and the world of work.

In addition to individual career counseling, career planning and placement offices also have available a wide variety of services, such as part-time and full-time job postings, student credential file materials for use with prospective employers, as well as workshops covering such topics as résumé writing, the job interview, and job search techniques. A career resource library may house a full complement of career and educational information for student use.

During the academic year, special events may include a general Career Day or an Allied Health Career Day. Employers from the full spectrum of the working world, including the military, are invited to the campus to discuss career and job opportunities with students. On-campus interviews may be held as an additional service. To further enhance student opportunities, some colleges have an Employer Advisory Board and an employer guest lecturer file that articulates the needs of the working world to help the student prepare to meet those needs.

Once the potential job is located, the application process begins. The job seeker can look at the recent outpouring of materials on résumé writing and interviewing techniques for help in the first step — writing the résumé or data sheet.

The Résumé

A résumé or data sheet is a brief summary of your education, your work experience and training, and any other special skills you might have. It is either sent with a cover letter to a prospective employer or brought to an interview. Bringing it to the interview is a good idea, even if you have already sent one.

Résumé writing workshops are offered to help career-oriented students in compiling accurate and proper résumés for their own use in finding employment. The following guidelines are basic.

1. Employers look at your résumé for strengths you may have to offer over those of other candidates for the same position.
2. To show those strengths, your résumé should point out clearly what you have done in the past that indicates potential success in the future.
3. The résumé is more than a brief history of your education, achievements, and experience highlighting your accomplishments. It is not, however, an autobiography and, therefore, should not contain your whole life's history. Its length will vary, growing longer as you grow older and have more jobs and experiences.
4. Be positive in your entries. Omit any weaknesses but always tell the truth.
5. If your hobbies and outside interests pertain to the job or indicate that you get along well with people, include them.
6. Photographs, unless required, are not included. Under the law, the times when they can be required are limited. For example, a photograph would be expected from an applicant for a modeling position but not from an applicant for a teaching position.
7. Personal information is optional. An employer can no longer demand to know your marital status except for your tax exemptions, or your sex and many other bits of personal information that used to be routine on all job applications. Such questions might be in violation of Title VII of the Civil Rights Act of 1964 or other laws pertaining to equal employment opportunities. You may volunteer as much as you care to, but you can refuse to give such information if asked.
8. References, if listed, should be on a separate sheet of paper. Usually a notation is made at the end of the résumé, "References available on request." Neither are school transcripts included. If employers want them, they will ask you to have them forwarded.
9. The résumé can begin with a summary statement of the specific kind of position you want.
10. As a graduating student with little or no experience, you may want to indicate what part of your college expenses you earned if the amount was significant, and any summer or part-time work you may have had to show a sense of responsibility and independence. Naturally any work experience relating to the job being sought should be given serious attention.
11. Each time you make a change — more education, promotion, job change, awards — you should add it to your résumé.

After compiling all your information, setting up your outline, and preparing to write the final draft, ask yourself these questions.

1. Does the résumé tell the whole story?
2. Does it emphasize my strengths without exaggeration or understatement?

3. Is it complete? Concise? Neat?
4. Does it contain any unnecessary information?
5. Does it sell me? Does it reflect my major accomplishments?

If you can answer these questions satisfactorily, you are ready for the final product. The following guidelines should help you do a good job.

1. Set up the format carefully. Be sure to include your social security number.
2. Type it accurately on good-quality white bond paper.
3. Be sure spelling and grammar are correct.
4. Leave wide margins and sufficient white space between entries.
5. Use offset printing or clean sharp photocopies as the least expensive ways of getting good duplicates.
6. Reread your résumé and show it to at least two businesspeople for an objective analysis. If those two people do any hiring, so much the better as you are looking for objective criticism, not compliments.

Chronological and Functional Résumés

There are two types of résumés: the *chronological* and the *functional*. The chronological is most often used, especially by those seeking their first job, those in the teaching profession, or those in any position where there are specific educational requirements. The functional résumé stresses work experience skills and other life experiences that might pertain to the position being sought. It is used more by those lacking advanced education, those who want to change jobs, or those whose educational background does not relate directly to the sought-after career.

The information in each type of résumé is similar, but the emphasis is different. Personal information, while not necessary, is often included, sometimes at the beginning and sometimes at the end. Photographs, unless specifically required, are not included.

If you hold a license for any profession such as for nursing, piloting, or bus or truck driver, the license number should be included even if it does not pertain directly to the position being sought.

Volunteer activities such as Red Cross Disaster Service, Water Safety, First Aid Work, Scouting, and other youth activities should be mentioned as an indication of a well-rounded individual able to get along with all types of people, committed to the community, concerned about others, and most importantly with a sense of responsibility and an ability to manage time. Although most students will be using the chronological résumé, examples of both kinds are given here. The order of information may vary depending on the individual's preference and the background required for a specific job. A basic outline for a résumé might look like this:

Name   Telephone number
Address
Social Security number
Job objective
Education
    Honors and awards
Experience
    Foreign language fluency and travel
Extracurricular activities
Personal
Interests and hobbies
Community activities
References

Study Examples 11–1 through 11–5 and notice the different formats. Note also that some résumés volunteer more information than is required by law. Consider the reasons such information may have been included.

The Letter of Application

The letter of application may well be the most important letter you will ever write. It is essentially a sales letter, and the products you are selling are you and your skills. The letter is usually the employer's first introduction to you. The old cliché, "First impressions are lasting impressions," was never more true.

Assuming you have all the required education, training, and abilities, your letter will be the deciding factor in whether you get a response and an interview. Thus, the function of the application letter is to establish in the reader's mind a favorable attitude toward you, to create in the reader a desire to meet you and discuss your qualifications, to convince the reader that you are the person he or she wants, and to stimulate the reader to action on your behalf.

The importance of the appearance of the application letter cannot be stressed enough. A search committee will very often refuse to consider any applicant whose letter is not typed or in which there are grammatical errors, regardless of the individual's qualifications. This is particularly true if the position being sought is one in which the applicant would represent the business to the public. Such carelessness in an application letter indicates carelessness in other areas.

Put yourself in the position of a prospective employer. You receive letters from eighty applicants seeking the one job you have advertised. As you go through the letters, perhaps sorting them into piles of no, yes, and possibly, you instinctively form an opinion of each writer from the appearance, content, and tone of the letter. Regardless of each applicant's qualifications, you will

EXAMPLE 11–1   Résumé

RÉSUMÉ OF DOROTHY BAKER KEANE

Address: 701 Greenwich Avenue
           Warwick, RI   00000
Telephone: (000) 000–0000
Social Security Number: 000–00–0000

Education

A.S.   Associate in Science (Medical Laboratory
                  Technology)
June 1982   Community College of Rhode Island

June 1975   High School Diploma — Technical Curriculum
                  Atlantic City (New Jersey) High School

Additional Education

1975–76   Completed one year nurse's training
                  Hahnemann Medical College and Hospital
                  Philadelphia, PA   00000

Experience

June 1976–   Research Assistant   Biological and Medical
January 1978   Sciences, Brown
                                        University
                                        Providence, RI   00000

                  During college years worked part–time for
                  William Jones, M.D., East Greenwich, RI as a
                  medical assistant

References available upon request

EXAMPLE 11–2   Résumé

```
Harriet M. Purdy            Social Security: 000-00-0000
302 Oxford Boulevard        MI License: RN-0000000
Mayberry, MI  00000         Telephone: (000)-000-0000
```

Professional Objectives

    To do general nursing duty at a community hospital, to continue my education part time, and to rise eventually to a supervisory nursing position.

Education

```
1970                    RN  General Hospital, Titusville, AL
                        (fourth in class of fifty)
```

Employment

```
1978 to present:    Salmon Creek Memorial Hospital
                    Salmon Creek, OR
1975-1977           U.S. Army Field Hospital, Korea
                    Rank — First Lieutenant
1970-1977           General Hospital
                    Titusville, AL
```

Personal

```
Health — excellent      Age — 35
Single — free to travel
Fluent in Spanish, French, and Portuguese
Active First Aid instructor ARC
```

References (by permission)

```
Major Charles Harkness    Dr. Bart X. Hodges
Chief of Staff            Salmon Creek Memorial Hospital
General Wood Hospital     Salmon Creek, OR  00000
Washington, DC  00000
```

EXAMPLE 11–3 Résumé

Résumé of James Carl Baxter   Social Security Number:
       703 Westbrook Lane   000–00–0000
       Harleysville, PA 00000   Telephone: (000)–000–0000

<u>Health</u>   Excellent   Need glasses for reading

<u>Sex</u>   Male   <u>Race</u> Caucasian

<u>Age</u>   29

<u>Religion</u>   Roman Catholic

<u>Marital Status</u>   Married, one child

<u>Education</u>

June 1982   AFA in Art
            Harleysville Junior College, Harleysville,
            PA 00000
June 1975   Graduate Atlantic City, NJ High School

<u>Additional Education</u>

1975–76   Completed courses in Beginning and Advanced
            Engineering Drawing — Sacramento, CA Junior Col-
            lege

<u>Experience</u>

Summer 1976   Apprentice Architectural Draftsman
              Haining & Jones Company
              Sacramento, CA 00000

1976 to present   Cartographer — Right-of-Way Division
              Pennsylvania Department of Transportation
              Norristown, PA 00000

<u>Additional Qualifications</u>:   Hold 88.9 Rating at GS–4 Level
                        Cartographic Assistant/
                        Technician
                        U. S. Civil Service — 11–82

EXAMPLE 11–4   Résumé

RÉSUMÉ

Jacqueline Fenstermacher
SS 000-00-0000

Home Address

592 Salem Street
Northburn, VA 00000

Phone   000-0000

Job Objective

To obtain a position writing advertising copy.

Education

1980 MS		Television/Radio Video University New York, NY
1978 MFA		Creative Writing Penstaff University Oglesby, GA
1976 BA		English/Speech Signal College Mt. Holly, NC
Honors		Phi Beta Kappa

Experience

1979–80	Teaching assistant, Video University. Taught basic writing for TV/Radio including news, commentary, drama.
1976–78	Part time. Wrote advertising copy for local merchants for Oglesby Weekly Chronicle. Writer/Editor, Oglesby Police Department. Wrote and taped public service announcements for local radio and TV. Wrote video scripts to train police and civilian personnel.
1974–76	News writer and announcer for Signal College radio station.

Languages

Fluent in French, Italian, and Spanish

EXAMPLE 11–4   *(continued)*

Personal

    Age 30
    Marital status Single

Hobbies

    Photography, travel, painting, and jogging.

References furnished on request.

EXAMPLE 11–5 Résumé

Henry Hilton Harlow   Married, no children

9 Walker Avenue   Age: 20

Williston, NC 00000   Health: Excellent

Tel: (000)–000–0000

CAREER GOALS   To work as an automobile mechanic in a large
                  garage servicing foreign cars and to own my
                  own garage someday.

EXPERIENCE

1978   Head mechanic at Grantroads Foreign Car Sales,
to present   Williston, NC — familiar with all major Brit-
                  ish, German, and Japanese sports cars.

1974–1978   Assistant mechanic, Michaelson's Service Sta-
                  tion, Lucasville, NC — worked on all makes of
                  American cars.

1972–1974   Apprentice mechanic part time and summers at
                  Havenor Garage, Williston, NC.

EDUCATION

1974   Williston Vocational High School — Diploma in
                  automobile mechanics.

INTERESTS   Sports car racing — member Sports Car Club of
                  America, driver and pit crew.

HOBBIES   Jogging, metal work, and photography.

automatically put those letters that are sloppily written, too self-centered in content, or pushy and overbearing in tone in either the no or maybe pile. You may even refuse to consider anyone whose letter is not typed. The candidates you will consider and eventually interview are those whose letters are neatly typed, indicating care in preparation, whose information is given briefly but completely, whose tone implies confidence but not conceit, and whose manner indicates an interest in what they can contribute to your company and not what you can do for them.

Realizing, then, the importance of the application letter, the next step is to decide what goes in it. What belongs there and what belongs in the résumé? Ask yourself the following questions and write down the answers in outline form. Then when you write the actual letter, discard any information that is not relevant.

1. Where did I learn about the job? Did someone suggest I write?
2. Do I understand what the position entails? Am I really qualified?
3. If my background does not apply directly, does the position offer on-the-job training?
4. What exactly are my qualifications, my education, skills, experience? Do they apply?
5. Do I have references available? Have I called or written for their permission to list them as references?

Generally, the letter itself should be three or four paragraphs long on a single page. It should mention the reason you are writing, the specific position you want, and where you heard about it (the classified ads, a business friend, or the college placement service). You should touch briefly on your interest in the company or business to which you are applying and tell how you believe your qualifications can be of benefit. If you have experience that applies directly to the job you are seeking, you should mention it.

How much or how little you say about your educational background in the letter will depend upon the kind of job you are seeking, whether such information is asked for, or whether you are a recent graduate with no work experience. You also refer the reader to the résumé.

In closing you express your wish for an interview, when and where you will be available, and the phone number at which you can be reached. If you are looking for work in a distant city, you should indicate your willingness to send any additional information that may be required.

Since the application letter is a cover letter for the résumé, you should be careful to repeat as little as possible the information in the résumé but refer to it.

Other factors governing the content of the cover letter are whether the application is in direct response to a job posting, whether the letter is unsolicited, or whether the letter is in response to hearsay that a position is open.

For Class Discussion

Study Examples 11–6 through 11–10. Be prepared to discuss the following questions in class.

1. Would you agree to write a reference for the writer in Example 11–7? Why? What is there about the letter that makes you want to do so?
2. Which application letters make the best impression? Why?
3. Which letters make the worst impression? Why? How would you change them?
4. How do you react to the tone of each letter?
5. How do you react to the content?
6. Are any of them incomplete? Are any too long?

The Interview

Despite an impressive résumé and cover letter, the interview can make or break the job applicant. Once again, appearance can be a deciding factor, all other aspects being equal. When interviewing applicants for positions in the English Department, we look for a number of different things in addition to educational background and experience.

We take it for granted that the individual has the necessary degrees in the academic discipline, or he or she would not be interviewed. Therefore, we look for the following qualities. Overall appearance is first. Neatness and good grooming are very important. A sloppy appearance often is an indication of sloppy ways. The classroom teacher has a captive audience and owes the students the courtesy of being as pleasant to look at as possible. Tone of voice is another point. To have to sit for an hour and listen to a squeaky, high-pitched voice can be torment, and voice modulation can be learned. Good enunciation is important. Students cannot learn if they cannot understand what the instructor is saying. Needless to say, correct grammar is vitally important. Poise is another consideration. Naturally anyone seeking a job is bound to be a bit anxious, but trembling hands can be clasped in the lap or kept under the table. The control the individual is able to exert over that anxiety is important. Students are the first to sense a nervous teacher and capitalize on that weakness. Last but not least is the question of whether the applicant will fit in with the rest of the faculty and have patience with the slower students. We ask many questions about attitude; for example, "How do you feel about in-service training? How do you feel about teaching composition? How do you feel about honoring office hours? Do you welcome students for extra help?"

While the above comments pertain to the teaching profession, many of the points under consideration apply equally well to any position in which the applicant meets the public, works in an office, or even in a shop. However well trained a secretary may be, he or she must still learn the system used in each new place of employment. Machinists must learn new procedures whenever

EXAMPLE 11–6 Letter Asking for a Recommendation

954 Parkway Street
Folly Landing, RI 00000
May 2, 198–

Ms. Erica Moser
Admissions Office
Quantum Community College
Quantum, RI 00000

Dear Ms. Moser:

For the past three-and-one-half semesters and in the intervening summer sessions I have worked under your supervision
as a Work-Study Student. During that time, I did typing, filing, used various office machines, answered the telephone,
delivered messages, and sorted mail.

In three weeks I will receive an associate degree, graduating
with high honors in secretarial sciences. I am now applying
at several business offices for a secretarial position.

Do you feel that you know me and my work well enough to write
me a letter of recommendation to be added to my dossier at
the Quantum Placement Office? If you do, would you please address your letter "To Whom It May Concern," and send it directly to the Placement Office. I have waived my right to see
the recommendation letters.

Thank you for your help.

Sincerely,

Sharon DeWitt

Sharon DeWitt

EXAMPLE 11-7 Application Letter

> Missy Lovecraft
> Forest Lane
> Salem, MA 00000
>
> August 8, 198—
>
>
> Chairman, Department of English
> Carstairs College
> Carstairs, CN 00000
>
> Dear Sir or Madam as the Case May Be:
>
> I am a dynamite instructor, full of enthusiasm and piz-
> zazz. I am just what you need to spice up your department and
> give the students a run for their money.
>
> I have a BA in English from Calamity Hill College in Ne-
> braska, and while I do not have a Masters I have scads of
> credits in graduate courses in Art, Music, and English.
>
> I have had ten years' teaching experience at the second-
> ary school level but this year was retrenched. You really
> can't afford to pass me by when I have so much to offer.
>
> I should tell you that I will teach any course, my back-
> ground is diverse, better than that of half of your current
> faculty. However, I teach composition only under duress.
>
> Don't wait too long to call me at 1-000-000-0000 as I am
> sure to be offered other positions.
>
> Sincerely,
>
> *Missy Lovecraft*
> Missy Lovecraft

EXAMPLE 11–8   Application Letter

---

29 Hover Avenue
Nebulous, ME 00000
10 July 198—

Mr. Herman Hochts
Personnel Director, Hochts Electronics
Overland Industrial Park
Overland, ME 00000

Dear Mr. Hochts:

The July issue of ELECTRONICS magazine carried your advertisement for an electronic engineering assistant. I am interested in that position.

A recent graduate of Excelsior Community College, I have an
Associate Degree in electronics. Prior to entering college
after three years military service, I had worked for six
years at Hover Electronics in Alliston, NH in the experimen-
tal laboratory. During that time I rose from assisting the
project engineers in various capacities to running my own
projects. I received awards for two inventions that saved the
company many thousands of dollars. The attached résumé provides more detailed information.

The combination of work experience and education meet the requirements specified in the advertisement. On that basis, may
I have the privilege of an interview at your convenience? I
can be reached at the above address by mail or at 000–000–
0000 by phone anytime between 9 a.m. and 5 p.m.

Sincerely,

Oscar Mason

Oscar Mason

EXAMPLE 11–9   Application Letter

756 Allen's Avenue
Norwood, MA   00000
11 May 198—

Zayner Toys, Inc.
Jefferson Boulevard
Warwick, GA   00000

Gentlemen:

The classified section of the May 10, 198— Centaur Bulletin carried your ad for a toy designer. This letter expresses my interest in that position.

After ten years in the same designing job, I feel it is time to move on. The design and manufacture of toys has always interested me, and Zayner Toy trucks are among the best I have seen. My experience and skill as an automotive body designer could easily be adapted to designing toy trucks, and I believe I have much to contribute to Zayner Company in that capacity. My various experiences in design and other areas are listed in the attached résumé.

I would appreciate an interview at your convenience. At that time I will bring a portfolio of my work, which will include a unique new toy truck design that I would like to offer Zayner Toys if I am given the opportunity.

I can be reached at work at 000-0000 between 8 a.m. and 3:30 p.m. and at home after 4:30 p.m. at 000-0000. My employers know of my interest in changing jobs and are aware that I am writing this letter.

Sincerely,

Mathew Hornby

Mathew Hornby

EXAMPLE 11–10   Application Letter

95 Essex Road
Huxley, PA 00000
August 30, 198—

Hastings Contractors
Fales Industrial Park
Perkiomenville, PA 00000

Gentlemen and Ladies:

Woodlines Building Supply had your ad for a finish carpenter posted on their bulletin board. Chet Woods, the owner, suggested I write to you and apply for the position.

I have fifteen years of experience in all areas of carpentry: from an apprentice in a cabinet shop, through rough carpentry in construction, to finish work. My résumé lists the firms I have worked for and the type of work I have done for each.

I have a truck, ladders, and all my own tools as your ad specifies, and I can come for an interview at any time convenient for you. You can reach me by phone after 5 p.m. at 000-0000.

Sincerely,

Harold C. Schultz

Harold C. Schultz

they change jobs or even move from one department to another within the same company.

Some do's and don'ts to remember when being interviewed. Do:

1. Try to be at ease.
2. Take pains with your appearance. Cleanliness and neatness are more important than makeup or expensive clothing.
3. Answer all questions honestly, briefly but completely.
4. Have any papers you bring to deliver or refer to in proper order so you can find them calmly and with a minimum of paper shuffling.
5. Establish eye contact as much as possible without actually staring.
6. Maintain a pleasant expression but feel free to react and respond to the interviewer. A deadpan is disastrous.
7. Show you know something about the business.

Do not:

1. Begin by asking about salary and benefits; save that until the end.
2. Chew gum. Nothing can turn a prospective employer against an applicant more quickly than gum snapping.
3. Smoke unless the interviewer should say, "If you smoke go ahead and I will join you."
4. Fidget, i.e., don't tap your feet, click ballpoint pens, or tap fingers on the chair. Such habits are extremely annoying.
5. Be late and don't overstay your time. The employer may have a whole day scheduled for interviews, and if you run late you inconvenience the next candidate as well as upset the interviewer's schedule.
6. High pressure the interviewer. Rarely does anyone get a job offer on the first meeting. If you are called back a second or third time, you know you are in the running. It is acceptable, however, to ask when you might expect to hear about when a decision will be made.

The Follow-up Letter

After an interview that you feel has gone well, write a follow-up letter. But before you begin to write, jot down the high and low points of the interview. Was there anything you forgot to add? Were there any questions you could not answer at the time? Were there any points you should have emphasized more?

In the follow-up letter you should briefly restate your interest in the company and the job. Point out again how your education and experience would fit in and be of benefit to the business. You should include information you did not mention but remembered after the interview. And, of course, thank the interviewer for the opportunity.

Sometimes a letter is not always necessary. For example, a follow-up letter is not written if an interview went badly or if you have discovered the job is not what you want or that you are not qualified for the position. Generally, however, the follow-up letter does create a favorable impression on the interviewer. Study the two examples below. How would you react to the letters if you were the interviewer?

1. Dear Mrs. Stimson:

   Thank you for the interesting tour of the offices at
   Bergers Secretarial Services, Inc. and for the privilege
   of an interview. I came away with an even stronger feeling
   that Bergers is where I want to work.

   At the time of our interview in describing my shorthand and typing skills and my familiarity with office machinery, I neglected to mention that I also am proficient
   in using word processing machines. With my extensive background and experience I believe I could contribute greatly
   to the efficiency of Bergers Services.

   Should you care to discuss my qualifications further,
   I am available at your convenience.

2. Dear Mr. Lyle:

   My visit to Gemini Cartographers convinced me that it
   is the ideal place for a serious and capable cartographer
   to work. Meeting the high standards of performance exhib-
   ited by those people I met presents the kind of challenge
   I look for. Because of my ten years' experience as a Navy
   cartographer and five years as a draftsman, I believe I
   can meet that challenge.

   Thank you for a most interesting and exciting meeting.

Accepting or Refusing a Job

Finally, you have been offered a job and must make the decision to accept or reject it. Whether you have been notified by letter or phone, a written response accepting or rejecting the position is necessary. The acceptance letter is probably the easiest, simplest, and most pleasant to write. In some instances this acknowledgment may be considered a legal contract. The rules are few. Let your enthusiasm show but don't emote. Acknowledge the position and the date of the letter offering it to you. Answer any questions you may be asked and acknowledge any forms you may have been sent. If you have not been given a date to report to work, ask if you could come in on a certain date to make arrangements. Here is a sample acceptance:

Dear Mr. Lyle:

I accept with pleasure and anticipation your offer of June 10 to work as a master cartographer at Gemini Cartographers beginning July 6.

Although I shall be out of state this weekend, I will have all the necessary papers on the way to you before I leave. I have also made arrangements for the required physical exam.

I look forward to seeing you again, to working with the Gemini Company, and to meeting the challenge you have offered me.

Occasionally you may have to refuse a position. Perhaps it was not just what you wanted, another job offer has arisen that pays more, you really don't want to move, or perhaps you just didn't like what you learned at your last interview. Whatever the reason, you must reject the position with tact. You may someday want to work there, and you do not want to create a bad impression. How would the tone of the following letter appeal to you if you were Mrs. Stimson?

Dear Mrs. Stimson:

Thank you for your kind offer of the position as a member of the secretarial pool at Bergers Secretarial Services, Inc. I am certain I would have enjoyed working there knowing there was the opportunity to work up to a supervisory capacity.

However, since my meeting with you I have been offered just that kind of supervisory position with another company. Since that position is exactly in line with my future goals, I must decline your offer of employment.

Thank you for the interest you have taken in me and for the time you spent showing me around Bergers Secretarial Services.

After reading this chapter, you now realize that finding the right job is not always going to be easy. It will be to your advantage then to make use of the various agencies designed to help with the job process. Start with the Career Planning and Placement office at your college and branch out from there. Be honest in your self-evaluation; take great care in writing your résumé and application letters; be neat, well groomed, polite, and, above all, prompt when you go to an interview. If you follow these simple rules, you cannot help but make a favorable impression on any prospective employer.

CHECKLIST

The Job Process

- Search for job openings through agencies, friends, social organizations, and college placement offices.
- Develop résumé.
- Get references.
- Compile dossier.
- Write application letters.
    a. Keep letter to one page.
    b. Don't repeat résumé details.
    c. Ask for an interview.
- Write follow-up letter after interview.
- Write acceptance/refusal letter if offered a job.

EXERCISES

1. Rewrite the following letters of application adding any information you feel is necessary to make the letters complete and correcting any errors.

    a.   I would like to apply for a public relations job at your business. I am an expert at PR as I have an AA degree from XYZ Junior College. I took journalism, speech and lots of psych courses. My friends say I could sell refrigerators to eskimoes because I talk so well.
    I want a full time position, at least 20 grand a year to start, and all benefits like Blue Cross, Delta Dental and the perscription plan.
    By the way, exactly what do you do at Hielsing Service Corp.? Call me at 000-000-0000 between 9 and 4:30. After that I will be either at the beach or on the town. Oh yes, my resume is attached.

    b.   I would very much like to work as a teacher aide at your school because I heard that handicapped students are mainstreamed there. My AA degree is in Education and Social Services from Sumpter Community College. I did my field placement at Saxon Elementary School, Wildwood, MA. under the supervision of Mr. John Doe. My resume is attached. Please let me know when I can come for an interview.
    Thanking you in advance, I remain
    Sincerely yours,

    c.   I read in a paper the other night that you are looking for a good data processer. Stop looking for here I am. I have a certificate in data processing from Hoot-Owl technicians school and placed first out of a class of 50. I worked during the summer for the White-Owl Bank under the supervision of Mrs. Jane Smith. Let me tell you, she was one tough boss.

```
Everything had to be done just right or else!
     I'll be in your area next Thursday afternoon
and will drop in to see you and tell you all about
myself. Take a good look at the attached resume and
you will see I am just the person you are looking
for.
```

2. You have just received an associate degree in Secretarial Sciences as an executive secretary. You see the following ad in the classified section of your local paper.

   Wanted: Executive assistant for small business office. Must be able to take shorthand, type, file, and run various office machines. Experience and some knowledge of word processing desirable but not vital. Will train. Pleasant personality and good telephone voice mandatory. Send letter and résumé to Box 21, Prov., RI.

   a. Write a letter of application, making up the name of the paper and the business office.
   b. Write a résumé.
   c. Describe in general terms how you would dress for the interview.
   d. Write a letter declining the offer of the job, making up your reasons.

3. As a retail management student at a two-year college you have completed your work experience at a big city department store where you worked directly with the men's wear buyer. You want to apply for an opening that you heard about from your immediate supervisor — that of a department manager at the store's branch in another city. The position will be ready a week after you graduate with an Associate degree in retail management.

   a. Write an application letter.
   b. Write a résumé.
   c. Write to your work supervisor asking if you may use his name as a reference.

4. You have a Master's degree in business administration and have been working for five years at X Company, a manufacturing company that is now undergoing management changes. You do not like the way the changes will affect your position and decide that now is the time to move on. You have heard via the grapevine that a position similar to the one you now hold will open soon with a rival company at their overseas branch in Paris. You are fluent in French, having come from a French background and having studied the language for four years in high school and four years in college. You have traveled extensively in Europe as you were stationed overseas during military service between the time you earned your Bachelor's and your Master's degrees. In your five years with X Company, you supervised six people and received an efficiency award for introducing a timesaving system for handling orders.

   a. Write a letter of application.
   b. Write a résumé.
   c. Write a follow-up letter after what seemed to you to be a very successful interview.
   d. Write a letter accepting the job.

5. Write your own résumé to keep for future reference and to be updated as necessary.

12

The Memorandum and the Memorandum Report

Memorandums, or memos, are essentially "inside" correspondence. Unlike letters, they are not directed to outside recipients; rather, they contain messages sent within an organization. They may travel in three directions:

1. *Upward* — Up the corporate ladder to superiors.
2. *Across* — Across to equals or counterparts, perhaps in another location.
3. *Downward* — Down to subordinates.

Because these messages often travel toward those in higher positions, memos exert influence on decision makers, the people who decide about salary raises and advancements. Therefore, good memo writers frequently get the promotions. Obviously, care in preparation is important; a poorly written memorandum is as unsatisfactory as an unacceptable letter.

Letters and memos are alike in that both strive to convey messages briefly, yet clearly and completely. Nevertheless, letters and memos differ in both format and content.

Memo Format

The internal message eliminates some of the formalities of the letter. Addresses are often not needed, especially within a small organization. Salutations and complimentary closes are not included. Although signatures may be omitted, some dictators do choose to have their name or initials typed two lines below the message. Others prefer a handwritten signature or initials either alongside FROM or after the body.

Preprinted forms are generally used to convey basic information quickly and concisely. A typical form is either one-half sheet (8½ × 5½) or a full sheet

(8½ × 11) in size. Some have letterheads (see Example 12–1); others do not (see Example 12–2). The most common printed guide words are TO, FROM, SUBJECT, and DATE. They may be arranged in an ascending order on the page (see Example 12–1) or in groups of two or more horizontally (see Example 12–2). To provide an orderly appearance, start typing the appropriate fill-ins two spaces after the longer (two-column arrangement) or longest (one-column arrangement) guide word. Retain the first typed word on the left as the left margin for the entire memo. Make the right margin equal to the left one. Skip four or more lines after the last guide word, depending on the length of the message, and then begin the body. Single space paragraphs; double space between paragraphs. Place reference initials, if used, two spaces below either the message or the dictator's typed identification, depending upon which is last. An enclosure notice may be placed two spaces below the reference initials.

Notice the importance of the SUBJECT line. It must clearly specify the theme of the memo, thereby eliminating the need for an introductory sentence or paragraph. Also, the SUBJECT line helps to limit the content, which should revolve around one idea or situation. Be sure that the subject line is complete and concise; it rarely is a complete sentence. All major words are capitalized.

EXAMPLE 12–1 Preprinted Memo with Letterhead

Barnstable Auto Works
65 Mercury Street
Avon, CO 00000

```
TO:       Bill Shea

FROM:     Joe Petrie

SUBJECT:  Your Order for Blue Paint

DATE:     November 15, 198—



          Westcott Paint Company just called to say that the
          order was shipped yesterday. Their truck is due
          here before noon tomorrow.
```

EXAMPLE 12–2 Full-sheet Preprinted Memo

```
TO:     All employees        SUBJECT:  Summer Pay Schedule
FROM:   Mary Alstead, Payroll  DATE:     June 1, 198—


        From June 6 through Labor Day, pay envelopes will be
        distributed as follows:

            First shift — Wednesdays before noon
            Second shift — Wednesdays, noon to 5 p.m.
            Third shift — Thursdays, 5 p.m. to 11 p.m.

        If you wish to get your check at a time unscheduled
        for your shift, a request in writing must be sent to
        the Payroll Office at least 6 days in advance. Request
        must have name, Social Security number, department,
        and shift.

MA/ljf
```

The TO line may be directed to an individual or to a group. It may also contain a list of two or more people; each of these may get a copy or may simply check off his or her name after reading the memo and send it on to the next addressee. Location or position follow the name if this is necessary for proper delivery. It is courteous to have the TO line precede the FROM line. Courtesy titles such as Mr. are used in the TO line, but not in the FROM line.

The FROM line should identify the person sending the message. Avoid an impersonal group designation such as *Payroll* or *Management*; instead, use an individual's name whenever possible. Addresses or positions are also appropriate if needed for identification.

As memos are generally composed, typed, and sent within a day, the DATE line is usually the date of all three. If the memo discusses an event occurring before or after the date of transmission, the date of this event should be mentioned either in the SUBJECT line or in the body.

Telephone Messages

Telephone messages may generate memos when a person is not available to accept a call. Most organizations use a formal telephone slip such as shown in Figure 12–1.

Be sure to fill in the sections and check the boxes accurately to make a return call simple. Always note carefully the name and telephone number, including area code if it is long distance. Time and date can be important when necessary to pinpoint whether the call was independent or in response to a message or previous call.

If call slips are not available, note names, date, time, telephone number, and message on a memo such as that shown in Example 12–3.

Memo Content

Memos are generally brief, usually one page or less, although short reports in memo form may be a bit longer. The subject matter does not have to be introduced in the body, for the recipient may be familiar with it and also will have the SUBJECT line for guidance. Thus, introductory and concluding paragraphs, such as those found in letters, may often be eliminated. The writer gets immediately to the heart of a clear and concise message.

Some memos are objective; they convey facts only. These memos usually concern such routine matters as information about policies or procedures. They may also answer questions posed by earlier memos. Example 12–1 is an informational memo.

Other memos are persuasive; their objective is to convince recipients to agree to proposals or to take specific actions. These memos are as challenging to write as persuasive letters and use the same techniques. The "You" attitude is essential in these messages; always keep the readers' needs and desires in

FIGURE 12–1 Preprinted Telephone Message

To Merry Robbins

Date 15 May 198- **Time** 12:37

While you were out . . .

M . rs Peg Riley

Of Blue Shield

Phone 000-0000

[x] *Telephoned*   [ ] *Please call*
[ ] *Called to see you*   [ ] *Will call again*
[ ] *Wants to see you*   [ ] *Rush*

Message Call her before 4:30

today

Bill Keane

Operator

mind. If you require a particular result, know what you want *before you write your memo,* and "sell" your recipient by stressing reader benefit.

When you do not foresee resistance to your request, lead off with your major idea or request; that is, use deductive order, and then follow with essential supporting details. This arrangement is successful when you are sure of reader agreement and acceptance. (See Examples 12–4 and 12–5.) If reader conviction is necessary, lead up to the request or major idea by first giving the necessary facts or reasons; that is, write your memo in the inductive order. This arrangement, with the important message at the end, is preferable when

EXAMPLE 12–3   Telephone Memo

TO: Merry Robbins

FROM: Bill Keane

SUBJECT: Telephone Call

DATE: 15 May 198—

          Mrs. Peg Riley, of Blue Shield, called at 12:37.
          Return her call before 4:30 today at 000-0000.

the reader must be persuaded to agree with a proposal or to take a specific action. (See Example 12–7.)

Courtesy is as important in memos as it is in letters. However, formality may vary according to both the type of message and the writer-reader relationship. Generally, a message to a superior, to a group, or to someone not personally known by the writer will be more formal than one written to a close associate or friend. An informally written memo will use the first- and second-person personal pronouns, such as *I, we,* and *you*; it may use slang or contractions and will be phrased in the more conversational active voice, such as "I've checked the cost of the new computer." First names or nicknames are often used (only if appropriate!) as in Example 12–1, and the memo may be hand-written. Informally written memos tend to concern routine matters.

A greater level of formality is usually appropriate in longer messages to superiors, to coworkers not personally known, or to groups. A more professional, objective, and impersonal note may be achieved by couching the message in the third person and in the passive voice; for example, "The cost of the new computer has been calculated." Although the passive voice is slower and wordier, it does emphasize what has been done rather than who has done it.

Formal memos are most often typed and usually address the recipients by their full names and titles. As complete formality may sound stodgy to many, modern memos are often written in a semiformal style, perhaps using the third person and the active voice. (See Examples 12–4 and 12–6.)

An appropriate tone or attitude is essential if a memo is to achieve the desired result. In order to appeal to a reader, and to gain approval, be sure to emphasize the message from his or her viewpoint. Notice how the first line of Example 12–4 does this. Maintaining the appropriate level of formality and a focus on the readers' interests are important for favorable reception. Positive and tactful wording are also important. Note how Example 12–5 uses *please* to introduce the list of required steps, rather than using a demanding tone in an expression such as *you must*. Always avoid a negative approach: state what *can* be done rather than what *cannot* be done. The closing paragraph of Example 12–4 would be much weaker if it said:

```
As the class size is limited to 25, you cannot participate
unless you fill in and return the enclosed enrollment card
immediately.
```

Establish rapport with a memo reader just as you would with a letter reader. Review the following principles discussed in Chapter 1:

1. Write in a reader-centered manner.
2. Use words with appropriate positive connotation.
3. Avoid antagonistic words.
4. Accentuate the positive.
5. Subordinate the negative.

Writing the Good Memo

First, decide exactly what you want your memo to do. Should it make a recommendation to your superior, discuss the results of a meeting, answer the questions posed by a memo you have received, or explain procedures or policies to other employees? Do you expect a reply? Remember to limit your discussion to one central idea; if you have several points to make, be sure they are all clearly related to the subject.

Next, list the points to be included and set them up in a logical, coherent order. Plan a separate paragraph, or at least a separate sentence, for each.

Write your SUBJECT line. As briefly as possible give a comprehensive overview of your topic. Write and rewrite until you are satisfied that it is as complete and concise as you can make it. Then, fill in the other guidelines.

Compose the body in clear and to-the-point language. Reread and revise if necessary to eliminate haziness, wordiness, or irrelevancies. Be sure to emphasize important ideas by placement, sentence structure, and by underlining or using all capital letters. Check for completeness. Only when you are totally satisfied should the memo be typed and sent.

The Short Memo

The following situation requires a brief (less than one page) informational and persuasive memo. How would you develop the ideas to convey a clear message?

You are Nancy B. Jones, Director of Personnel for the Superior Insulated Wire Company, 400 Payne Boulevard, Somersville, NY 00000. A fifteen-week business writing course taught by faculty from Somersville Junior College will be offered, starting September 15, to all office and management-level employees. Tuition and book costs will be paid by the company. Meetings will be held on Tuesdays from 5 p.m. to 7:30 p.m. in Conference Room L. The workday ends at 4:45 p.m. The course, which will be limited to 25 students, carries three credits toward an Associate of Arts degree.

First, what do you want your memo to do? You want it to explain the details of the course offering; you also want to encourage enrollment. You expect replies from those who are interested, so you will enclose an enrollment card.

Now, list the points to be made in an appropriate order. Newspaper format (Who? What? Where? When? Why?) will be helpful.

1. *Who?* Nancy B. Jones, Director of Personnel, Superior Insulated Wire — this should be covered by the letterhead or the FROM line.
   Office and management-level employees — the TO line must clarify this.
2. *What?* A business writing course taught by Somersville Junior College faculty. You also want to specify that the company will pay for books and tuition.
3. *Where?* Conference Room L.
4. *When?* Fifteen Tuesdays from 5 to 7:30 p.m., starting on September 15. You do not have to tell them what they already know, that the workday ends at 4:45 p.m.; this would add unnecessary wordiness.
5. *Why?* They will receive three credits toward the A.A. degree. Also show why they should sign up quickly — the course is limited to 25 students.

What would be an appropriate SUBJECT line for this memo? To simply use *Business Writing Course* would be too vague and incomplete. Wouldn't *Fall In-Building Business Writing Course Given by SJC* be better? Although the latter seems wordy, these facts are needed to introduce the subject adequately.

Read Example 12–4, the memo written around this situation. Does it handle the problem clearly, briefly, and adequately? Would you make changes, additions, or deletions? If so, where?

More short memos. Example 12–5 is a memo concerning procedure. A view of letters giving instructions (Chapter 4) might be helpful in writing this type

EXAMPLE 12–4   Short Memo

SUPERIOR INSULATED WIRE COMPANY

Memorandum

TO: Office and Management—Level Employees
FROM: Nancy B. Jones, Director of Personnel
SUBJECT: Fall In—Building Business Writing Course
          Given by SJC
DATE: August 1, 198—

Earn travel—free course credits this fall!

A business writing course taught by Somersville Junior College faculty will meet in Conference Room L, from 5 to 7:30 p.m., for fifteen Tuesdays starting September 15.

The company will pay all tuition and book costs.

Students will earn three credits toward the Associate of Arts degree.

As the class size is limited to 25, please fill in and return the enclosed enrollment card to me immediately if you wish to participate.

Nancy B. Jones

fc

Enclosure

EXAMPLE 12–5   Short Memo Giving Instructions

```
TO:    All Staff              SUBJECT:  Summer Paychecks
FROM:  May Simms, Payroll     DATE:     June 12, 198—


       If you wish your paychecks from July 2 through August
       27 to be mailed, please:

       1. Using a 4 x 6 file card, print on three separate
          lines (a) your name, (b) your Social Security num-
          ber, and (c) your department.

       2. Attach 5 stamped, addressed envelopes to the card.

       3. Bring these to the payroll office before June 23.

       4. Sign the sheet marked Summer Check Mailing posted
          on the left inside the door.

       5. Have a wonderful vacation!

                             MS


bg
```

of message. Some memos, like Example 12–6, clarify policies. Other memos, such as Examples 12–7 and 12–8, ask for recommendations or reply to these requests.

The Informal or Memorandum Report

Although the formal report is several pages long and contains numerous components (see Chapters 13 and 14), many briefer, less formal reports may be in memo form. The informal or memorandum report is usually shorter, and has fewer components, than a formal report. The body of a memo report generally is one to five pages long; full-sized pages, rather than the typical half-size sheets of brief memos, are used. If the informal report is more than one page, it needs second-page headings like those in letters, including addressees' names, page number, and date. The headings (TO, FROM, SUBJECT, DATE) replace the title page and letter of transmittal of the formal report; the table of contents and synopsis are eliminated, and rarely is a bibliography required in this long memo. The memorandum report, thus, is less repetitious than a formal report as the long memo contains only the body or essential elements of the message.

The informal report probably deals with more routine, less complex subject matter or research and is usually prepared more quickly than the formal report. It may have fewer readers and most likely will be read within the organization, possibly only at the writer's level within the chain of command. Formal reports, on the other hand, may circulate outside the organization or may be written for higher-level management within the organization. Memorandum reports may analyze or solve relatively simple internal problems or proposals, as well as make suggestions. They may also concern progress within a brief period, trips, accidents, or individual hiring and firing decisions. Like shorter memos, they can be informational or persuasive. Some just present facts; others summarize, conclude, or recommend.

Memorandum reports contain only the essentials:

1. *Introduction* — If inductive order is used, here the subject and purpose are stated, unless the SUBJECT line gives sufficient information. If deductive order is chosen, the recommendations and conclusions may be here.
2. *Body* — This section contains a complete account of the subject matter, including visual aids if necessary.
3. *Ending* — This summarizes the findings if deductive order is used. If inductive order is used, the conclusions and/or recommendations are here.

The sections sometimes are set off by headings; the headings may be eliminated when the text clearly indicates the subject matter.

Example 12–9 is an informal report that provides information compiled by one person concerning a relatively simple problem that required some, but

EXAMPLE 12–6   Short Memo Clarifying Policies

Roberts Department Store
Simmstown, AL 00000

TO: New Employees   SUBJECT: Reporting
                                           Departures
FROM: John Golden, Security   DATE: January 2, 198—

All employees must report to Security before leaving the store.

If before closing time, they must sign out at the Security Office at the bottom of the east stairway in the basement level.

If after closing time, they must leave by the Main Street door, where names will be checked by security officers.

Please follow these regulations which contribute to efficient operations.

                        JG

rto

EXAMPLE 12–7   Short Memo Requesting Recommendations

WINGATE MANUFACTURING COMPANY

TO: Barbara Mills, Burton Bracci, Marge Miller
FROM: Samuel Orrs, President *SO*
SUBJECT: Possible Employee Choices for Cutting Costs
DATE: August 3, 198—

Because last quarter's sales were 30 percent below average, the Board of Directors has voted to curtail production. Which of the following cost-cutting methods do you consider most satisfactory for our employees?

1. Closing the entire plant for two weeks.

2. Asking for volunteers to take payless leaves.

3. Laying off on a last-in, first-out basis.

4. Shortening the work day to six hours.

Please poll your staffs and let me know by August 15.

SO:wrs

EXAMPLE 12–8   Short Memo Replying to Request for Recommendations

---

WINGATE MANUFACTURING COMPANY

TO: Mr. Samuel Orrs

FROM: Barbara Mills *BM*

SUBJECT: Billing Department Choices for Cutting Costs

DATE: August 13, 198—

A combination of volunteers for payless vacations
and shorter workdays is most acceptable.

In this department two of the 85 members would take
leaves; most others feel a pay cut for all is
fairer than a loss of pay for some.

We would appreciate knowing the final decision and
the effective date for starting shorter work days.

---

not extensive, research. The report, organized inductively, concludes with a recommendation.

Example 12–10 is a periodic progress report, containing information probably compiled by several people, although the memo is signed by an individual. It shows changes over a specific time interval and is organized deductively, with the summary and recommendations preceding the body of the report.

Memos and memo reports are important messengers within an organization. They omit some letter formalities such as the salutation and complimentary close; however, like good letters, memos and memo reports are positively worded and reader-centered. Guide words help to convey information quickly and concisely. The memo, usually less than one page in length, gives facts, clarifies policies, asks for or replies to recommendations, or persuades. The memo report, generally one to five pages long, covers progress or analyses or solves relatively simple internal matters. Test your memo writing skills by completing the Exercises at the end of this chapter.

EXAMPLE 12–9 Informal Report, Organized Inductively

FLUSS ENTERPRISES

TO: Mr. Charles Morton   SUBJECT: Revision of Our Form
                                                  Letters

FROM: Jim Cleary   DATE: 4 April 198—

I have been in touch with H.C. Smith Associates about the terms under which they will revise our form letters. The fee is $15,000 for one year's service, including the following:

1. Reviewing and rewriting where necessary the form letters of all departments.

2. Preparing of a correspondence manual for use by all those who dictate. (The cost of printing is not included in the fee.)

3. Meeting for six one-hour instructional sessions with all letter-writing personnel.

4. Distributing of the <u>Smith</u> <u>Better</u> <u>Letters</u> <u>Bulletin</u> biweekly to all persons in the program. A sample is attached.

After one year, continued service will be provided for $3,000 yearly. This fee will include reviews of all new form letters, three group meetings, and distribution of the <u>Smith</u> <u>Better</u> <u>Letters</u> <u>Bulletin</u>.

Mr. Griswold, with whom I spoke, said his company could begin at any time upon one month's notice. He gave as references three recent clients:

      The United Bank and Trust Company
      The Amalgamated Petrol Company
      The Universal Machine Works

EXAMPLE 12–9   *(continued)*

Charles Morton   Page 2   4 April 198—

    I recommend that we sign a one-year contract with H.C.
Smith Associates as the references spoke very highly
of their service. We should reassess our needs for re-
newal next March.

Jim Cleary

JC:gh

Enclosure

EXAMPLE 12–10   Periodic Progress Report, Organized Deductively

---

MILLBORN ASSOCIATES DRILLING COMPANY

```
TO:       Board of Directors
FROM:     Rowena S. Leguire, President
SUBJECT:  Progress, First Fiscal Quarter, 198—
DATE:     April 15, 198—
```

First Quarter Earnings Double

Results for the first fiscal quarter show continued
gains for Millborn Associates Drilling Company. Net
income for the three months ending March 31, 198—,
was $186,000, more than double the $71,000 of the
previous quarter. Revenues in the most recent quarter totaled $540,000 compared to $127,000 during
the preceding three months. Earnings per share were
.03 versus .02.

Broadened Drilling Effort Recommended

As planned, we should raise our exploration and development spending to $6 million in fiscal 198—.
Current softness in oil and gas prices has signifi-
cantly broadened the drilling exposure we can cap-
ture with these funds. Lease rates on rigs and
other drilling equipment have dropped by 25 percent, and the cost of land has come down substan-
tially. These lowered costs and broadened exposure
will result in increased profits; by year's end,
the company's proven reserves are expected to be
approximately $50 million.

Outstanding Drilling Results Achieved

During the first quarter, all of the wells in which
the company participated were successfully completed. Significant discoveries were made in the
Waterloo Basin:

Barry #2--Drilled to 12,500 feet; tested 500 bar-
         rels of oil per day.

Sammy #18--Drilled to 8,300 feet; completed for 589
         barrels of oil per day.

EXAMPLE 12–10   *(continued)*

Board of Directors   Page 2   April 15, 198—

      Rowna #3—Drilled to 5,100 feet; completed for
           420 barrels of oil per day.

      Bob Ray #6—Drilled to 8,200 feet; completed for
           650 barrels of oil and 2,500 Mcf of gas
           per day.

198— Prospects

We are confident about the prospects for a record
year for fiscal 198—. Earnings for the first quarter doubled those of the previous quarter. Lower
costs, increased investment, and participation in
successful wells should provide increased earnings
as the year develops.

CHECKLIST

Writing Memos

- Limit the message to one central idea.
- Decide on the desired result.
- Outline or list the essential points in a logical order.
- Write a complete, clear, and specific SUBJECT line.
- Fill in the other guidelines: TO, FROM, and DATE.
- Use the appropriate level of formality based on type of message and writer-reader relationship.
- Write a positively worded message.
- Check for completeness, clarity, and conciseness.

EXERCISES

1. How might the following messages be improved? Rewrite them according to the ideas presented in this chapter.

   a. TO: Whomever it may concern   SUBJECT: Hours
      FROM: Management   DATE: September

   ```
   Your work hours are now 9:00 a.m. to 5:00
   p.m. We would like to change them to 8:30
   a.m. to 4:30 p.m. for the summer months.

   You can let us know if you don't like this
   idea.
   ```

   b. TO: Mr. Riggs, Boss
      FROM: Bob Newell
      SUBJECT: Vacation
      DATE: January 18, 198–

   ```
   I'd like to tell you in this memo about when I would
   like to go on vacation in the spring, maybe March or
   April.

   The reason I want to go then is because my brother
   has invited me to visit him in Florida.

   I hope you don't give Bill Butts first choice be-
   cause he took the time I wanted last year. And, any-
   how, I was here before he was. I don't like being
   treated unfairly.
   ```

   c. TO: Miss Lane Adler   SUBJECT: Thank You
      FROM: Lyle Bascom   DATE: July 10, 198–

   ```
   This is to thank you for helping me to clean
   ```

out the file cabinets. I never would have
gotten out of the mess without you.

As you are so efficient, I hope that you will
take over my job while I'm on vacation next
week. Mr. Rahway has given his permission for
you to do so.

Hoping to hear from you in the near future, I
remain,

Sincerely,

Lyle Bascom

Lyle Bascom

d. TO: Lillian Means, Accounting
FROM: George Rawley, Sales
SUBJECT: Money
DATE: 18 June 198—

Please answer me within three days.

I want to know why my request for payment
hasn't arrived. I requested fare and other
expenses for a trip I took last month. It
was to Las Vegas. For a furniture sales
convention. Please answer as I asked
above. You owe me $432.55. Can I get paid
for the convention in Los Angeles in September? Also, when will my commissions for
May be coming? Thanks.

e. TO: Milly Weill   SUBJECT: Telephone Call
FROM: Sadie Flack   DATE: November 15, 198—

You got a telephone call when you were at
lunch from some guy with a long name beginning with an <u>S</u>. He said it was very important
and that you should call back immediately. I
think he said that he was calling long distance, but I forgot to ask for a telephone
number. You probably know who he was anyhow.

f. TO: Mr. Raymond Suits, President
FROM: Walter Zacks, Merchandise Manager
SUBJECT: Joining the Retail Merchants Club
DATE: 15 February 198—

You asked me to answer your five questions
about joining the Retail Merchants Club.
Yes, we should. Some very high-class owners belong. I forgot to ask about yearly

```
dues and when the meetings are, but we can
always find that out.
```

2. Write appropriate memos for the following situations.

    a. You are a salesperson for Top Notch Office Products. Your sample case is falling apart and you need a replacement before you leave in two days for your next sales trip. Write a memo to Ms. Gail Cartella, Supply Department, asking that a new case be ready for you the day after tomorrow.

    b. Mr. Orrin Nason, the president of Simple Auto Parts, has asked you, the purchasing manager, to check with Billings Tire Company about an order for 500 snow tires which should have arrived last week. You have found out that Billings' truck carrying the tires had an accident and all the tires were destroyed. A new shipment left yesterday and will arrive tomorrow. Write an informational memo to Mr. Nason.

    c. You are the personnel manager for Kates Industries. Because there has been much confusion over lunch and coffee breaks, you have decided to devise a clear-cut policy and relate it to the employees. All office workers will have coffee breaks from 10–10:15 a.m. and will have lunch from 12:30–1:15 p.m. Laboratory personnel and the maintenance crew will have coffee breaks from 9:30–9:45 a.m. and lunch from 11–11:45 a.m. Machinery operators will have coffee breaks from 9:45–10 a.m. and lunch from 11:45–12:30 p.m. Write a memo that will clarify this schedule.

    d. You are the merchandise manager for Quirk's Department Store. Lately you have discovered that many sales clerks are not appropriately handling sales involving Charge-A-Cards. They must first fill out a Charge-A-Card slip, have the customer sign it, and then check its number against their list of lost and stolen cards. Next they should fill out a Quirk's sales slip and ring up the amount of the sale. Then they should staple the original copies of both slips and place them in the cash register. Finally, the customer must be given the carbon copies, also stapled together. Write a clear, concise memo explaining this procedure.

    e. You are secretary of the Board of Directors of the Zilch Corporation. At its October 15 meeting, the Board discussed the possibility of having an employee Christmas party this year rather than distributing turkeys as has been the custom previously. Send a memo to the heads of the five departments asking for their opinions about this change.

    f. You are manager of the Personnel Department of the Zilch Corporation. You answer the memo written for problem e, disagreeing with the change. Give your reasons.

    g. You are the supervisor of the Plating Department of the Zilch Corporation. Agree with the proposed change discussed in problem e in a memo that states the reasons why you believe employees will be in favor of it.

    h. Your supervisor, Darrell Pinkerton, at Megan Electronics is interested in offering a course in business mathematics to all employees. He wants to know whether the school you attend would have such a course, and, if so, whether it could be taken after working hours, from 5:30 p.m. on. He also needs a breakdown of tuition fees and the cost of books as the company plans to pay all expenses of employees taking the course. He asks you to research what would be taught to be sure that this course would benefit the staff. Finally, he wants your recommendation as to whether the company should, indeed, carry through with this project. Write an informal report, using your college catalogue for reference.

i. Mr. Pinkerton has decided, on the basis of the report you wrote for problem h, to offer the business mathematics course to Megan Electronics employees. Write a memo to them, informing them of the details and asking them to notify you if they are interested in participating.

j. Sandra Sturgess, a Megan Electronics typist, would like to take advantage of the free tuition offer; however, she has already taken the math course. She wants to know whether she can take a shorthand course instead. Write her memo to Mr. Pinkerton asking about this possibility.

13

The Formal
Business Report

Getting It All Together

The word *report* comes from the Latin word *reportare* (*re* plus *portare*). *Re* means "back" and *portare* means "to carry." Thus, a report is the carrying back of information. In business, both informal and formal reports are written by reporters who work with the concerns of one or more people and who research the solutions objectively by collecting and organizing factual information. These facts, which must be both complete and correct, are then organized into accounts that convey and possibly interpret the data.

The informal, or memo, report discussed in Chapter 12 is the most frequent mode of expression. Why, then, do we need a more formal document? If a rather simple single-phase problem needs analysis quickly, the memo report is both very efficient and very effective. Generally shorter than its formal counterpart, the memo report can deal with the ideas in the simple three-part format of an introduction, body, and ending.

However, not all questions that arise are uncomplicated and speedily investigated. Complex problems, such as an important project or major reorganization, demand considerable time and research. Top-level executives are typically the authorizers and potential readers; they may not work in the same location or even know the writer(s). For these recipients, the format of the formal report, with its numerous required specific components organized in an orderly pattern, makes the message clearer and easier to follow. Because formal reports are often long and require secondary research, documented evidence, and visual aids, they would become unwieldy if not broken down into segments.

Thus, although an informal memo might adequately handle the problem of choosing a new employee, the question of opening a new plant in another city would probably necessitate a formal report. As formal reports are major projects, much time and care in gathering data and writing the report are required.

Both informal and formal reports are divided into three major categories. Length, complexity, and individual preference determine which form is chosen.

1. *Periodic* — They are issued at specific time intervals. A company's annual report or a salesperson's monthly report are examples. They may also be progress reports.
2. *Progress* — They also may be issued at specific times and be combined with a periodic report, or they may be issued as needed to show developments of chosen aspects of a particular segment or activity of an organization. A laboratory's report about its advances toward perfection of a drug or a builder's report on progress toward completion of a building are examples.
3. *Special* — They deal with specific questions or problems that require appraisal. Often they are one-time investigations, such as an analysis of changing the packaging of a product or of adding a new line of products or services. An informational report gives facts only; an examination report not only gives data but also analyzes and interprets them. An analytical report additionally draws conclusions and often makes recommendations. Because the analytical special report is the most comprehensive, containing all possible segments, a sample of this type will be presented in Chapter 14.

Planning and Researching

After you or a superior decides that some matter needs investigation, your systematic examination and gathering of facts must be planned and developed step by step.

Defining the Problem Clearly

To determine your objective, you must understand the purpose of the investigation. What type of report is expected? Should it contain facts only or also conclusions and recommendations? Perhaps terms such as *less time* or *reasonable profit* require clarification. *Ask questions* until you are positive that you understand what is wanted. Remember, a report that does not perform the desired task is useless. What questions would you ask if you were told, "Go to Riddlesburg and see how a new factory would go there" or "Have the new computers made our payroll department more efficient?" List additional information you would need in order to define these problems clearly.

Writing a Statement of Purpose

When you are confident that you know the scope of the project, write a statement of purpose that defines the assignment and its boundaries. Refer to this statement often as you develop your report. Note how the following statements of purpose provide a guide to research and writing. The first is written for an examination special report, the second for an analytical special report.

> The purpose of this report is to compare production of the payroll department the year prior to and the year following introduction of the SX 273 computer.

> This report compares production of the payroll department the year prior to and the year following introduction of the SX 273 computer so as to determine whether the Foresight Company should continue to rent it from Saville Electronics.

Giving Your Report a Tentative Title

After you have defined the problem and have written your statement of purpose, give your report a tentative title. A good title will adequately cover the subject to be addressed and will define the limits. A complete title page should answer the questions Who? What? Where? When? and possibly Why? Some of the answers will be provided by the title, the rest by other sections of the title page (see Chapter 14). Notice how the following titles help limit the report boundaries.

> A REPORT ON THE FEASIBILITY OF OPENING A 200,000 SQUARE FOOT DYEING PLANT AT 400 WISDOM ROAD, RIDDLESBURG, OH, BY JANUARY, 198—

> AN EVALUATION OF THE EFFECT OF THE SX 273 COMPUTER ON PAYROLL DEPARTMENT EFFICIENCY AFTER ONE YEAR

Allowing for Time and Money Limitations

Now begin to plan your research. Again, *ask questions.* How soon must the report be presented? Budget your time so that you will have adequate opportunity for investigation and organization. Must the payroll department figures be ready for inclusion in the annual report, which goes to the printer in three weeks?

What expenses do you foresee? Will you have to travel or stay overnight at another location? Will experts need to be hired or estimates prepared? Unless you are given *carte blanche* financially, clarify monetary requirements before you begin. For example, how much will it cost you to fly to Riddlesburg and stay two weeks?

Listing Required Information and Organizing a Tentative Outline

To ensure an accurate report, you must gather complete and correct data. Study the problem, decide what you need to know, and make a list of all the questions that should be explored. Be flexible; you may have to add to this list as you get more involved with your work. If, for instance, original plans for the Riddlesburg plant call for a one-story building and cost is prohibitive, you may also want to explore the expense of two-level construction. Organize your questions into categories and arrange them logically into a tentative outline.

Gathering the Information: Primary and Secondary Sources

After the tentative list of questions and the outline are prepared, you will probably discover that you can use both first-hand (primary) and second-hand (secondary) sources of data. Those facts which you obtain yourself through such methods as checking your company records, experimenting, observing, and surveying either by interview or questionnaire are considered primary evidence. Secondary evidence is material that has already been compiled and recorded by others. Although much secondary data can be found in a library, other sources are booklets and manuals. Records of other companies, city halls, and chambers of commerce are either primary evidence if obtained directly or secondary evidence if incorporated and summarized in a report by someone else.

Secondary information. Begin by acquainting yourself with available secondary information. If someone else has done part of the chore, you can save time and perhaps money. If the project warrants it, go to the library. Traditional alphabetized card catalogues or records kept on microfilm, microfiche, or computer list helpful books and reference volumes. Indexes to periodicals, which list the contents of magazines, journals, trade publications, and certain newspapers, may also be of help. Or use a guide to *Books in Print*, which lists all available books, including some that are perhaps not in your library. And, certainly, enlist the aid of a librarian if the wealth of written material seems confusing; he or she will make the task much easier by quickly assessing your requirements and guiding you toward helpful material.

The following list is a partial sampling of library holdings that can prove invaluable to a report writer.

Reference Books

Ammer, Christine, and Dean S. Ammer. *Dictionary of Business and Economics.* New York: Free Press, 1977.

Brownstone, David M., and Gordon Carruth. *Where to Find Business Information.* New York: John Wiley and Sons, 1979.

Daniels, Lorna M., comp. *Business Reference Sources,* rev. ed. Boston: Harvard Graduate School of Business Administration, 1979.

Hayel, Carl. *The Encyclopedia of Management,* 2nd ed. New York: Van Nostrand Reinhold Co., 1973.

Moore, Norman D. *Dictionary of Business, Finance, and Investment.* Dayton, Ohio: Investor's Systems, 1975.

Selden, Maury, ed. *The Real Estate Handbook.* Homewood, Ill.: Dow Jones-Irwin, 1980.

Washington Researchers. *How to Find Information About Companies.* Washington: The Researchers, 1979.

Wasserman, Paul, and Joanne Paskar, eds. *Statistics Sources,* 4th ed. Detroit: Gale Research Company, 1974.

Wasserman, Paul, Charlotte Georgi, and James Woy, eds. *Encyclopedia of Business Information Sources,* 4th ed. Detroit: Gale Research Company, 1980.

The library reference section also usually contains current and back issues of such annually published volumes as: *The Dow Jones-Irwin Business Almanac,* Dun and Bradstreet's *Million Dollar Directory, Moody's Manuals,* The Department of Commerce's *Statistical Abstract of the United States,* and many of the numerous handbooks put out by such government agencies as the Department of Commerce.

Indexes to Periodicals

Applied Science and Technology Index. New York: The H.W. Wilson Company.

Bibliographic Index. New York: The H.W. Wilson Company.

Business Periodicals Index. New York: The H.W. Wilson Company.

New York Times Index. New York.

Reader's Guide to Periodical Literature. New York: The H.W. Wilson Company.

Wall Street Journal Index. New York.

Guides to Books

Cumulative Book Index: A World List of Books in the English Language. New York: The H.W. Wilson Company.

Subject Guide to Books in Print. New York: R.R. Bowker.

Primary sources. When you have exhausted the relevant secondary sources of information, decide what primary research is required. Here you may well obtain the major portion of your data. The three basic methods for gathering first-hand information are observation, experimentation, and interrogation.

Observation, the act of noting and recording facts, may be done either informally or formally. The records of your company or organization are a good place to begin. Facts and figures found there may be extremely helpful and may save valuable time and effort. Casual or informal observation might be conducted by a potential store owner who walks around a mall on one or two occasions, checking sales activity in competitive stores. If the owner, or others, pursued a systematic survey of traffic patterns over an extended time, including representative hours, days, and seasons, the observation would be more formal and more informative.

Experimentation, testing in an orderly manner, is another useful source of data. An experiment is performed when one factor of a situation is methodically manipulated while all the other factors are kept unchanged. If this is done appropriately, the effect of the manipulated factor can be assessed. For example, a chain of stores might offer discounts on cash purchases in one unit to analyze the effect on sales volume. Or a manufacturer might try a new piece of machinery in one section of a department to compare production figures with and without it.

Interrogation, asking questions, ranges from the simple one-to-one interview to elaborately constructed questionnaires. Obviously, the honesty and reliability of respondents affect the accuracy of data obtained by this method. Interviews are conducted with those who are knowledgeable about a matter under consideration. The potential mall store owner may ask present owners about their experiences at this location; the owner might also wish to question the mall manager. If you decide to interview others, set up an appointment, prepare a comprehensive list of questions, and be prepared to take notes.

The questionnaire, done by telephone, mail, or in person, is a more formal type of interrogation used to elicit the same information from a number of people. If the group is small, you can poll all its members. The thirty members of a payroll department could all be questioned about their experiences with a new computer. However, when the reactions of a larger group are required, the general law of sampling will be used. This law assumes that a sufficient number of studies, taken at random or by some systematic method from a larger number, will display the same characteristics as the larger group. Again, a comprehensive list of questions must be prepared, and each respondent must be queried in exactly the same form to assure valid results. Be sure that your questions

1. Are easy to understand.
2. Ask for only one factual answer each.
3. Are not leading, that is, do not suggest an answer. Thus, instead of asking, "Is television your favorite form of entertainment?" ask, "What is your favorite form of entertainment?"

4. Ask only for easily remembered information.

5. Do not touch on personal pride, prejudices, or privacy.

Choose wording so that a check mark or a brief response is sufficient. Arrange the questions in a logical order, moving from the simplest to the more difficult ones. A questionnaire is included in Example 14–9.

Recording the Information

You will probably begin this procedure while you are gathering your information. As you research and find material for your presentation, systematically record it and its origin. Take down everything you might need. (It is easier to delete than to search frantically for something you wish you had recorded.) Photocopy relevant long passages or entire articles and underline or make notes. Be sure that you have complete bibliographic information for each selection.

A good method for note taking uses a combination of 3 × 5 and 4 × 6 note cards. Because cards can be easily shuffled and rearranged, they make it easier to write drafts, especially if reorganization of the tentative outline is required. Each 3 × 5 card should contain one bibliographic item, set in appropriate form to facilitate writing of the final bibliography. Take notes on the 4 × 6 cards, putting only one item of information on each to simplify reorganization. Label each card to indicate the type of information it contains; also indicate in abbreviated form the source of secondary material, including page numbers, for documentation. Write legibly in ink, as pencilled writing blurs. If possible, use the front of the card only; if necessary to write on the back, write the word *over* on the bottom front so that you will not overlook any notes. Put directly quoted passages in quotation marks on both your cards and in your report. You may also paraphrase (restate in your own style the thought or meaning using approximately the same number of words as the original passage) or write a précis (condense or summarize in a briefer form). Do remember that all *three* require documentation, i.e., a footnote. It is plagiarism to offer the words or ideas of another as your own; you must footnote quoted, restated, and summarized material.

Notice how Figures 13–1 through 13–4 follow the above advice.

Organizing the Information

After you have gathered the data necessary to answer your questions (and any others that may have arisen), arrange your cards and photocopied material. Tabulate any questionnaires and organize interview notes. Reread the statement of purpose to assure adequate coverage; rewrite the statement if necessary. Then, rearranging notes as required, change your tentative outline into a clear, logical blueprint that will guide the writing of your report.

The arrangement of your outline will be affected by your choice of organizational pattern. If you choose the logical or inductive pattern, you will

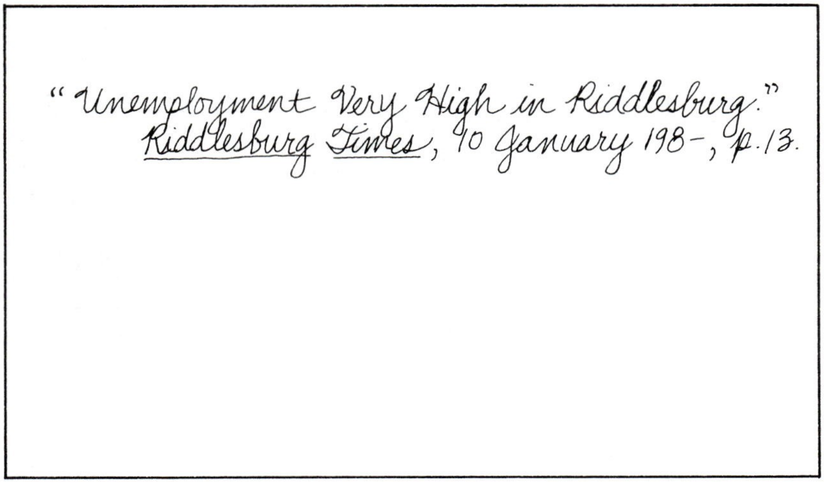

"Unemployment Very High in Riddlesburg."
<u>Riddlesburg Times</u>, 10 January 198–, p. 13.

FIGURE 13–1 Bibliography Card

Type of information   Source in abbreviated form
↓   ↓

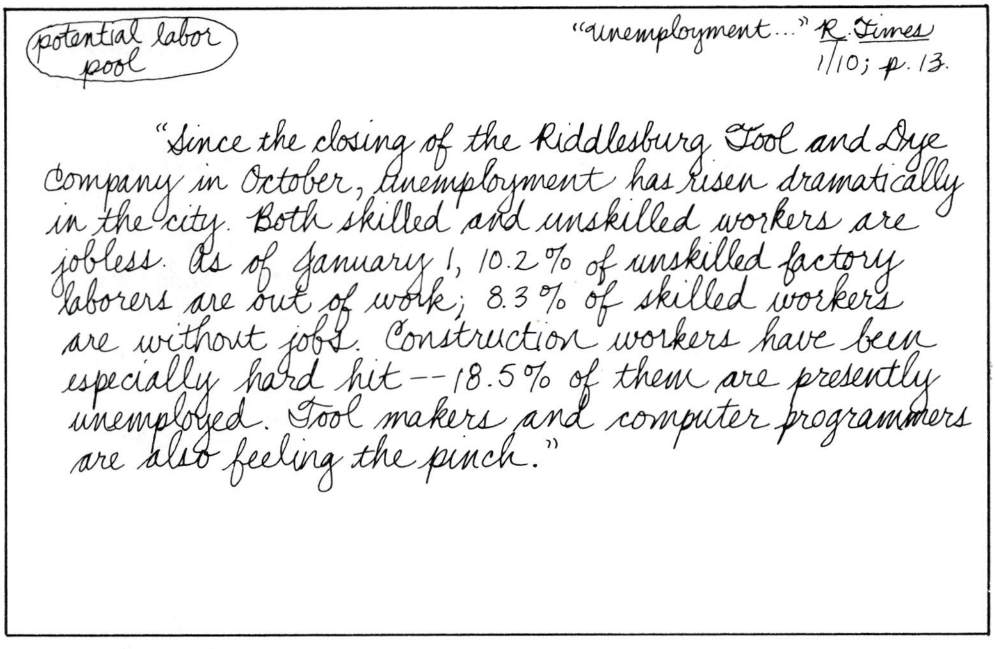

(potential labor pool)   "unemployment..." R. Times
                                                     1/10; p. 13.

   "Since the closing of the Riddlesburg Tool and Dye Company in October, unemployment has risen dramatically in the city. Both skilled and unskilled workers are jobless. As of January 1, 10.2% of unskilled factory laborers are out of work; 8.3% of skilled workers are without jobs. Construction workers have been especially hard hit -- 18.5% of them are presently unemployed. Tool makers and computer programmers are also feeling the pinch."

FIGURE 13–2 Note Card: Direct Quotation

potential labor pool

"Unemployment..." R. Times
1/10; p.13.

Unemployment has risen a great deal in Riddlesburg since the tool and die plant there closed in October. According to the Times, both skilled and unskilled workers are seeking jobs. The jobless figures are: 18.5% of construction workers, 10.2% of unskilled factory laborers and 8.3% of those with skills. Tool makers and computer programmers are among the jobless skilled.

FIGURE 13–3   Note Card: Paraphrase (Restatement)

potential labor pool

"Unemployment..." R. Times
1/10; p.13.

Because of a plant closing, unemployment in Riddlesburg is high:
18.5% — construction workers
10.2% — unskilled factory laborers
8.3% — skilled laborers
Many tool makers and computer programmers are jobless.

FIGURE 13–4   Note Card: Précis (Summary)

begin with introductory comments; will proceed to give the information; and will end with a summary, conclusions, or recommendations. Your reader will be led step-by-step through the material. This is the more traditional way of presenting a report. Many readers, however, want to know the major message, usually the summary, conclusions, or recommendations, immediately. For them a report written in the direct or deductive pattern would be more satisfactory. A report written with this arrangement would "begin at the end." It would lead off with the summary, recommendations, or conclusions and then present the supporting data. The two arrangements are often combined by the addition of a synopsis, organized deductively, which is placed in the preliminary section of the report, immediately preceding the report proper. A detailed discussion of the synopsis or abstract is provided in Chapter 14 and is also included in the précis section of Chapter 15.

Providing Accurate Documentation

When you use the words or ideas of others, credit must be given to the originator. If your notes were carefully documented, this will be a simple mechanical process. Follow the format of a current style manual such as the *MLA Handbook* (New York: Modern Language Association, 1977), or the one followed in this book: Kate L. Turabian, *A Manual For Writers,* 4th ed., (Chicago: The University of Chicago Press, 1973).

Footnotes, needed for all borrowed items, may be placed at the bottom of the appropriate page or in one list after the report proper. They are numbered consecutively throughout the paper by Arabic numerals placed slightly above the line both after the borrowed material and just before the footnote. If footnotes appear at the page bottom, they are separated from the text by an unbroken line, starting at the left margin, twenty spaces long. They are typed single spaced starting two lines below this, with double spacing between the individual entries. The first line is indented five spaces or the same number of spaces as paragraph indentation in the report. The same format is used with end-of-report placement. The first reference to a source gives the basic information, as shown in the sample documentation that follows. Second or later references either use a shortened form of the information (Hardwick, pp. 18–20), or may use *ibid.* if references to the same work are consecutive. Although *ibid.* is considered outdated by many, some banks and older firms still use this term.

The bibliography, or list of reference sources, is placed at the end of the report. Sources are listed in alphabetical order, according to the author's last name. If no author is given, the title is used to guide placement. Bibliography entries are placed with the first line at the left margin; the succeeding lines, with single spaces between, are indented a definite number of spaces, usually five or six. Double spacing is used between entries. They also contain specific information as shown in the samples.

Sample documentation.

(F) = Footnote
(S) = Second footnote entry
(B) = List of sources or bibliography entry

Book, one author

(F)   ¹Robert C. Hardwick, <u>The</u> <u>Effective</u> <u>Report</u> (New York: Valiant Press, 198–), pp. 18–20.

(S)   ²Hardwick, pp. 18–20.
or
         ²<u>Ibid</u>. (if this immediately follows the complete footnote)

(B) Hardwick, Robert C. <u>The</u> <u>Effective</u> <u>Report</u>. New York: Valiant Press, 198–.

Book, two or three authors

(F)   ³James C. Ball, Walter Rudd, and John Wills, <u>Good</u> <u>Management</u> (Boston: Puritan Printing Company, 198–), p. 352.

(B) Ball, James C., Walter Rudd, and John Wills, <u>Good</u> <u>Management</u>. Boston: Puritan Printing Company, 198–.

Book, more than three authors

(F)   ⁴Rodney Abel et al., <u>Communication</u> (Chicago: Chicago Publishing Company, 198–), pp. 305–342.

(B) Abel, Rodney, C. Allen, F. W. Bond, and J. Rawls. <u>Communication</u>. Chicago: Chicago Publishing Company, 198–.

Book, no author

(F)   ⁵<u>The</u> <u>Bosses</u> (London: Robeson, Ltd., 1902), p. 37.

(B) <u>The</u> <u>Bosses</u>. London: Robeson, Ltd., 1902.

Book, edited

(F)   ⁶R. L. Smythe, ed., <u>Word–Perfect</u> <u>Letters</u> (San Francisco: Cable Car Printers, 198–), pp. 73–78.

(B) Smythe, R. L., ed. <u>Word–Perfect</u> <u>Letters</u>. San Francisco: Cable Car Printers, 198–.

Book, institution, or association as "author"

(F)   ⁷Writing Researchers Institute, <u>Directory</u> <u>of</u> <u>Secretarial</u> <u>Schools</u> (New York: Writing Researchers Institute, 198–), pp. 1–82.

(B) Writing Researchers Institute. <u>Directory</u> <u>of</u> <u>Secretarial</u> <u>Schools</u>. New York: Writing Researchers Institute, 198–.

A chapter in a collective work

(F)   [8]Roland Wilkes, "The Apology Letter," in <u>Letters</u> <u>in</u> <u>Action</u>, ed. Susan Field (Providence: Roger Williams Press, 198–), p. 181.

(B) Wilkes, Roland. "The Apology Letter." In <u>Letters</u> <u>in</u> <u>Action</u>, edited by Susan Field, 179–182. Providence: Roger Williams Press, 198–.

Published report, author named

(F)   [9]Laura L. Bentley, <u>Report</u> <u>on</u> <u>Injuries</u> <u>to</u> <u>Women</u> <u>in</u> <u>Electrical</u> <u>Plants</u> (Los Alamos: Roberts Researchers [198–]), p. 22.

(B) Bentley, Laura L. <u>Report</u> <u>on</u> <u>Injuries</u> <u>to</u> <u>Women</u> <u>in</u> <u>Electrical</u> <u>Plants</u>. Los Alamos: Roberts Researchers, [198–].

Published report, committee chairman named

(F)   [10]<u>Report</u> <u>of</u> <u>the</u> <u>President's</u> <u>Committee</u> <u>on</u> <u>Financial</u> <u>Aid</u> <u>to</u> <u>the</u> <u>Blind</u>, by Richard Leaf, Chairman (Washington, D.C.: Government Printing Office, 198–), pp. 1–5.

(B) <u>Report</u> <u>of</u> <u>the</u> <u>President's</u> <u>Committee</u> <u>on</u> <u>Financial</u> <u>Aid</u> <u>to</u> <u>the</u> <u>Blind</u>, by Richard Leaf, Chairman. Washington, D.C.: Government Printing Office, 198–.

Unpublished report

(F)   [11]Roberts Realty Company, "Locations for Potential Malls in the Louisville, KY Area," Louisville, Ky., May 198–, mimeographed.

(B) Roberts Realty Company. "Locations for Potential Malls in the Louisville, KY Area." Louisville, Ky., May 198–, mimeo.

Journal article

(F)   [12]Selma Ritter, "Better Office Management," <u>The</u> <u>Executive</u> <u>Quarterly</u> 38 (May 198–): 102.

(B) Ritter, Selma. "Better Office Management." <u>The</u> <u>Executive</u> <u>Quarterly</u> 38 (May 198–): 100–110.

Magazine article

(F)   [13]Leslie Lee, "Polish Your Typing Skills," <u>Better</u> <u>Homemaking</u>, October 198–, p. 87.

(B) Lee, Leslie. "Polish Your Typing Skills." <u>Better</u> <u>Homemaking</u>, October 198–, pp. 80–88.

Unsigned encyclopedia article

(F)   [14]<u>Encyclopedia</u> <u>Canadiana</u>, 198– ed., s.v. "Shorthand."

(B) <u>Encyclopedia</u> <u>Canadiana</u>, 198– ed. S.v. "Shorthand."

Newspaper article

(F)   [15]"New Plant Opening Predicted," <u>Bilkno Times</u>, 7 April 198–, p. 3.

(B) "New Plant Opening Predicted." <u>Bilkno Times</u>, 7 April 198–, p. 3.

Yearbook

(F)   [16]U.S. Department of Forestry, <u>Yearbook of Forestry</u>, 198– (Washington, D.C.: Government Printing Office, 198–), p. 752.

(B) U.S. Department of Forestry. <u>Yearbook of Forestry</u>, 198–. Washington, D.C.: Government Printing Office, 198–.

Interview

(F)   [17]Interview with Marian A. Keene, Tax Assessor, Ralls, RI, 15 March 198–.

(B) Keene, Marian A. Tax Assessor, Ralls, RI. Interview, 15 March 198–.

Government publication

(F)   [18]U.S. Congress, House, <u>An Act to Amend the Estate Taxation Act of 197–</u>, Pub. L. 00–000, 100th Cong., 3rd sess., 198–, H.R. 0000, p. 3.

(B) U.S. Congress, House. <u>An Act to Amend the Estate Taxation Act of 197–</u>. Pub. L. 00–000, 100th Cong., 3rd sess., 198–, H.R. 0000.

Letter

(F)   [19]Letter from Nancy Perkins, President, Natco Company, to Ruth Bills, 18 August 198–.

(B) Perkins, Nancy, President, Natco Company. Letter to Ruth Bills, 18 August 198–.

Supplementing with Graphic Aids

A well-known saying states: "One picture is worth a thousand words." Although this saying may be an oversimplification, words alone are usually inadequate to tell the report story. Graphic devices must never replace written discussion; however, they supplement and emphasize the text by clearly and concisely picturing the facts. Graphics should be chosen carefully to illustrate points that require clarification by effective restatement. Good graphic presentations are not decoration; they benefit a report by simplifying ideas and relationships for the reader. If taken from secondary sources, they must be documented like all other borrowed materials. Most of your visuals, however, will be original, created to tie in with your presentation.

Not only must aids illustrate effectively, but also they must be correctly interpreted by the writer. Therefore, do not merely present a table or figure; also comment on its significance. Place aids where, combined with text, they will contribute to presenting a clearer picture than words alone can present. Verbal discussion should highlight implications and generalizations and should analyze relationships where necessary.

If a graphic aid illustrates a particular section of a report, it should be placed as near that discussion as possible. Always put aids where they won't stop the reader's train of thought, but readers should not have to search frantically to find the aid being discussed. A full-page graphic may immediately follow the related text, or it may face the text on the back of a blank, but numbered, page. A smaller table or figure may be on a page surrounded by the writing that refers to it or may come just after that passage. The appendix will contain any general or summarizing presentations that have no logical place within the report proper.

Graphic aids must be labeled concisely and accurately to indicate contents. Introduce them either by referring to them and their roles within the text or by a brief introductory passage immediately preceding the table or figure. Generally, graphic aids are divided into two groups defined on the following pages: figures and tables. Table titles are usually placed above them, numbered consecutively using Roman numerals, e.g., *Table I*. Titles of figures are placed below them. Figures, such as charts, diagrams, maps, and pictures are grouped together and numbered consecutively and consistently with either Roman or Arabic numerals, e.g., *Figure I* or *Figure 1*.

Keep the graphic aids simple to comprehend by avoiding unnecessary or confusing details or coverage of more than one point. Highlight by bordering and by leaving enough space around and within the graphics to facilitate reading. Use color, shading, and pattern variations to emphasize differences.

Figures

Pie charts.   Pie charts are relatively simple to construct and easy to understand. They are circles, or pies, with the parts or segments divided into slices sized according to percentages of the whole. A pie chart can only be used to represent a whole and its parts, which add up to 100 percent. Percentages, rather than amounts, are shown; not only are relationships between parts depicted but also the relationship of each part to the whole.

As pie charts cannot show changes over time or compare unrelated figures, they do have limitations. Each slice must be identified, including percentage; sometimes varied colors or patterns are used to further separate the segments. A compass and protractor are used to divide the circle correctly. Often the largest component is placed starting at the 12:00 position and is then followed clockwise by the other parts in descending size order. Note how clearly Figures 13–5 and 13–6 tell their story.

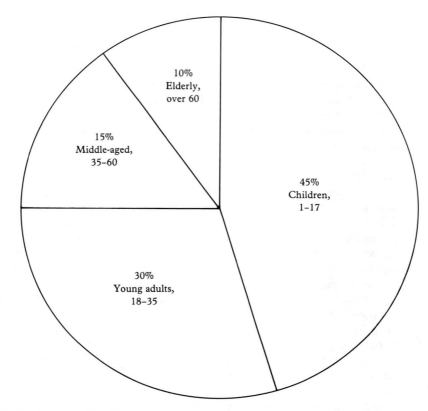

10%
Elderly,
over 60

15%
Middle-aged,
35–60

45%
Children,
1–17

30%
Young adults,
18–35

FIGURE 13–5   Pie Chart Showing Patronage by Age Group at Funland Amusement
Park, 198-

Line charts.   The line or curve chart uses two scales: one horizontal, the other
vertical. This graph most efficiently depicts changes in measurable quantities
that continue over a period of time. Amount of change is generally shown on
the vertical scale from bottom to top; time is shown on the horizontal scale
from left to right. Graph paper is usually used to enhance clarity. Curve charts
may contain a single line or several lines of different colors or patterns. Multiple-line charts compare two or more factors using the same basis of measurement. Figure 13–7 employs graph paper with equally spaced lines (tick marks)
to indicate numbers of patients attending a clinic (vertical scale) over twelve
months (horizontal scale). Figure 13–8, on unlined paper, is another simple
line chart. A multiple-line chart is shown in Figure 13–9.

Bar charts.   Simple bar charts use one set of horizontal or vertical parallel
bars of different lengths or heights to compare magnitudes of one variable
factor. More complex bar graphs use several sets of bars, or subdivided bars,
for comparison of two or more variables. These variables are distinguished
from each other by different colors or patterns. One dimension or scale lists

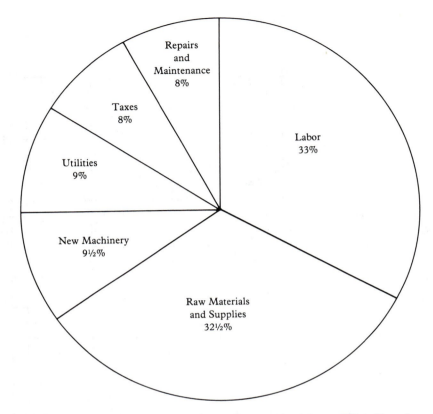

FIGURE 13–6 Pie Chart Showing Operating Costs Breakdown, Wiley Manufacturing Co., 198-

the items being measured; the other scale measures and compares. Bars must be of equal width and use an appropriate scale starting at zero so that all columns fit within the chart.

Figure 13–10 is a simple bar chart with the items to be measured listed at the bottom and the measurement scale in a column at the left. A simple horizontal chart is shown in Figure 13–11. Figure 13–12 is a horizontal chart that measures and compares two variables: the incomes of residents of two different living complexes. Note the explanatory legend at the right. Figure 13–13 uses subdivided bars with the legend at the bottom and the measurement scale at the top.

A pictograph, especially popular in magazines and newspapers, is a bar-type chart in which representative symbols and pictures are used rather than bars. Variation can be shown either by length (number): see Figure 13–14; or by size (magnitude): see Figure 13–15. Pictographs may be either horizontal or vertical. Because these symbols or pictures expand in two dimensions simultaneously, the message is easily distorted. Great care must be taken, or a pictograph will deliver an incorrect message.

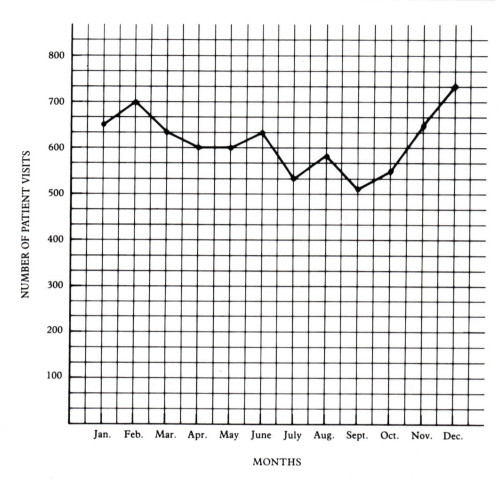

FIGURE 13–7   Simple Line Chart Showing Monthly Patient Visits at the Rhodes Clinic, 198-

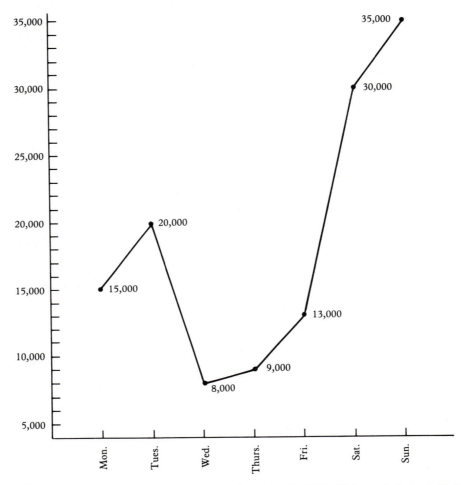

FIGURE 13–8   Simple Line Chart Showing Average Daily Visitors, Lakeland Mall, 198-

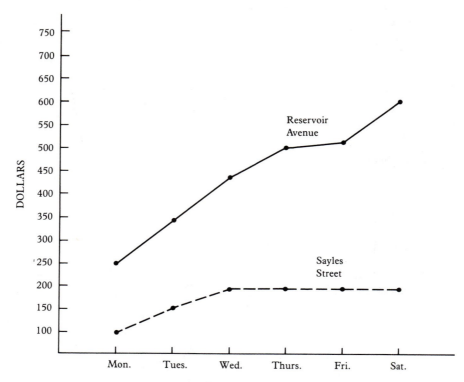

FIGURE 13–9 Multiple Line Chart Showing Gross Daily Income, Reservoir Avenue and Sayles Street Stores, Week of June 25

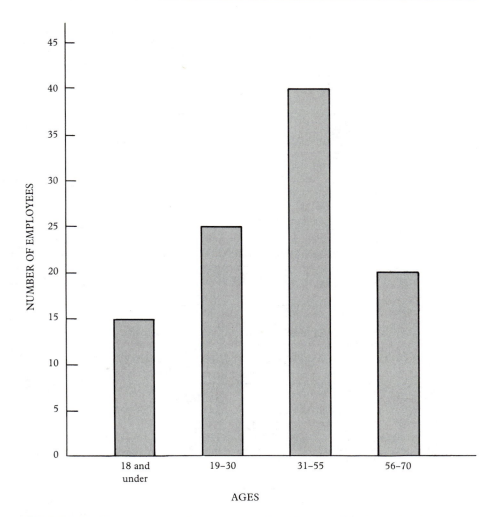

FIGURE 13–10 Simple Bar Chart Showing Breakdown of Employees by Ages, Sills Department Store

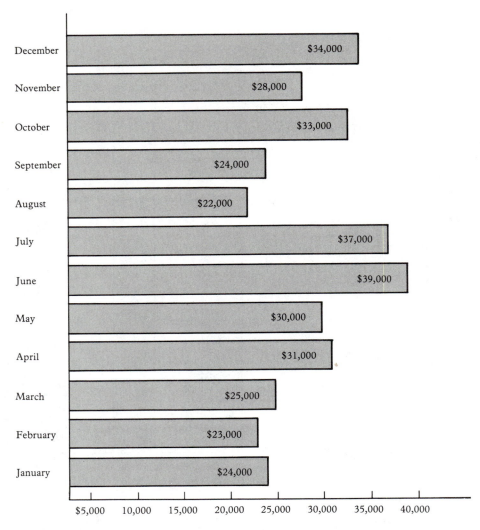

FIGURE 13–11 Simple Horizontal Bar Chart Showing Anticipated Monthly Gross, Avon Beauty Salon, First Year of Operation

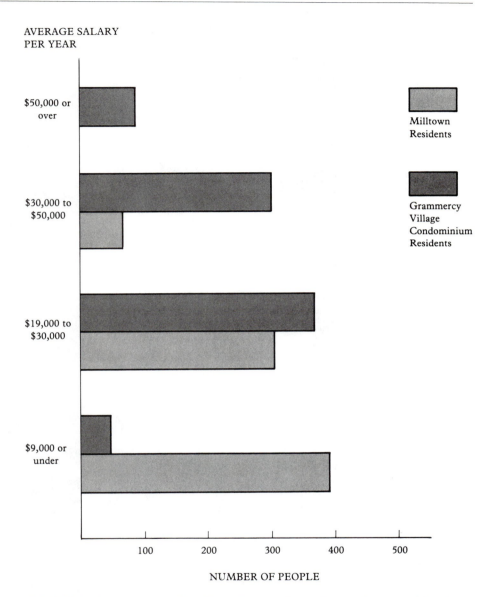

FIGURE 13–12 Horizontal Bar Chart Showing Comparison of Incomes of Residents of Milltown Apartments and Grammercy Village Condominiums

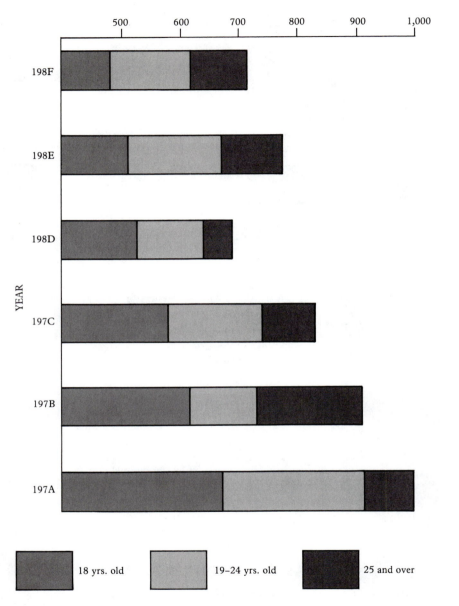

FIGURE 13–13 Bar Chart Showing Ages of Women Marrying for the First Time, Last Six Years

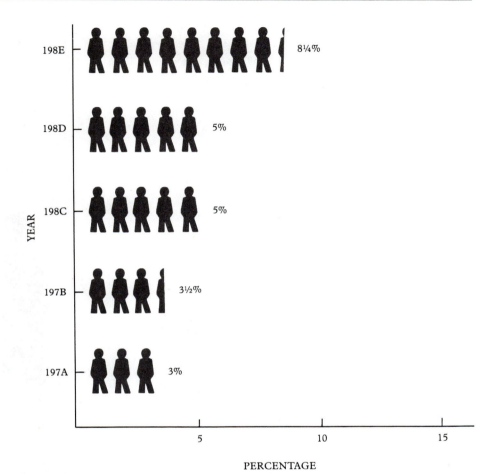

FIGURE 13–14   Pictograph Using Length to Show Percentage of Employees Retiring Yearly, Lumb Products Company

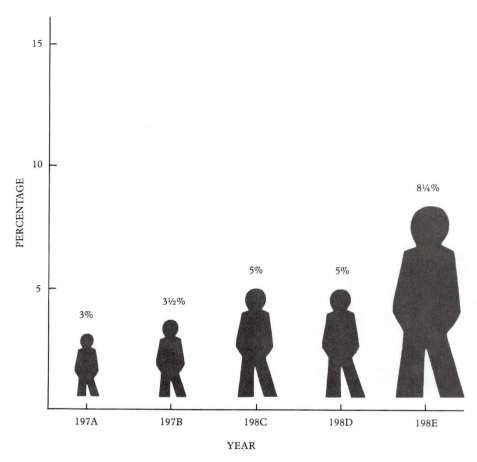

FIGURE 13–15   Pictograph Using Size to Show Percentage of Employees Retiring Yearly, Lumb Products Company

Tables

Tables are composed of columns or rows of systematically arranged information, most often numbers. Because exact figures can be presented, they may be eliminated from the report proper, thus saving space. As tables do not present data in graphic form, they are not technically visual aids. They give facts but do not show relationships; therefore, it is left to the reader to make any necessary comparisons and contrasts. Headings for the columns and titles at the left (the stub) are essential to clarity. Logical order also aids reader comprehension.

Table I is a simple table with only two columns: one listing months and the other listing gross estimated profits. Table II is more complex; it lists three sets of figures, each for a different year, across from the list of items in the stub.

TABLE I

Estimated Monthly Gross,
Lake Lodge, 198–

Month	Gross
January	$25,550
February	25,900
March	27,650
April	26,950
May	28,000
June	37,500
July	37,800
August	37,800
September	26,400
October	27,100
November	25,200
December	24,150
Total Estimated Gross Income	$350,000

TABLE II

Financial Brackets of the Guests at Lake Lodge,
Last Three Years, 198A–198Y

Income	Percentage in Bracket		
	198A	198B	198C
$25,000 and over	2	22	29
21,000–24,999	3	18	25
16,000–20,999	55	26	28
12,000–15,999	7	9	7
9,000–11,999	14	10	5
7,000–8,999	10	9	4
under 7,000	9	6	2

Ensuring Accuracy

Because visuals must convey information accurately, great care should be used in creating them so that they do not misinform or mislead. The same information scaled differently can give a different impression. Use a scale that shows the relative importance of differences or changes. For example, an increase of twenty students in a class numbering 200 is less dramatic than the addition of five students in a class of ten. To avoid misinforming, begin quantitative scales at 0 on charts unless there is a definite reason for doing otherwise. If you consider it necessary to begin at a point other than 0, make this fact clear. Be sure that all bars in a bar chart are the same width (only the length should vary). In a two-scale figure, such as a line chart, be sure that both scales are the appropriate relative size and ratio and that distances between the grids are equal.

Figures 13–16 and 13–17 illustrate how a message can be distorted if visual aids are not carefully created. Figure 13–16 gives an inaccurate picture of the increase over four semesters of the number of students enrolled in Business Writing I. The quantitative scale does not start at 0 and, thus, is collapsed. It appears that a large increase in registration has taken place. Figure 13–17 gives an accurate picture of the same changes.

Other visual aids.   If relevant, visual aids other than graphics may add to a presentation or clarify the message of a report. Maps help a reader to picture

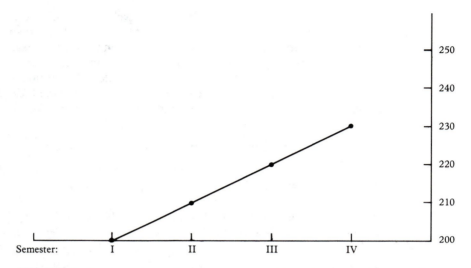

FIGURE 13–16　Line Chart Used Inaccurately to Show Number of Students Enrolled in Business Writing I

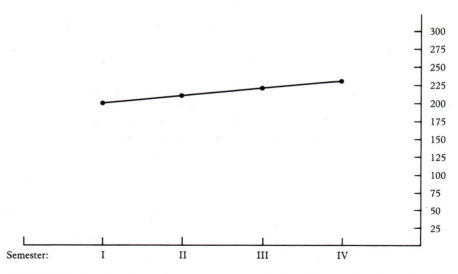

FIGURE 13–17　Line Chart Used Accurately to Show Number of Students Enrolled in Business Writing I

locations, distances, and their relationships as well as visualize routes and specific areas. Well-chosen photographs are often more helpful than verbal descriptions. Diagrams or drawings can show building layout or describe assembly or operations. Organizational charts and flow charts are other auxiliary visuals required in some reports. Although a detailed description of these specialized aids is not within the scope of this book, they, like graphics, should be used only when they supplement and highlight the written information.

Suggestions for Further Reading

For more complete treatment of the topics discussed in Chapters 13 and 14, the following books are helpful.

Andrews, William D., and Deborah C. Andrews. *Write for Results.* Boston: Little, Brown and Company, 1982.

Berdie, Douglas R., and John F. Anderson. *Questionnaires: Design and Use.* Metuchen, N.J.: Scarecrow Press, 1974.

Carr-Ruffino, Norma. *Writing Short Business Reports.* New York: McGraw-Hill, 1980.

Emory, C. William. *Business Research Methods,* rev. ed. Homewood, Ill.: Irwin, 1980.

Holcomb, Marya W., and Judith K. Stein. *Writing for Decision Makers.* Belmont, Calif.: Wadsworth, Inc., 1981.

Lesikar, Raymond V. *Report Writing for Business,* 6th ed. Homewood, Ill.: Irwin, 1981.

Spear, Mary Eleanor. *Practical Charting Techniques.* New York: McGraw-Hill, 1969.

Treece, Malra. *Effective Reports.* Boston: Allyn and Bacon, Inc., 1982.

The writing of a formal business report requires both time and care. First, the purpose of the investigation must be clearly defined; then complete and accurate factual information must be gathered and correctly documented. Graphic aids must also be created to supplement the text. The following Checklist gives a step-by-step formula for developing an effective presentation.

CHECKLIST

Planning and Researching the Report

- Define the problem clearly.
- Write a statement of purpose.
- Give the report a tentative title.
- Allow for time and money limitations.

- List the required information.
- Organize a tentative outline.
- Gather the information.
- Record the information, accurately documented.
- Organize the information.
- Create necessary graphic aids.

EXERCISES

1. Read the following business report assignment and complete the tasks below.

You have been authorized by Mrs. Joan Searles, president of the Toujours L'Amour Bridal Salons, Inc., 2025 Seventh Avenue, New York, NY 00000 to investigate the possibility of opening a salon and providing complete clothing and accessories for both male and female members of bridal parties at a mall near your home or school. You are to send your report to Mrs. Searles, who wants to know whether this would be a profitable venture for the company. She wants the answer within three months; she expects to pay all travel and other necessary expenses.

   a. Define your problem clearly and write a statement of purpose.
   b. Write a tentative report title.
   c. List the information you need and organize it into a tentative outline.
   d. Use your school library to compile a list of possible helpful secondary information sources.
   e. Record your secondary information on 3 × 5 bibliography cards and 4 × 6 note cards.
   f. What primary data might you obtain through observation? Write a detailed description of your plans.
   g. How might you use experimentation in the other five Toujours L'Amour salons to determine whether to operate this new salon as a discount, cash-only operation or as a full-price store offering credit privileges?
   h. Develop a questionnaire that you could send to all the couples whose engagement announcements have appeared in the local newspaper within the last six months.
   i. You wish to interview the owner of a clothing store catering mainly to men and women in their teens and early twenties at the mall. Decide what helpful information you might obtain. List the questions you plan to ask.
   j. Record your primary information on note cards and bibliography cards.
   k. Organize the primary and secondary data you have recorded and develop it into a clear outline after deciding what type of organizational pattern you will follow.
   l. Write your bibliography in proper form. Set up footnotes for the information on your note cards.
   m. Create at least three different graphic aids from the following lists to help tell your report story.
      (1) Table
      (2) Pie chart
      (3) Line chart

       (4) Bar chart

       (5) Pictograph

   n. Describe at least one of the following that would enhance your report.

       (1) Photograph

       (2) Map

       (3) Diagram

2. Read the following business report assignment and complete the tasks below.

During current union negotiations, the management of Reuter Technologies, Inc. has agreed to give life insurance policies equal to one year's pay to all employees. Ralph Riley, the president, has asked you, the personnel manager, to research the cost of this benefit for the company. He wants to know what ten of the largest insurance companies in the area would charge. He asks that your examination report be completed in six weeks so that a decision can be made within the next three months.

   a. Define your problem and write your statement of purpose.

   b. Write a tentative report title.

   c. List the information you will need and organize it into a tentative outline.

   d. List potential sources of secondary data. Does your library offer possibilities? What secondary information might the insurance companies provide?

   e. Gather and record the secondary information on 3×5 bibliography cards and 4×6 note cards.

   f. What primary sources might be helpful? List them.

   g. Develop a questionnaire to send to the insurance companies.

   h. You have decided to interview the presidents or personnel managers of two other organizations that already offer this benefit. List your questions.

   i. What primary information might be obtained from records of your company?

   j. Record your primary information on bibliography cards and note cards.

   k. Organize your primary and secondary data and develop them into a clear outline.

   l. Write your bibliography in proper form. Set up footnotes for the information on your note cards.

   m. Create at least three different types of graphic aids from the list below to tell your report story.

       (1) Table

       (2) Pie chart

       (3) Line chart

       (4) Bar chart

       (5) Pictograph

3. Read the following report assignment and complete the tasks below.

The administration of your college is considering raising tuition fees 15 percent. The Dean of Students has asked you, her assistant, to write an informational report on comparative charges at five similar schools within a three-hundred-mile radius. Your information will be presented at the President's Council in five weeks.

   a. Define your problem and write your statement of purpose.

   b. Write a tentative report title.

   c. List the schools you will consider and the information you will need. Organize a tentative outline.

d. Use your school library as a source for secondary material.

e. Record your information on 3 × 5 bibliography cards and 4 × 6 note cards.

f. List sources of potentially helpful primary information.

g. You have decided to include student reaction to the proposed increase through personal interviews. Develop a questionnaire that would be used with a representative random sample of five percent of the total student body.

h. Record your primary data on bibliography cards and note cards.

i. Organize your primary and secondary information and develop a clear outline.

j. Write your bibliography in proper form. Set up footnotes for the information on your file cards.

k. Create at least three graphic aids from the following list to help you tell your report story.

  (1) Table
  (2) Pie chart
  (3) Line chart
  (4) Bar chart

14

The Formal Report

Creating the Final Product

The final product is created after all the preliminaries discussed in Chapter 13 have been completed. To follow this process, assume that you have been given the following assignment.

> You, Jo Ann Billings, are the investment analyst for Laurel Real Estate Associates, a company that invests in and manages multi-unit dwellings. You have been authorized by Mr. Robert Leonard, the president, to investigate the possible purchase of a 24-unit brick apartment building at 38 Nicholas Road, Chelsea, ND 00000. Mr. Tom Lamson, the present owner, has set a price of $485,000. Mr. Leonard wants a formal report concerning the building's potential as a profitable investment. Mr. Leonard defines *profitable investment* as a 10 percent yearly return on actual money invested (here, the downpayment) after all expenses, including mortgage costs, are met.

> You first define the problem as that of determining whether this investment will meet Mr. Leonard's requirement for profitability; thus, the purpose of your report is to discover whether this investment should be made by Laurel Real Estate Associates. Before you compose a statement of purpose, determine the boundaries or scope of the problem. Limit the investigation to answering only the problem under consideration; for example, you are not concerned here about the possibility of converting the property into a medical office building or dormitory. Formulate a statement of purpose:

The purpose of this report is to determine whether the purchase of the 24-unit apartment building at 38 Nicholas Road, Chelsea, ND 00000 would be profitable, that is, produce a 10 percent annual net return, for Laurel Real Estate Associates.

Next, write a tentative title:

A REPORT ON THE FEASIBILITY OF PURCHASING THE 24-UNIT APARTMENT BUILDING AT 38 NICHOLAS ROAD, CHELSEA, ND 00000

Now list the facts that you plan to explore. Keep in mind the extent or scope of the inquiry.

1. Condition of building; apartments; and plumbing, heating, and electrical systems.
2. Suitability and potential of location, including comparison with other apartment buildings in area.
3. Past gross and net revenues.
4. Mortgage—minimum available downpayment and interest rate.
5. Anticipated operating expenses.
6. Gross and net revenues required for "profitable investment."
7. Anticipated vacancy rate.
8. Potential for acceptable rent increases.

After you have gathered and recorded the answers to these questions and any others that may have arisen during the investigation, organize the report.

The final report, depending upon category, will contain most or all of the following parts in one of the two orders listed below.

Preliminary section
Title page
Letter of transmittal
Table of contents
List of illustrations
Synopsis
Report proper, inductive order
Report body
  Introduction
  Report findings
  Summary and/or
  Conclusions
  Recommendations
List of references (bibliography)
Appendix (if used)

Or:

> ***Report proper, deductive order***
> Report body
>> Summary and/or
>> Conclusions
>> Recommendations
>> Introduction
>> Report findings
> List of references (bibliography)
> Appendix (if used)

These elements cannot all be written in the order of presentation. Parts of the preliminary section cannot be completed until the report proper is done. A good method is to write the report body first, then the appendix and bibliography, and finally the preliminary section.

Elements of the Business Report

The following sections present each element in the final order of a special analytical report fulfilling the assignment introduced at the beginning of this chapter. This report is organized inductively, with the synopsis organized deductively. Although you would write the report body first, it is discussed here in its place in the formal arrangement of parts.

Title Page *(See Example 14–1)*

The title page quickly and efficiently introduces the report by answering the questions Who? What? Where? When? and possibly Why? The first and most important element is the title itself. Like the subject line of a memo, it must be brief but complete, giving a clear and comprehensive overview of the report contents. The tentative title and statement of purpose developed earlier should be helpful. The title should be typed in all uppercase letters and placed so as to provide for a balanced appearance of this page.

The next element, usually centered with first letters capitalized, is the authorizer's identification, preceded by *prepared for*. Included here are name(s), position(s), company, and any other information, such as address, necessary for complete identification.

Prepared by followed by the writer's identification is placed lower on the page in the same form as the authorizer's identification.

The final section contains the date of submittal.

Letter of Transmittal *(See Example 14–2)*

The letter of transmittal is a personal communication from writer to reader. It provides a permanent dated record of transfer along with a short message reviewing authorization information and writer identification. In direct style it briefly mentions the purpose and scope of the report and may refer to special features or problems encountered during research. An expression of appreciation for assistance or for the opportunity to write the report is sometimes included. The major report data or recommendations should not be previewed here unless the report will not contain a synopsis.

The final paragraph usually closes with an invitation for comments and suggestions. The writer may also offer to meet and further discuss the report with the authorizer.

The letter of transmittal appears as an actual letter, single-spaced within paragraphs and double-spaced between paragraphs. The date always appears; however, the return address is omitted if this is an intra-company message.

Table of Contents *(See Example 14–3)*

A table of contents cannot be completed until the report is in its final form. It outlines the presentation and serves as both a guide and preview for the readers. Generally listed are major sections, except the title page, as well as headings and subheadings for the body. The table's length and complexity will depend upon those factors in the report itself. Short reports with few illustrations often combine the table of contents and the list of illustrations by making the list a continuation of the table of contents page.

Headings and subheadings are worded and typed exactly as they appear in the report, using the same system of capitalization and underlining. Titles of major sections begin at the left margin; subheadings are indented to indicate the degree of subordination. Double-spaced dots, or leaders, from the typed headings to the page numbers are useful reading aids. Double space between each entry.

List of Illustrations *(See Example 14–4)*

The list of illustrations contains the listing of all graphic and visual aids, such as figures, tables, charts, maps, photographs, and diagrams. An extensive paper with many illustrations may separate tables from the other visuals. The list of illustrations is set up in the same form as the table of contents. The figure or table number is placed first; next the title is given. Leaders, or dots, connect the identifications with the page numbers. Double space between entries.

Synopsis *(See Example 14–5)*

The synopsis, or abstract, presents the major facts, analyses, and conclusions of the report in a brief summary, or précis, approximately one-fifth to one-tenth of the length of the report body. It serves as an overview for a reader unable to read the entire report immediately and as a review for a reader who wants to refresh his or her memory. It must contain significant information and not simply describe what type of data will be found in the report. Obviously, it cannot be prepared until the body of the report has been completed.

A synopsis may be ordered inductively or deductively. If the report body is developed inductively (from introduction to findings to summary, conclusions, and recommendations), the synopsis, as in the sample report in this chapter, is often developed deductively, leading off with the conclusions and recommendations. No matter how it is organized, the synopsis should emphasize results. The largest portion of the synopsis should be devoted to the summary or the conclusions and recommendations. Condense the main ideas of each major division into one paragraph by elimination of all but the most basic facts. Write your synopsis in good English and complete sentences. Note how Example 14–5 effectively summarizes in deductive order the major ideas, conclusions, and recommendations of the report. For more on writing abstracts, précis, summaries, or synopses see Chapter 15.

Introduction *(See Example 14–6)*

The introduction marks the beginning of the inductively ordered report proper and is placed on a page with the Arabic numeral 1 at the bottom. This section, like the first paragraph of a business letter, tells what the report is about; it defines the scope of the report. It delineates both the problem and the purpose for researching the problem. If knowledge of background or history would aid in understanding, they are included. Helpful definitions may also be given. The writer usually explains where and how data were obtained. Some introductions review authorization details, although they are adequately covered by the title page and letter of transmittal. Finally, the writer previews the report findings through discussing the order to be followed and possibly by giving reasons for the choice of organization.

A long introduction may be divided into subheadings such as *Purpose, Scope, Plan for Presentation, Sources and Methods of Collecting Data, Background,* and *Definitions*. However, most reports do not require this type of subdivision.

Writing the Formal Report

Prepare to develop the formal report in its final form for presentation. You may begin by creating the appropriate graphic aids, or you may choose to develop the aids as you note the need for supplementing or emphasizing parts of the report story.

Because your report will be judged not only by its accuracy and adequate coverage but also by its polished presentation, concentrate on verbal skills. First, write a rough draft, getting your ideas down on paper. Let this draft "cool" overnight, or longer if possible. Then reread and revise, deleting unnecessary material, adding evidence, rearranging to clarify relationships, and checking for spelling and punctuation errors.

The main components of the report are words, sentences, and paragraphs. Before beginning to write, review Chapters 1 and 2 and apply the principles discussed there. Remember the following:

1. *Completeness* — Include all necessary information (but eliminate all that is irrelevant, even if it means discarding information that you spent hours gathering).
2. *Clarity* — Use exact words, ordered logically in sentences.
3. *Conciseness* — Use short simple words that contribute to meaning. Keep sentences and paragraphs short and readable.
4. *Concreteness* — Avoid generalities or vagueness.
5. *Correctness* — Check spelling, punctuation, grammar, and word usage.
6. *Courtesy* — Use the "You" attitude and a positive approach.

Report Findings *(See Example 14–6)*

The report findings section is the focal, and usually longest, part of a business report. Therefore, it must be planned, researched, and organized first, as all of the other sections revolve around it. Here, the complete and correct data and pertinent visual aids are objectively presented, analyzed, and applied to the problem.

Using your carefully organized outline and recorded information as guides, write the first draft of your findings. Open directly with a sentence or paragraph that arouses interest and begins the topic development. Provide for ease of reading by logical order and division of the material into appropriate subheadings. Rearrange your cards or photocopies and add or delete information and graphics as necessary. Set up and place your footnotes in proper form and location.

When you have completed and reread this draft, revise and rewrite by eliminating any unnecessary material and adding any pertinent evidence and aids. Check for errors in sentence structure, word choice, punctuation, and footnote placement. Now the draft is ready to be typed in its final form as discussed later in this chapter.

Summary, or Conclusions and Recommendations *(See Example 14–7)*

This subdivision is so important that it is placed first when report findings are arranged deductively. It is an objective and impartial presentation closely related to the statement of purpose and title. There should be no new information here; the content is based on data contained in the other sections of the report findings.

The content of this section varies according to report type. An informational report, which only provides data, concludes with a summary of the material presented. Usually longer and more detailed than the synopsis, it repeats all the major ideas and statistics in about one-quarter the space allotted in the findings. No conclusions or recommendations are offered.

An examination report, which also analyzes and interprets the presented information, may end with a summary or with a section of conclusions. The conclusions analyze the data and must be logically supported by the facts. Here the writer interprets the findings and indicates what they imply about the given problem. Conclusions must be objectively based on facts already presented. They are a summarization and may reiterate data presented earlier in the report. They do not specify what should be done as a result of these findings.

In an analytical report, both conclusions and recommendations appear. They may be developed in two separate sections but are usually combined. Recommendations go a step further than conclusions. They make one or more suggestions for action or alternatives, based on the conclusions. Presented as suggestions, not commands, the recommendations must be specific and clear; the reader is still free to react or to choose one of the alternatives presented. If alternatives are given, the writer should state any preferences and may also point out the consequences of acting upon a particular suggestion.

Reference Sources
or Bibliography *(See Example 14–8)*

The reference sources section lists the sources that provided the primary and secondary information used in the report. The term *bibliography* is generally not used when many data are supplied by interviews and other non-printed sources. Review the format of this section in Chapter 13.

Appendix *(See Example 14–9)*

The appendix, if included, contains supplementary material that supports the findings but is too bulky, too long, or has no logical place within the report findings section. Some possible contents of an appendix are copies of questionnaires or correspondence, tabulations, computer printouts, and summary graphic aids. The word *Appendix* is typed on a separate numbered sheet, with the appropriate supplements on the pages following.

Format

Leave 1½-inch margins on the top and left of pages and 1-inch margins on the right and bottom. Double space or single space consistently within columns; double space between paragraphs. Center and type the titles of the main sections either in all capitals or with the first letter of each word (except for prepositions and conjunctions) capitalized. Separate these titles from the text by four spaces above and below. Second-degree titles, subheadings under the main sections, should be underlined with the first letters of major words capitalized. They are placed at the left margin four spaces below and two above the text. If third-level titles, subheadings under second-level titles, are used, they follow the specifications for second-level titles except that there are only two spaces above, they are followed by a period, and the following text is placed on the same line. (See Figure 14–1.)

The pages of the preliminary section are numbered at the bottom in lowercase Roman numerals. Although the title page is page i, do not put a number on it; start placing the numbers on page ii, the letter of transmittal. The first page of the report proper has the Arabic numeral 1 at the bottom. Numbers of the second and succeeding pages of this section, and also the appendix and bibliography when included, belong in the upper right-hand corners. Review footnote and reference source format discussed in Chapter 13.

Some Highlights of the Sample Report

The sample report contains all of the major sections of a typical formal presentation. It is a special report because it concerns a one-time investigation; it is an analytical report because, in addition to presenting and interpreting data, it draws conclusions and makes recommendatons.

The title page clearly identifies the problem under consideration as well as both the authorizer, Robert Leonard, and the writer, Jo Ann Billings. The letter of transmittal mentions the date the investigation was assigned and refers to the inclusion of conclusions and recommendations. As is traditional, the letter of transmittal invites discussion of the material. To facilitate reading, a table of contents and a list of illustrations are included. Thus, if Mr. Leonard wants to read the conclusions and recommendations first, he can locate that section of the report quickly and easily.

The synopsis is organized deductively; it begins by making the recommendation that the building under discussion should not be purchased. This deductive organization, giving the reader an immediate answer to the major question, is especially effective when the report findings section is inductively

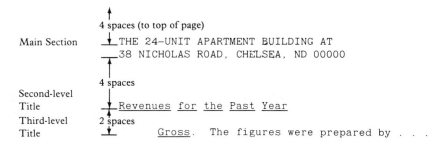

FIGURE 14–1 Format for Formal Business Report Titles

ordered. Next the synopsis, in précis or shortened form, gives the major facts and figures that have led to the recommendation.

The introductory section of the report proper limits the scope of the report by specifying the exact purpose of the study, briefly telling where necessary information was obtained, and defining the term *profitable investment*. It also indicates that this section will be developed inductively; it will first give data and end with conclusions and recommendations.

Starting with a general description of the area and the building, the findings section moves on to specifics about the property. Wherever facts have been obtained from secondary sources, these sources are documented. Past revenue and operating expenses, again documented, are given. Next, indicating step-by-step how the figures have been arrived at, the report gives anticipated operating costs and compares them with past costs by a line chart. A pie chart pictures the breakdown, by percentage, of the anticipated expenses. The revenue from rentals required to realize acceptable profit, as previously defined, is computed and compared with current rentals, using a bar chart. The results of a tenant questionnaire are discussed to measure tenant reaction to substantial rent increases. Finally, rents for comparable apartments in the area are given.

Analysis of the presented facts is contained in the conclusions. Here, using the figures already provided, three major conclusions are made about the results of purchasing the apartment building:

1. Operating expenses would rise dramatically.
2. Rents would have to be raised 65.6 percent to provide the required profit.
3. Many tenants would move, and the apartments would be difficult to rent because the proposed charges would not be competitive.

Based on these conclusions, it is recommended that Laurel Real Estate Associates not purchase the building at 38 Nicholas Road.

In alphabetical order, the sources of information are listed in the next section. There are fifteen items.

Finally, the appendix contains two items that are relevant to the report but have no logical place within the findings section because they would have interrupted the flow of thought. They are:

1. The inspection report, in memo form, from Klements Building Contractors.
2. A sample of the questionnaire mailed to all tenants.

After the tasks outlined in Chapter 14 have been completed, the report proper is written. When this section, including graphic aids, is in its final form the appendix, bibliography, and introductory elements are created and placed. Now the formal business report is ready for presentation. Use the sample report in this chapter and the Checklist as guides for preparing your report assignment for presentation to your instructor. The end-of-chapter Exercises contain possibilities for your investigation.

EXAMPLE 14–1 Title Page

A REPORT ON THE FEASIBILITY OF PURCHASING

THE 24-UNIT APARTMENT BUILDING AT

38 NICHOLAS ROAD, CHELSEA, ND 00000

Prepared for

Mr. Robert Leonard, President
Laurel Real Estate Associates
164 Butler Avenue
Brighton, ND 00000

Prepared by

Jo Ann Billings
Investment Analyst

October 8, 198–

EXAMPLE 14–2 Letter of Transmittal

October 8, 198–

Mr. Robert Leonard, President
Laurel Real Estate Associates
164 Butler Avenue
Brighton, ND 00000

Dear Mr. Leonard:

In accordance with your authorization of August 1, 198–, I
have investigated the feasibility of purchasing the 24–unit
apartment building at 38 Nicholas Road, Chelsea. The results
of my study, as well as my conclusions and recommendations,
are to be found in the accompanying report.

Mr. Tom Lamson, the building owner, was very helpful in sup-
plying data and allowing me access to both the building and
the tenants. Mortgage information was provided by Mr. Raul
Turner of the Citizens Bank.

When you have had an opportunity to examine the report, I
should appreciate your comments. I would be very glad to discuss them with you at any time.

Sincerely,

Jo Ann Billings

Jo Ann Billings
Investment Analyst

Enclosure

ii

EXAMPLE 14–3   Table of Contents

```
                        TABLE OF CONTENTS


LETTER OF TRANSMITTAL ........................................ii

TABLE OF CONTENTS ..........................................iii

LIST OF ILLUSTRATIONS ......................................iv

SYNOPSIS ....................................................v

THE 24-UNIT APARTMENT BUILDING AT 38 NICHOLAS ROAD, CHELSEA,
ND  00000 ...................................................1
     Purpose and Scope .....................................1
     Sources of Data .......................................1
     Definition ............................................2
     Plan of Presentation ..................................2
     An Overview of the Property ...........................3
     Operating Expenses for the Past Year .................5
     Revenue for the Past Year ............................6
     Anticipated Expenses for
        Laurel Real Estate Associates .....................6
     Summary of Anticipated Yearly Operating Expenses .....11
     Required Revenue for Profitable Investment ...........11
     Comparable Rents in the Area .........................15


CONCLUSIONS AND RECOMMENDATIONS ...........................17

REFERENCE SOURCES .........................................19

APPENDIX ..................................................21
     Building Inspection Report from Jay Klements .........22
     Sample Questionnaire Mailed to All Tenants ...........25




                            iii
```

EXAMPLE 14–4 List of Illustrations

EXAMPLE 14–5   Synopsis

SYNOPSIS

    Laurel Real Estate Associates should not purchase the
building at 38 Nicholas Road, Chelsea, ND 00000, as this
would not be a profitable investment. Our anticipated yearly
operating expenses of $103,727 plus required profit of
$12,125 are $84,192 more than the operating costs ($31,660)
of the present owner who netted $38,300 this past year. The
difference can be attributed to increased costs of taxes, insurance, utilities, and maintenance from $31,660 to $45,020
plus annual mortgage payments of $58,707.

    These increased costs would necessitate rental raises of
65.6 percent, resulting in loss of tenants. The projected
rates are not competitive with either similar or more luxuri-
ous units in this area. The location has also become undesirable because the railroad tracks adjacent to the property are
being used for transporting dangerous gases.

v

EXAMPLE 14–6 Introduction and Report Findings

THE 24-UNIT APARTMENT BUILDING AT

38 NICHOLAS ROAD, CHELSEA, ND 00000

<u>Purpose</u> <u>and</u> <u>Scope</u>

The purpose of this report is to determine whether the
purchase of the 24-unit apartment building at 38 Nicholas
Road, Chelsea, ND 00000 would be a profitable investment.
The study compares present expenses and revenue with anticipated first-year expenses and required revenue if the property were purchased. A recommendation is made as to the feasibility of this venture for Laurel Real Estate Associates.

<u>Sources</u> <u>of</u> <u>Data</u>

Information was obtained from interviews and correspondence with Mr. Tom Lamson, the owner; Chelsea town officials;
the manager of the Citizens Bank of Brighton; and insurance
and gas company personnel. Laurel Real Estate Associates records were also consulted. A thorough inspection of the property was made. Tenants contributed helpful information
through their replies to a questionnaire. Finally, secondary
sources provided some data.

<u>Definition</u>

<u>Profitable</u> <u>investment</u> is the sum necessary for the real-
ization of a yearly 10 percent return on money invested.

<u>Plan</u> <u>of</u> <u>Presentation</u>

After a general informational overview of the property,
the report presents current operating expenses and revenue.
It then details anticipated expenses and the revenue needed

1

EXAMPLE 14–6 *(continued)*

2

to produce the required profit. Rentals are shown for comparable units in the area. The report concludes with a recommendation based on these findings.

An.Overview of the Property

This 18-year-old brick veneer building, for sale for $485,000, is on Plat 53, Lots 102, 103 and 104 (24,382 square feet)[1] in the northeast section of Chelsea. It is three blocks from a small shopping center with a supermarket, clothing store, and repair shops; it is one and one-half miles from a major highway, Route 125. Homes and commercial buildings in the neighborhood appear well maintained. Other than five apartment buildings owned by Laurel Real Estate Associates, the residences are one-, two-, and three-family houses.

The 24 apartments are on three floors. There are 2 efficiencies; 12 three-room, one-bedroom units; and 10 four-room, two-bedroom units. All have air conditioners, stoves, refrigerators, and intercom systems linked to the outside front door. The hallways and stairs are well lighted and, like the apartments, all of which I have seen, appear to have been painted recently. There are twenty-five parking spaces at the front of the building on Nicholas Road. A grass area extends twenty feet from the rear of the building to a chain link fence separating this property from adjacent railroad tracks.

Jay Klements, of Klements Building Contractors, inspected the property on August 15. His memo report (see Appendix) evaluated the structure, and the heating, plumbing, and electrical systems. He found everything but the roof in good condition and recommended its immediate replacement at a cost of $6,800. The building is equipped in compliance with Chelsea's fire laws.

---

[1]Chelsea, ND, Bureau of Statistics, Plat and Lot Records, 1900–198–, 10:73.

EXAMPLE 14–6   *(continued)*

3

   Heat, as well as hall and outside lighting, is provided
by the owners; tenants pay for the electricity used within
their own apartments. Mr. Tom Lamson, the owner, says that
all tenants are long-term occupants; there have been no va-
cancies during the past year. He also says that he has never
had a problem collecting rents.[2]

Operating Expenses for the Past Year

   Mr. Lamson summarized operating expenses for the past
year as:

```
        Property Taxes--------------------------------$9,360
        Insurance------------------------------------ 4,684
        Fuel----------------------------------------- 8,324
        Electricity---------------------------------   902
        Water---------------------------------------   855
        Maintenance and Repairs--------------------- 7,535
                                                    $31,660
```

   Property taxes are based on the present assessment by
the town of Chelsea of $110,000 for the building and $20,000
for the land.[3] There is no mortgage on the property, which is
insured for $324,000.

   As Mr. Lamson is retired, he does much of the maintenance work without charge. He takes care of the lawn, does
the snow removal, cleans the halls and foyer, and performs
minor repairs.

---

   [2]Interview with Mr. Tom Lamson, 10 August 198–. The figures in this and the next section were given at this meeting.

   [3]Chelsea, ND, Tax Assessor's Office, Tax Assessment Records, 198–, p. 78.

EXAMPLE 14–6   *(continued)*

4

Revenue for the Past Year

Gross

```
 2 efficiency apartments at $175/mo.--------$4,200
12 three-room apartments at $240/mo.-------34,560
10 four-room apartments at $260/mo.-------31,200
                                         $69,960
```

Net

```
$69,960----Gross Revenue
-31,660----Expenses
$38,300----Net Revenue
```

Anticipated Expenses for Laurel Real Estate Associates

I foresee major increases in operating expenses if
Laurel Real Estate Associates purchases this property.

According to Mrs. Rhoda Mills, Tax Assessor for Chelsea,
the building would, if sold, be reassessed and taxed at 41
percent of the sales price.[4] If the building were purchased
for $485,000, the new assessment would be $14,317 at the
present rate of $72 per thousand.

The property should be insured for at least 80 percent
of its value,[5] or $388,000. Presently it is insured for
$324,000. Insurance fees would be approximately $5,325, including a potential increase in commercial rates.[6]

----

[4]Interview with Mrs. Rhoda Mills, Tax Assessor, Chelsea,
ND, 21 August 198—,

[5]William Polle, *Effective Real Estate Management* (Boston: Lively Press, 198—), p. 22.

[6]Telephone interview with Marcy Wright, Gaspee Insurance
Associates, Brighton, ND, 23 August 198—.

EXAMPLE 14–6   *(continued)*

5

Fuel prices have been rising steadily for the past few years; therefore, a 10 percent increase over the previous cost should be assumed.[7] Electric rates have also increased; the Chelsea Electric Company recently announced a 5 percent fuel surtax, effective September 1.[8] Water usage charges are expected to remain constant.

Maintenance and repair costs will rise considerably, as Mr. Lamson's labor was not included in the figures he gave us. According to Laurel Real Estate Associates company records, our costs for interior maintenance and minor repairs for a similar building, the 25–apartment Rosemont Gardens in Chelsea, were $200 weekly for the past year. We also spent $3,975 last year for exterior maintenance (gardening and snow removal) at Rosemont Gardens.[9] Using these figures, maintenance and repair costs would nearly double at 38 Nicholas Road, to $14,375. This figure does not take into account potential increases in future years; our experience at Rosemont Gardens has indicated that we must anticipate constant rising costs as indicated by Figure 1, page 6, which shows the rise in maintenance expenses over the past eight years.

Laurel Real Estate Associates' customary policy of acquiring property by putting down the smallest possible downpayment and carrying the largest possible mortgage will also greatly increase expenses. On August 25, 198– I spoke with Raul Turner of Citizens Bank, Brighton, who suggested two ways for mortgaging the building. The first would be through personal financing by the owner. He suggested that we ask Mr. Lamson to accept a 25 percent downpayment and a 14 percent

---

[7]Selma Simms, "What Will Happen to Fuel Prices Next Year?" Financial Times, March 18, 198–, pp. 75–82.

[8]"Fuel Surtax Announced," Chelsea Chronicle, 8 August 198–, p. 1.

[9]Laurel Real Estate Associates, Expense Sheets for Rosemont Gardens, 197X–198Z.

EXAMPLE 14–6   *(continued)*

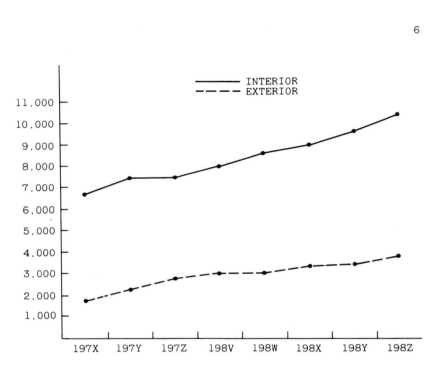

Figure 1.   INTERIOR AND EXTERIOR MAINTENANCE COSTS, ROSEMONT
GARDENS, 197X–198Z

mortgage with monthly payments for thirty years.[10] Unfortunately, Mr. Lamson refused this offer as he intends to rein-
vest the money from the sale in Florida property.[11] He also
stated that the asking price is not negotiable.

---

[10]Interview with Mr. Raul Turner, Manager, Citizens
Bank, Brighton, ND 00000, 25 August 198—.

[11]Interview with Mr. Tom Lamson, 26 August 198—.

EXAMPLE 14–6   *(continued)*

7

    The second method for mortgaging is through a bank. Mr. Turner presented the following figures on September 12, for the maximum 30-year mortgage at 16 percent interest with a minimum downpayment of 25 percent.[12]

```
        Cost of Property----------------------$485,000
        Downpayment--------------------------- 121,250
        Mortgage Note Payable------------------$363,750

        Monthly Payments----------------------- $4,892.25
        Annual Payments-----------------------$58,707.00
```

Summary of Anticipated Yearly Operating Expenses

```
        Property Taxes------------------------$14,317
        Insurance-----------------------------  5,325
        Fuel----------------------------------  9,156
        Electricity---------------------------    992
        Water---------------------------------    855
        Maintenance and Repairs-------------- 14,375
        Mortgage Payments-------------------- 58,707
                                             $103,727
```

    Figure 2, page 8 shows the breakdown of these anticipated expenses by percentage.

Required Revenue for Profitable Investment

    To realize the required profit of 10 percent on actual investment after all expenses are paid, revenue for the first year must be:

```
        Anticipated operating expenses-----------$103,727
        10% return on $121,250 downpayment-------  12,125
        Required revenue, first year-------------$115,852
```

---

    [12]Letter from Mr. Raul Turner, Manager, Citizens Bank, Brighton, ND to Laurel Real Estate Associates, 12 September 198–.

EXAMPLE 14–6   *(continued)*

8

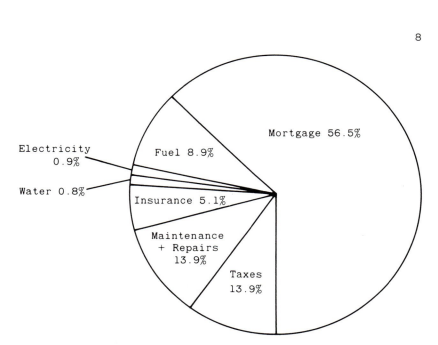

Figure 2.   BREAKDOWN OF ANTICIPATED OPERATING EXPENSES BY
           PERCENTAGE

    If rents were raised 65.6 percent, a yearly total of
$115,992 would be realized, assuming that no vacancies oc-
curred.

<u>Projected Rentals</u>

    Efficiencies---------------------------------$290
    Three-room units----------------------------- 398
    Four-room units----------------------------- 431

Figure 3, page 9 compares present and projected rental rates.

    A questionnaire was sent to all tenants to gauge reac-
tion to possible rent increases (see sample in Appendix).

EXAMPLE 14–6   *(continued)*

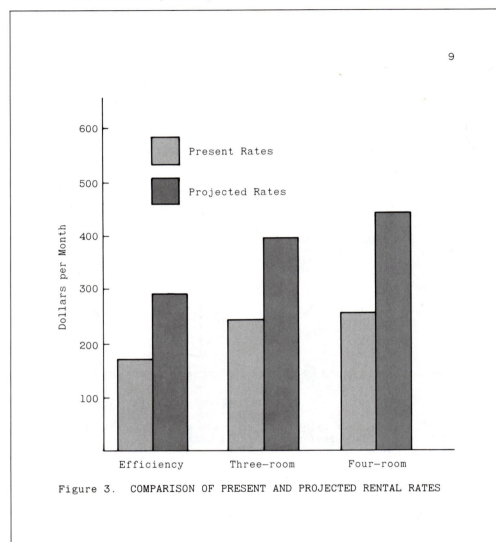

Figure 3.   COMPARISON OF PRESENT AND PROJECTED RENTAL RATES

EXAMPLE 14–6   *(continued)*

10

Twenty (75 percent) of those questioned responded, including
both efficiency occupants, ten of the twelve three–room unit
tenants, and eight of the ten four–room unit renters. Five of
their leases expire within three months, twelve within three
to six months, and three leases continue from six months to a
year. Rents cannot be raised until after the expiration dates
of these leases. None of the occupants said that they would
definitely remain if the building changed ownership; eighteen
said they might remain; two said that they would definitely
move. However, nineteen of the twenty responded that they
would probably not stay if rents were raised by 50 percent or
more.

   Three tenants also commented, in the section provided,
about concern regarding the railroad tracks located behind
the rear chain link fence. They said that the Chelsea Gas
Company has recently received exclusive rights to the tracks
for the transportation of highly volatile liquid gas to a new
refinery located just three miles south of the building. Tenants recently had to be evacuated from their apartments for
an entire evening when one of the cars carrying the dangerous
gas went off the track just behind the building.

   Mr. Roland Fannon, vice–president of the Chelsea Gas
Company, confirmed that the company has exclusive rights to
the tracks and that the tenant evacuation was a necessary
safety precaution. He could not promise that a similar incident would not happen again.[13]

   One tenant said that friends rented a one–bedroom apartment like hers in what she termed "a more desirable neighborhood" for only $5 more monthly, including enclosed parking.

   Another said that he felt entitled to a $10 monthly rent
reduction as he does not use a parking space.

---

   [13]Telephone interview with Mr. Roland Fannon, vice–president, Chelsea Gas Company, Chelsea, ND, 28 September 198–.

EXAMPLE 14–6 *(continued)*

Comparable Rents in the Area

Rental charges in the five apartment buildings in this area owned by Laurel Real Estate Associates were researched in company records. All are of similar caliber in comparable locations. The monthly price ranges are:

```
Efficiencies----------------------------$160-$200
Three-room-----------------------------$225-$300
Four-room------------------------------$350-$425[14]
```

The only other apartments located in the vicinity are in an 85-unit complex under construction by J and B Realty at 149 Ludlam Place. These apartments feature central air conditioning and a swimming pool. Rentals will be:

```
Efficiencies---------------------------$200-$225
Three-room-----------------------------$260-$325
Four-room------------------------------$350-$425
Five-room------------------------------$450-$500[15]
```

---

[14]Laurel Real Estate Associates, Rental Records for 41 Unity Street, 65 Vinal Street, 3 Appian Way, 138 Gano Street, 53 East Avenue, 198—.

[15]"New Apartments Now Renting," Chelsea Sunday Chronicle, 15 September 198—, p. 10.

EXAMPLE 14–7 Conclusions and Recommendations

CONCLUSIONS AND RECOMMENDATIONS   12

In order to realize a 10 percent yearly profit of
$12,125 on the required downpayment of $121,250., rents at 38
Nicholas Road would have to be raised by 65.6 percent. This
raise would be necessitated by an increase in operating expenses from the present $31,660 to $103,727 the first year
for the following reasons:

1. Because of sales price and inflation, taxes, insurance, and fuel and electricity rates would increase
   from $23,270 to $29,790 for the year.

2. We would have to hire employees to replace Mr. Lamson
   who did not include the cost of his time and labor in
   his operating figures. Thus, maintenance would nearly
   double during our first year of ownership, from
   $7,535 to $14,375. It would probably rise in succeeding years.

3. No mortgage payments were included in last year's
   figures. At present rates, our payments would be
   $58,707 yearly.

These figures do not include any potential major repairs, such as roof replacement estimated at $6,800.

Rental increases would cause most of the tenants to
move. We might be left with empty apartments that would be
extremely difficult to rent at the required rates as:

1. The recent development of the use of nearby railroad
   tracks for the transportation of dangerous gases
   makes the location undesirable.

2. The rents would not be competitive with similar
   apartments in the area or even with newer, more luxu-
   rious units.

It is therefore recommended that Laurel Real Estate Associates not purchase the property at 38 Nicholas Road, Chelsea, ND 00000 as it would not be a profitable investment.

EXAMPLE 14–8 Reference Sources

13

REFERENCE SOURCES

Chelsea, ND. Bureau of Statistics. <u>Plat</u> <u>and</u> <u>Lot</u> <u>Records</u>,
    <u>1900–198–</u>, vol. 10.

Chelsea, ND. Tax Assessor's Office. <u>Tax</u> <u>Assessment</u> <u>Records</u>,
    <u>198–</u>.

Fannon, Roland. Vice–President, Chelsea Gas Company, Chelsea,
    ND. Telephone Interview, 28 September 198–.

"Fuel Surtax Announced." <u>Chelsea</u> <u>Chronicle</u>, 8 August 198–,
    p. 1.

Lamson, Tom. Owner, 38 Nicholas Road, Chelsea, ND 00000. In-
    terview, 10 August 198–.

_____. Interview, 26 August 198–.

Laurel Real Estate Associates. Expense Sheets for Rosemont
    Gardens, 197X–198Z.

_____. Rental Records for 41 Unity Street, 65 Vinal Street,
    3 Appian Way, 138 Gano Street, 53 East Avenue, 198–.

Mills, Rhoda. Tax Assessor, Chelsea, ND. Interview, 21 August
    198–.

"New Apartments Now Renting." <u>Chelsea</u> <u>Sunday</u> <u>Chronicle</u>,
    15 September 198–, p. 10.

Polle, William. <u>Effective</u> <u>Real</u> <u>Estate</u> <u>Management</u>. Boston:
    Lively Press, 198–.

Simms, Selma. "What Will Happen to Fuel Prices Next Year?"
    <u>Financial</u> <u>Times</u>, March 18, 198–, pp. 75–82.

Turner, Raul. Manager, Citizens Bank, Brighton, ND 00000. In-
    terview, 25 August 198–.

EXAMPLE 14–8 *(continued)*

14

_____. Letter to Laurel Real Estate Associates, 12 September 198–.

Wright, Marcy. Gaspee Insurance Associates, Brighton, ND. Telephone Interview, 23 August 198–.

EXAMPLE 14–9   Appendix

15

APPENDIX

EXAMPLE 14–9   *(continued)*

Klements Building Contractors
165 Blue Street
Brighton, ND 00000

16

TO: Laurel Real Estate Associates
FROM: Jay Klements
DATE: 15 August 198—
SUBJECT: Inspection of Property, 38 Nicholas Road,
          Chelsea, ND 00000

I have analyzed the above property as follows:

General Construction
Excellent workmanship
Good—quality materials

Exterior
Bricks recently repointed
Wood trim recently repainted
Roof: tar and gravel construction; in poor
      condition, but no apparent leaks
      Areas down to base of roof and covered
      with tarpaper only
      Recommend immediate replacement

Interior
Dry wall construction in good condition
Recently repainted
Hardwood floors throughout
Well soundproofed
Fireproofed in accordance with Chelsea fire
      laws
Smoke detector system throughout
No signs of termites
Basement dry, no signs of leakage

Heating System
Oil—fired hot water system
Baseboard radiation with individually con-
      trolled thermostats
Boiler well maintained
High—efficiency burner installed one year ago

EXAMPLE 14–9   *(continued)*

17

<u>Electrical</u> <u>System</u>
Circuit—breakers, 100 amp. system each unit
Meets town and state codes
Appears in good condition

<u>Plumbing</u>
All copper tubing
No apparent signs of defects

In accordance with your instructions to include es—
timates for any major repairs, we propose to strip
the entire roof and replace all paper, tar, and
gravel at a charge of $6,800. We offer a ten—year
guarantee on this job.

JK:fh

EXAMPLE 14–9 *(continued)*

18

Questionnaire Mailed to all Tenants:

LAUREL REAL ESTATE ASSOCIATES
164 BUTLER AVENUE
BRIGHTON, ND 00000

As Mr. Tom Lamson has informed you, the property at 38 Nicholas Road, Chelsea, is being offered for sale. We are considering purchase and would like to have you continue as a tenant. Your answers to the following questions, and any comments you would like to make, will be very helpful. We shall appreciate your returning this, as soon as convenient, in the stamped, addressed envelope.

1. How long have you lived at 38 Nicholas Road?

   Under 2 years   2–5 years   5–10 years   Over 10 years
   ☐   ☐   ☐   ☐

2. What size apartment do you have?

   Efficiency   Three–room   Four–room
   ☐   ☐   ☐

3. When does your lease expire?

   Within 3 months   3–6 months   6–12 months
   ☐   ☐   ☐

EXAMPLE 14–9 *(continued)*

19

4. Do you use the parking facilities provided?

<u>Yes</u>   <u>No</u>

☐   ☐

5. Do you use the grass area behind the building for relaxation or recreation?

<u>Yes</u>   <u>No</u>

☐   ☐

6. Would you remain if the building had new owners?

<u>Definitely</u>   <u>Possibly</u>   <u>Probably</u> <u>not</u>

☐   ☐   ☐

7. Would you remain if your rent were increased by 50 percent
or more?

<u>Definitely</u>   <u>Possibly</u>   <u>Probably</u> <u>not</u>

☐   ☐   ☐

We welcome any comments you may have. Please use the space
below.

Name (optional)

CHECKLIST

Creating the Final Report

- Write a rough draft of the report proper.
- Reread and revise, creating a polished final product complete with appropriate graphic aids.
- Complete the other sections, so that your report contains:
  a. Title page.
  b. Letter of transmittal.
  c. Table of contents.
  d. List of illustrations.
  e. Synopsis.
  f. Report proper.
  g. List of references (bibliography).
  h. Appendix (if needed).
- Present the report to authorizer(s).

EXERCISES

1. Write complete formal business reports around the following problems.
   a. Complete problem 1, Chapter 13.
   b. Complete problem 2, Chapter 13.
   c. Complete problem 3, Chapter 13.
   d. You have just learned that your deceased uncle, J. Robert Safier, has left you $250,000. However, he has left the money with some strings attached. You must use this money to establish a small business for yourself, one which you can prove to his lawyers will be a profitable and worthwhile investment. You will not inherit the money until you have submitted a satisfactory formal report of your plans to his lawyer, F. Nancy Miller, of Miller and Lees, Attorneys at Law, 155 Relish Square, Hamburg, VA 00000. Some possibilities might include a small manufacturing enterprise or a retail store. Choose a business possibility to research and write the report that you will submit to Ms. Miller. Some of the matters you might consider are:
      (1) Cost of setting up the business (such costs as inventory, fixtures, modernization, machinery).
      (2) Cost of running the business (wages, rent, utilities, etc.).
      (3) Potential (business trends, growth).
      (4) Location.
      (5) Advertising.
      (6) Potential income. (You might want to consider inventory turnover here.)
      (7) A contingency fund. (Would it be wise to hold back some of the money to provide income for a while, until the business is established?)
   e. You have been authorized by Mr. Robert Smith, president of the Top Value Furniture Outlets, 3005 Seventh Avenue, New York, NY 00000 to make the following investigation.

As the business manager of the chain of stores, you are to investigate the possibility of opening a store specializing in cash-and-carry inexpensive to moderately priced furniture and accessories in or near one of the malls in your home city. The store, if approved, should open no later than next September. You may choose both the possible location and store site. These factors will affect your estimated costs. Research this business possibility and write a formal report of your findings. It will be sent to Mr. Smith, who wants to know whether or not this will be a manageable and profitable venture. Conclude and recommend. Your report should consider the following:

(1) Location.
(2) Available stores (size, rental costs, lease requirements).
(3) Cost of equipping store.
(4) Cost of stocking store.
(5) Competition.
(6) Business and growth potential in area.
(7) Business trends in area.
(8) Costs of operation (hours of operation, employees needed, other overhead costs such as utilities).

f. You have been authorized by Mr. Henry Gibson, president of the Read Rite Book Company, 389 Logos Street, Los Angeles, CA 00000 to make the following investigation. You are director of development for the company.

For several years the Read Rite Book Company has successfully operated bookstores, generally located in shopping malls in various large cities. Mr. Gibson is now interested in expanding the scope of operations by taking over college bookstores in which articles other than books are sold. One of the stores in which he is interested is the one at your college. You are to investigate the possibility of taking over and managing this store.

You have learned that you must rent the facilities on a year-round basis, with a two-year lease; monthly rental is $1,000. You will be expected to continue to carry all the items the bookstore now carries, and you may want to add some lines of your own.

Research this business possibility and prepare a formal analytical report to be sent to Mr. Gibson. Be sure that your report includes the following:

(1) The hours of operation, including special hours at the beginnings of semesters.
(2) Average gross and net incomes.
(3) Number of employees needed.
(4) Overhead (operational costs including salaries, rental, cost of merchandise, etc.).
(5) Conclusions and recommendations.

g. You have been authorized by Mr. Syle Wilson, president of Economy Bus Lines, 118 Silver Street, your city, to make the following investigation. You are to investigate the possibility of offering regular private bus service from various points within the commuting area of your campus. The busses would run hourly both to and from the campus. You are to investigate whether or not this would be a profitable venture for the company. You are the business manager.

Write a formal report on your findings, including conclusions and recommendations. Your report should consider the following:

(1) The hours that the busses should run in each direction (remember to take class hours into consideration).

(2) The number of busses needed.

(3) Cost per trip to company.

(4) The exact routes that should be planned for both profit and convenience.

(5) Fare charges (versus expense of other transportation methods).

(6) Number of riders needed to break even or make a profit.

(7) Number of potential riders.

h. You have been authorized by Mr. Bradford Beans, president of the Quick-and-Easy Copy Service, 589 Lotus Place, Atlanta, GA 00000 to make the following investigation. You are the director of development for the company.

The Quick-and-Easy Copy Service has 100 copy centers in malls and shopping centers all along the Atlantic coast. They are now interested in expanding to your city. The location they have chosen to investigate is a shopping center near your college. You must research the possibility of opening a profitable center at this location. Research this possibility and prepare a formal report, including conclusions and recommendations, to be sent to Mr. Beans. Your report should include the following:

(1) Cost of setting up and equipping center.

(2) Cost of running (rent, hours, number of employees needed, cost of supplies, utilities, etc.).

(3) Competition. How might it affect possible profit?

(4) Traffic at shopping center. What is the potential customer population?

i. You have been working for Plug-It-In, a wholesale appliance firm, as an assistant manager in the branch in your city at 895 Bloure Boulevard, for the past year. The main office is at 354 Wright Avenue, Tulipville, CT 00000. The branch in which you work is presently the only one in your area. Because business has been increasing, the company has decided that it would like to establish two more branches in two nearby cities (City A and City B).

Since the members of the Executive Board will be meeting with the manager of your branch in December, they have asked for analytical reports on both proposed branches for that time. Your supervisor, Ms. Sylvia Pease, has assigned the City B report to you. She has arranged a meeting with the City B Development and Business Council and with the real estate agent handling the building proposed for this branch. You attend the meeting and will write a report including conclusions and recommendations on the possibility of opening a branch at the proposed location. Miss Pease has indicated that you might be recommended to become the manager for this branch on the basis of your report.

Among the interesting facts you learn during your visit to City B are the following:

(1) The building was originally an ice-cream warehouse, which would necessitate major renovations. The owners would allow your company to make any desired changes.

(2) Through a slip of the tongue on the part of the real estate agent, you learn that the owners of the building are Miss Pease's sister and brother-in-law. The home office is not aware of this.

(3) This building is, however, the only one available that is large enough for a branch for your firm. In addition, the owners are so anxious to rent the building that they have offered to rent it for less than the going rate.

(4) There is only one other firm in City B that would offer competition, Gorman's Appliance Shop, which is primarily a retail store. Mr. Gorman's brother is the president of the City B Development and Business Council.

Some of the following factors should be considered in your report, as well as the above information:

(1) Location.

(2) Competition.

(3) Business potential in the area.

(4) Rental and renovation costs.

(5) Estimated sales.

(6) Estimated profit.

(7) Overhead costs.

(8) Possibility of building or buying own building rather than renting.

(9) Possible problems that may result because of the conflicts of interest you have discovered.

j. You have been authorized by the president of the Student Senate of Mount Lilly College, Mitton, MS to make the following investigation. You are vice-president of the Student Senate.

The purpose of this report is to determine whether students at the college should be offered the choice of being graded on a pass/fail basis as well as by the present A, B, C, D, and F system. Yours is the only community college in the state that does not offer these alternatives. Last May the faculty voted against introducing this new choice. Research this situation, using both primary and secondary sources, and present a formal report, including conclusions and recommendations, to Lila Sumner, Student Senate president. Your report should consider the following:

(1) Reasons for faculty disapproval.

(2) Faculty reaction at other schools.

(3) Opinions of students at Mount Lilly.

(4) Reaction and opinions of students at other schools.

k. Assume the position of administrative assistant to Gregory A. Thompson, sales manager for John Roth, Inc., manufacturers of men's suits. You have been asked to investigate two retail outlets as possible dealerships for John Roth suits. Each of the two stores has indicated an interest in handling your line, but both are located in the same general area, and one dealer to an area is Roth's policy. Martin Lowe, Ltd., is located in the Round Hill Mall; the London Shop is in the Blues Corner Mall.

You have been asked to gather all pertinent information on the two stores. As you analyze your findings, you should keep in mind Roth's reputation for selling a prestige product. As Roth suits are somewhat conservatively styled and in the higher price range ($300 and up), they appeal primarily to the successful professional man. Quality customers, however, are not your only consideration in selecting an outlet. You want one that can bring about quantity sales. And you want one that gives the kind of service that is consistent with Roth quality. Using local shopping areas, write a report considering the following factors:

(1) Store location.
(2) Social and economic standing of customers.
(3) Other stores in the areas and the customers they attract.
(4) Quality and type of merchandise carried by each store.
(5) Competition (other stores in the areas that carry comparable lines).
(6) Present financial situation of each store and the growth potential of each.
(7) Physical facilities.
(8) Store reputation.
(9) Type and amount of advertising done by each.

15

Other Forms of Communication: Oral and Written

Oral Communication

Whatever your job may be, you can be sure that the spoken word will be the major means of communication. Since most students in business-related programs must take one or more oral communication courses before graduating, the emphasis here will be on the various uses of speech in the day-to-day world of work.

An individual's voice can reveal more about feelings and attitude than any other form of communication. How many times have you said or heard someone else say, "I didn't like her tone of voice when she made that remark." Or, "His tone of voice was insulting!" What was actually spoken may have been harmless enough, but the way the words were uttered, the tone of voice, changed the meaning.

A poor speaking voice can so annoy listeners that they will mentally close out the speaker. How many times have you been unable to understand someone because he or she spoke too fast, had poor enunciation, or mispronounced words? How often have you been irritated by a nasal, squeaky, or whiny voice? How many times have you had to strain to hear what was being said because the speaker's voice was too soft?

An effective voice is easily heard without obvious strain or effort. It fits with the speaker's personality and message. Above all, the voice, if not actually pleasant to hear, is at least not abrasive. The volume is appropriate to the size of the room and the number of people in the audience, while the speed and tone of delivery are determined by the message.

Voices are as unique as fingerprints, and no two are identical. In fact, voice prints are being used more and more in criminal investigations. However, we are not doomed to live forever with a bad voice. Bad habits can be corrected; pitch can be raised or lowered; enunciation can be improved. Most minor faults can be eliminated at home by anyone willing to put in some concentrated effort. The process takes time but is not necessarily difficult nor expensive. Other problems can be overcome in oral communication or voice and articulation classes. Serious problems may require speech therapy.

To begin self-improvement, listen to yourself on a good-quality cassette tape. Better yet, have someone listen with you. Ask yourself the following questions as you listen and discuss them with your helper.

1. Does my voice suit what I am saying?
2. Is my voice too high? Too loud or too soft?
3. Do I speak in a monotone?
4. Is my voice too nasal, squeaky, or whiny?
5. Do I enunciate clearly, or do I slur my words?
6. Am I a "dese, dem, and dose" speaker?
7. Is my voice pleasing to the ear?
8. Do I vary the tone, pitch, volume, and timbre to fit the various parts of my message?

After doing this analysis, listen to radio and TV announcers, newscasters, sportscasters, and commercials. Determine the reasons you like certain voices and dislike others. Notice the different types of voices in commercials. The housewife advertising bowl cleanser has a very different tone from that of the sultry young beauty selling expensive perfume. Notice the faster pace of the sportscaster as compared with the slower, deliberate pace of the newscaster when the news is bad. Listen carefully to the upbeat tone when a funny human interest story is the subject.

Having decided on the kind of improvements you want to make, go back to the tape recorder and try to adapt those speaking characteristics to your own voice. Don't try to imitate, but work to overcome your bad habits. Practice will help make your daily oral communication with others more effective at work as well as in your personal life.

Oral Presentations

Planning

Without doubt, at some time in your professional or private life, you will have to make some kind of oral presentation. It may be simply expressing your opinion at a meeting, making an explanation or a formal report, giving a speech, or even training a new employee. How well you perform will depend not only on your knowledge and experience but also on your speaking ability.

The basic preparation of all planned oral presentations whether they are short reports or longer formal speeches is much the same in that they are all developed with an introduction, a body, and a conclusion. But the length and manner of presentation differ markedly and require varying degrees of preparation and formality in presentation.

Types of Presentations

The oral report is, perhaps, one of the easiest to prepare because the content is already at hand. The research has been completed and the report written. The presenter's job is to condense the essentials, keeping in mind the following outline.

1. Define the purpose of the report and how it will be presented.
2. Briefly describe the background and methods of investigation.
3. Report the findings.
4. Summarize the conclusions and implications.

The extemporaneous speech is planned and rehearsed but is not written in detail. The speaker uses note cards, an outline, or just a listing of topics to jog the memory. Most informal presentations are extemporaneous.

The memorized speech is written out completely and committed to memory. It is rehearsed in much the same way an actor learns a part in a play. If the speaker is good, the memorized speech can sound spontaneous and easily hold the audience's attention. Often, however, memorized speeches sound stilted. They do not allow for audience feedback, and a forgotten line can mean ruin.

Some speeches are meant to be read and are written accordingly. Literary papers are usually presented in this way as are technical papers where accuracy is mandatory. High officials, afraid of being misquoted, regularly resort to reading prepared scripts. Minutes of meetings and treasurer's reports are also always read.

Delivery

For the first-time speaker, nervousness can be traumatic. Even experienced speakers at times suffer from stage fright. If uncontrolled, the physical signs of nervousness can ruin the most carefully planned presentation. One of the most effective controls is to concentrate on the message, not the messenger. Using cards instead of paper for notes can camouflage trembling hands as can gently grasping the sides of a lectern.

When the subject matter permits, visual aids can be effective and enhance your delivery, but only if they are simple, clear, and uncluttered, easily visible, and help explain or answer questions. When using them, remember to address the audience and not the graphics. When using a projector, a pointer is invaluable as it allows the speaker to stand to the side of the projected material, face the audience, and point out key sections for emphasis or direction.

Another very important aspect of public speaking is maintaining eye contact. Everyone has at one time seen a picture of an individual whose eyes seem to stare directly at the viewer no matter where he or she moves in the room. A speaker can achieve the same effect quite easily. Simply look straight down the middle of the room about mid-way, focusing alternately slightly to each side of center. Each individual in the audience will think you are looking directly at him or her. Then, occasionally pan the room with your eyes looking directly at individuals, much as the camera operator does when photographing a crowd or the audience at a TV show. This technique is particularly effective when speaking to a small group, as it makes your presentation seem more intimate and personal.

Experienced speakers know that audience reaction serves as a good indication of performance. Just as a barometer reflects changes in the weather, so does audience response tell you when it is time to vary your delivery. The cues may be subtle or obvious and can always be used to your advantage. For example, murmuring or leaning forward to hear better can mean you need to speak louder. Stifled yawns can mean you are boring, or speaking in a monotone. Frowns or puzzled expressions can mean you are not being understood. Smiles and concentrated attention can mean you are successful in getting your message across.

Telephone Usage

As important as good speech is in face-to-face communication, it is even more important when you cannot see the listener. Whatever your job may be, you will undoubtedly use the telephone. When the listener can see you, your facial expressions and gestures help make your meaning clear. When using the telephone, you must rely on your voice alone to present an image of yourself and your business. Your voice may be the only personal contact the caller ever has with you. Therefore, telephone etiquette is very important. Applying the "You" attitude with courtesy toward the caller will automatically promote a pleasant image.

"Speak with a smile in your voice," a motto once used in training telephone operators, applies equally well to anyone using the telephone, especially in a business office. When answering the telephone on the job, don't make the caller ask, "Is this Sturdy Plastics Co.?" State the company's name, and, if it is company policy, your own name as well. The following are good examples.

> "Good morning. Sturdy Plastics Co., John Staner, Sales Manager speaking."
> "Good afternoon. Sturdy Plastics Co., Mr. Staner's office, Mrs. Smith speaking."

Should the caller not volunteer identification, there are several ways to ask politely.

"May I ask who's calling please?"
"May I have your name please?"
"Who shall I say is calling?"

If you are taking a message and do not understand the caller's name, politely ask how to spell it.

"Would you please spell your last name? I want to be sure I have it written down correctly."

Businesses receiving many calls may put the caller on hold until a line is open. Sometimes the wait is very long. This is particularly true when calling reservations offices, where the individual must hold on or lose his or her place in line. In most businesses, however, if the wait is long, the operator or secretary will check with the caller every thirty or forty seconds to find out whether the person wants to continue holding, to call back later, or to have the call returned when the desired individual is free.

Many of these same rules apply when making calls. Identify yourself and your business. If the call is confidential, say so. For example:

"Good morning. This is Mrs. Harlow. I would like to speak to the credit manager about an error in my bill."

Or:

"Good afternoon. This is John Staner of Sturdy Plastics Co. I would like to speak to Sam Wilson about a charge in our order of June 16."

Or:

"Hello. This is John Staner of Sturdy Plastics returning Sam Wilson's call. Is he in?"

Each organization will have its own rules governing telephone use and the handling of messages. Most offices have printed pads just for that purpose (see Example 12–3). While designs may vary, the information required is much the same everywhere.

Some businesses keep records of all calls, while others may note only long-distance calls depending on the type of phone service. Each business will have its own rules.

When time is important, there is no better way of doing business than by telephone with follow-up correspondence for the permanent records.

Here are some guidelines to follow for maximum efficiency in making business calls.

1. All business calls should be planned.
2. Time changes must be considered in all long-distance calls. Ten a.m. in your state may be 7 a.m. in San Diego, CA or 8 a.m. in Flagstaff, AZ.

3. Reference material should be at hand along with writing materials if you plan to take notes.
4. Always identify yourself promptly.
5. State your business briefly and completely.
6. Remember: in business time is money, and time wasted is costly.

Conducting a Meeting

At some time, you may be called upon to conduct a meeting. Whether it be a college club, a social organization, or a business meeting makes little difference. The procedure is much the same, and a knowledge of parliamentary law is important. Most organizations in this country use *Robert's Rules of Order*. How closely the rules are followed is determined by the organization and the degree of formality with which the meetings are conducted. Copies of the book are easily available, quite inexpensive, and a good investment for anyone planning to enter the business world or join social groups and clubs.

The conduct of a meeting has considerable influence on the attitudes and interest of those attending. You have no doubt heard such comments as, "I hate those meetings. Mr. Lancaster does such a poor job as presiding officer." Or, "You'll enjoy this meeting. Ms. Symonds does a fine job. She keeps things moving yet lets everyone have a say."

A presiding officer has several responsibilities. If the organization does not have a regular time and place for a meeting, such as the third Tuesday of the month at 8 p.m. in the first floor conference room, the presiding officer is responsible for setting the time, place, and date. In all instances, the preparation and distribution of the agenda are his or her responsibility. The presider is also responsible for calling the meeting to order, following the agenda, controlling the members yet allowing those who wish to speak to do so, and ending the meeting on time. Perhaps the hardest task for any presider is to cut off a speaker who monopolizes the floor. Tact is essential. One way to avoid the problem is to set a time limit at the beginning of the meeting for each speaker. If discussion becomes heated or a member gets out of line, the only recourse may be to bang the gavel and demand order. For details on the order of business usually followed, look at the next section on minutes of a meeting, as the organization of the minutes generally follows the sequence of business.

Written Communication

Business Meetings: Minutes

Minutes are the official records of any club, organization, or business meeting. While each group has its own particular version of format and style of writing minutes, some basic rules govern them. Minutes are a summary of all that occurs. In many organizations and businesses, a printed copy is sent out to all members as soon as possible after a meeting, and the original is kept on file. Minutes are legal documents and can be used as evidence in a court of law. At a succeeding meeting, they may be read, amended if necessary, then accepted. If the minutes of the previous meeting have been sent out to members prior to the current meeting, a motion may be made to dispense with the reading and the minutes approved as written.

Most organizations use *Robert's Rules of Order* in conducting their meetings, but the strictness with which the rules are followed depends on the degree of formality of the organization.

The person writing the minutes must be careful to keep out personal opinion and avoid interpretation. Motions must be written down exactly as stated. Usually the names of the people who made and seconded the motion are recorded as well as whether the motion was passed, defeated, withdrawn, or tabled. Occasionally in the case of a controversial issue, the vote count will also be recorded.

The basic parts of the minutes of a meeting are as follows.

1. The organization's name, the date, time, and place of the meeting; its purpose or the subject of the meeting if it is specially called; the name of the presiding officer. Whether you list the names of those in attendance or just the number to be sure of a quorum is a matter of organizational preference. (A quorum is the minimum number of members who must be present in order to have a legal meeting and conduct business, usually stipulated in the group's by-laws.) All the above information can usually be found in the opening sentence. For example:

   The regular monthly meeting of the Board of Directors of Eastern Gold Company was held at the Belltown, PA Company Executive Suite at the Belltown Plant on January 5, 198–. Called to order at 1:30 p.m. with the Chairman of the Board, James Pyrites, presiding, thirty members responded to roll call.

2. Approval and amending if necessary of the minutes of the previous meeting.
3. Approval of the treasurer's report.
4. Old business. This is unfinished business from the previous meeting.
5. Standing and *ad hoc* committee reports.
6. New business.
7. Correspondence and announcements: date, time, and place of next meeting.
8. Time of adjournment.

The report is always signed by the recording secretary and in some organizations also by other officers.

The order of the procedures described may vary depending on the customs of the organization, or members may vote to change the procedure for any one meeting only, depending upon circumstances.

The physical format of the minutes will be determined by each organization, but the form presented in Example 15–1 is a general one.

The Abstract, Précis, Summary, or Synopsis

In any business or profession, the occasion arises when you will be asked to summarize an article, a report, or even a meeting you have attended. The abstract, précis, summary or synopsis are ways of so doing. While the four terms are often used interchangeably, there are some minor differences among them.

Abstract: "Something that concentrates in itself the essential qualities of anything more extensive or more general, or of several things." Usually about one-fifth to one-tenth of the original in length, the abstract is an abridgement of the whole report or article highlighting the key points. It recapitulates the purpose, methodology, and results. A topical abstract presents only the points discussed in the longer piece, while the informative abstract gives the findings on each topic along with the conclusion and recommendations.

Précis: "A condensation or digest." A precise condensation of a writer's words and ideas, the précis is about one-tenth of the original in length, capturing the author's tone, vocabulary, and style. When writing this type of summary, look for topic sentences, thesis statements, primary and secondary support statements, and concluding statements. Put the author's ideas in your own words whenever possible, trying to maintain the original order, tone, and mood. To do this, ask yourself the following questions.

1. Why did the author write this? What is the point the writer is trying to make?
2. What are the main ideas?
3. How is the material arranged?
4. Have I picked out enough of the author's key words so that the précis retains the style, mood, and tone of the article?
5. Have I cut the article down to about one-tenth of the original length without losing any of the essential meaning?

Synopsis: "A brief or general statement giving a general view of some subject. A compendium of heads or short paragraphs giving a view of the whole." The synopsis is much like the abstract but is more complete and detailed, usually presenting a paragraph for each major division.

Summary: "A brief, comprehensive condensation of a longer piece of writing." The summary is like an outline in paragraph form presenting the key ideas in the same order as the original writing and is usually only one paragraph long.

EXAMPLE 15–1 Board Meeting Minutes

**Eastern Gold Company
12 Gold Standard Street
Belltown, PA 00000**

<u>Minutes of the Board of Directors</u>

The regular monthly meeting of the Board of Directors of Eastern Gold Company was held in the executive suite of the Belltown Plant on January 5, 198—. The meeting was called to order at 1:30 p.m. with all thirty members present, Chairman James Pyrites presiding.

The secretary's report was read and accepted.

The treasurer's report was read, accepted, and placed on file.

<u>Old Business</u>

Donald Golden described the progress of the new plant under construction in Smalterstown. Based on his report, the consensus of the board was that construction was on schedule.

<u>Reports</u>

The retirement committee chair reported that four men and three women, all supervisors in their respective departments, had requested retirement as of July 1. As the company policy was to present each retiree with a gift, the chair had authorized the usual vouchers for the personnel division.

May Zenith, the purchasing agent, presented pictures of the office furnishings for the new plant, explaining that they were different from the ones now in use at the Belltown Plant because she was able to get a better price, saving $500 altogether.

Sandy Bellows, chief designer, showed models of the new line of gold chains just starting production.

EXAMPLE 15–1 *(continued)*

Minutes of the   2   January 5, 198—
Board of Directors

New Business

    Chairman Pyrites brought forward a request from the
Mayor of Belltown asking the company to submit designs for a
centennial plaque to be used in the tercentenary celebration
in ten years.

    A motion by Sarah Carson and seconded by Sam Tinker that
the project be given to the design department was approved.
The secretary is to write a letter to the mayor explaining
the action taken on his request.

    Myron Salter's motion that the Belltown Plant close down
completely for vacation during the July 4 week rather than
have the usually staggered vacations was seconded by Dora
Merchant.

    After lengthy discussion the motion was tabled to allow
time for a committee to investigate the effect of such a
change in procedure. The chairman appointed Myron Salter,
Dora Merchant, Daniel Filings, Harvey Session, and Suzanne
Welden to serve on that committee and charged them to have a
report for the next meeting.

    There being no further business, the meeting was ad-
journed at 3:55 p.m. The next meeting will be held on February 8, 198— at 1:30 p.m. in the same place.

Respectfully submitted,

Janice Furlow

Janice Furlow, Secretary

The brief view each type of summarization presents saves time for the person who needs to be aware of the material but may not have the time to read the whole. These summarizations can also serve as a basis for oral reports.

While the following are really examples in deflating pompous prose, they also illustrate how to extract the essence of meaning from longer pieces of writing. The next statement can be reduced to the ten words that were originally spoken by the late President Franklin D. Roosevelt.

I visualize in my mind 33.3333 percent of this grand and glorious nation of ours deprived of the needed amount of adequate and comfortable dwelling places in which their families, lacking most terribly in the number and type of bodily coverings apropos to modesty, good appearance, and comfort, and the necessary quantity of nutritious, well-balanced edible substances mandatory for the maintenance of good health . . .

The ten words are:

I see one-third of the nation ill-housed, ill-clothed, and ill-fed.

Cutting through the gobbledy-gook of this next statement, we find a quotation from the late Sir Winston Churchill.

The British Empire anticipates that as always every loyal subject will do his utmost under all circumstances pleasant or unpleasant to fulfill his obligations to the crown in every way humanly possible.

The message?

England expects every man to do his duty.

Notice how each word in the original quotation represents whole phrases, yet the meaning is clearer and more precise and the impact much more powerful.

Refer to Chapter 14 for use of the various forms of condensations in business reports.

Telegrams

Telegrams are used when mail will be too slow or when a telephone call cannot handle the matter satisfactorily. Because wording is limited, clarity is essential. While businesses usually telephone their telegrams, they also keep a copy of the message on file just as they do copies of all other forms of correspondence.

Telegraph rates vary, but the general pattern is a set fee for a set number of words with each word thereafter at extra cost. Clusters of numerals make up one number and count as one word. Normal punctuation is used, but all words are kept to the minimum necessary for a clear message. Articles and personal pronouns are usually omitted.

Three types of telegrams are in general use. The *regular telegram* is the fastest. When the message reaches the telegraph office at its destination, the message is telephoned to the recipient. A copy of the message will be mailed upon request or if it cannot be delivered by phone. The telegraph boy on a bicycle as seen on television reruns of old movies is long gone. The *day letter* is longer, wordier, slower to arrive, and less expensive than the regular telegram. There is a minimum charge for a given number of words. The *night letter* is similar to the day letter, except it is sent overnight to be delivered in the morning. More economical than the day letter, it also has a minimum fee for a given number of words.

Cables

Cablegrams are basically telegrams sent overseas by underwater cable. The *full-rate cable,* which is the fastest, has a fee for each word. Thus businesses that regularly send and receive cables develop code words to represent groups of words or whole sentences. The address is also a code word often made up of five letters taken from the company's name or product. For example: Moon Products Manufacturing Company of Clarendon, VT might have MOMAN Clarendon as a cable address. The cable address, if there is one, is included in a company's letterhead.

The *letter cable,* slower than the full-rate cable, is similar to the domestic night letter. A fee is charged for a set number of words. The message is sent overnight for delivery the next day.

Ship radiograms are, as the name implies, messages sent to and from ships on the open seas. They also may be in code. Money can be sent by either domestic telegram or cable for a fee that varies according to the amount of money sent.

In whatever kind of employment you may find yourself, you will, at some time, be called upon to use one or more of the other forms of communication discussed in this chapter. Whether it be nothing more complicated than using the telephone or, depending upon your position, doing everything from conducting meetings to sending cables, a few simple guidelines will help you perform at your best. Practice the "You" attitude in everything you do. To paraphrase the "Golden Rule," consider others as you would like to be considered. Think of the listener when speaking just as you do the reader when writing letters. Try to make your voice pleasant to hear just as you try to make your letters pleasing to the eye. Be tactful, courteous, and honest, often a very difficult combination to effect, but one that can do much to help you create the right impression and gain the respect of others.

CHECKLISTS

Oral Communication

- Oral presentations.
  a. Know your material.
  b. Know what you want to say.

      c. Plan the presentation carefully.
      d. Present it clearly.
      e. Maintain eye contact and voice control.
      f. Use audiovisuals properly.
      g. Speak with, not down to, the audience.
      h. Be neat and well-groomed.
      i. Avoid distracting habits.
- Telephone use.
      a. Be courteous.
      b. Practice the "You" attitude with a smile in your voice.
      c. Identify yourself and your business.
      d. Take messages accurately.
      e. Control your tone of voice and enunciate clearly.

Minutes

- Present organizational information and opening time.
- List committee reports.
- Record all motions.
- Mention old and new business.
- Note time of adjournment.

Précis and Synopses

- Condense original material to about one-tenth.
- Use author's vocabulary, tone, and style.
- Avoid commentary.
- Avoid opinions.
- Present main ideas.
- Follow author's arrangement.

Telegrams

- Be brief.
- Omit all unnecessary articles and pronouns.
- Be clear.
- Use normal punctuation.
- Keep a copy for the records.

EXERCISES

1. Put the following information into the proper form for minutes of a meeting.

Organization:	Loyal Order of Red Eagles, Lodge #4
Regular meeting date:	The first Monday of the month at 8 p.m.
Place:	Red Eagle Lodge, Slobridge, New Hampshire
President:	Henry P. Jones
Secretary:	Yourself

The meeting began late at 8:30 p.m. The president presided. Secretary's report read and accepted with no corrections. Treasurer's report showed balance of $55 in checking account and $1,000 in savings. Twenty-seven members were present. Twenty needed for a quorum.

Committee Reports:

The Dance Committee: Orchestra hired for Valentine's Day dance, Saturday, 13 February. Favors have been ordered, tickets are now on sale, and the caterers have signed a contract. Door prizes will be solicited from the local merchants. A permit from the Town Council has been received, but two policemen must be hired. The dance is to be held at the hall in which the meeting takes place. The committee chairman, Elsworth Riley, requests $100 for incidental expenses. Melvin Sweeney so moves, and the motion is seconded by Harry Holstein. Following a short discussion, the motion is passed unanimously.

The House Committee: Vandals have broken three windows in the back of the hall. The Hoftsteader Insurance Company has been notified, and the damage has been repaired.

Old Business:

The purchase of a new stove, which had been tabled last month pending investigation, is now brought up. The committee doing the investigation has not yet had time to get prices. The motion that the matter again be postponed is made by Leonard Johnston, seconded by James Jones, and passed with unanimous approval.

The sale of Valentine candy, which began six weeks ago and ended the week before the meeting, is brought up. The sale netted $75, which is to be turned over to the Slobridge Home for the Aged to buy small transistor radios for the bedridden. This home is the Club's pet charity, and they have at least three charity drives a year for it.

New Business:

Lincoln Sharpe makes a motion that a permanent janitor be hired so that the members will not have to clean the hall themselves. This provokes heated discussion after it was seconded by Stanley Hoffman. The motion is defeated by a 20 to 6 vote.

Correspondence:

A request for rental of the hall by the local Fire Department for a training session to be held on 1 March 198– is read and placed on file. The decision is left to the House Committee. A thank-you note is read from the Slobridge Boy Scout Troop for the use of the hall on January 30 and placed on file.

The president announces that the next meeting of the Executive Committee will be on 3/3/8– at the hall. Time is 7:30 p.m. sharp. Jeffrey Salvas moves adjournment at 9:55 p.m.

2. Study the following paragraphs. Determine their essential meaning and condense them into as few sentences as possible.

Time in the Soviet Union does not seem to have the same meaning as it has in the United States when it comes to flight schedules. There appeared to be no regular times for Aeroflot to leave the airport in Paris for Leningrad. When we were two hours late arriving in Paris because of the air controllers' slowdown at Heathrow in England, we were certain we had missed our connecting flight. Much to our amazement we made the Soviet connection because Aeroflot simply held its flight, one of two daily, for the arrival of the plane from England. It did not, however, wait for our luggage, which caught up with us in Moscow a week later.

Comfort doesn't seem to be as important either, especially on planes. The planes used for international flights were not too bad, but those used within the country left much to be desired. Used to the comfort of the large, wide-body jets of American and British airlines, we found the smaller Soviet planes functional but spartan and uncomfortable. They looked like flying school buses on the inside, narrow with no individual air vents, seat lights, or overhead racks; and they were very noisy. The seats were so close together that even the shortest people aboard found their knees pressed into the back of the seat in front. The ceilings were so low that only a very few passengers could stand upright in the center aisle. However, they got us to our destination safely, which was the important factor.

3. Write a précis of a newspaper editorial.

4. Write a précis of a magazine article.

5. Condense the following messages to 15 words or less for a Western Union telegram.

   a. You want to reserve a room at the Biltmore Hotel, Providence, RI, 00000 for a visiting salesman, Harvey Jencks, from the Chicago branch of the J. P. Eggleston Manufacturing Company. You want a single room with bath.

   b. The John C. Spear Co. wants a rush order sent collect by Chivers Express Company for one gross ivory-handled steak knives from the Peerless Cutlery Company, Inc., 6970 Ives Ave., Halite, NV, 00000. The Spear Company's address is 731 Scituate Cove, Forestry, CT, 00000. The stock number of the knives is IK 793, cost @ $1.00 or $10.00 per dozen or $100.00 per gross.

   c. Your arrival date for a speaking engagement on 8 January 198– has been changed from 10 a.m. to 2 p.m. on 7 January. You are to be met by a Miss Nancy Hollister, 72 Orchard Lane, Bryndale, RI, 00000 at the T. F. Green Airport in Hillsgrove.

   d. A damaged shipment of china, stock #C-X12, is being returned to Liverpool, England, The Royal Dalton Co., 10 Thomas Ave. by air freight. Shipment will be made on TWA leaving New York on 11/29/8– to arrive in Liverpool on 11/30/8–. The order number is 010-901, and the insurance number is NY-602. You want the damaged lot replaced with good china to be returned collect the same way (air freight) as soon as possible. Your company is the Ivy China Shop — Imported China Only, 695 Fifth Avenue, New York, NY, 00000.

   e. Order one Armature Stock Number 5669. You want shipment by Parcel Post and will make full payment upon delivery.

   f. Tell one of your customers that the motor, stock #79-OX, called for in his order #4197 is being shipped to him by the Merchants Express Company to reach him on Tuesday, 5 April.

Appendix

Directions for Letter-Writing

1. Always mention the state in which the town or county is situated, from whence your letter is dated. This is necessary in all countries, but more especially in the United States, in which so many towns and counties are called by the same names. It will be still more necessary when a letter is dated from a gentleman's country seat.
2. Subscribe your first and second names in a plain legible style, without any flourish above or below it. Many letters have remained unanswered, in consequences of the names of the writers of them being illegible. Names thus written are most easily counterfeited, a fact which is not generally known. Affectation therefore in subscribing them, should be avoided upon this account, as well as others.
3. Take care to leave a vacant space in that part of your letter in which the seal or wafer is to be fixed. — By neglecting this caution, very important words in a letter have often been effaced.
4. In directing a letter, mention the state in which the person resides to whom it is addressed, except he lives in a large town, or in the capital of a state. — From a neglect of this caution, many letters have been delayed or perished in a post-office.
5. Never fail to pay the postage of your letters, when you write upon your own business. Be assured your business will be done the better for attending to this direction. The contrary practice is presuming, indelicate and unjust.

Postal Services

Postal services are many and varied, with the cost and regulations subject to constant change. Businesses can keep up to date with a monthly publication, free of charge, that advises mailers of changes as they occur. It can be ordered by writing to:

Memo to Mailers
P.O. Box 1
Linwood, NJ   08221

The *Mailers Guide* is an indispensable source of information about postal services for the individual as well as for businesses. This booklet can be obtained from your local Postmaster, who can also answer any specific questions about regulations and services. According to the *Mailers Guide* (PUB 19), July 1980, the six major classifications of mail service are Express Mail Service, First-Class Mail, Priority Mail, Second-Class Mail, Third-Class Mail, and Fourth-Class (Parcel Post) Mail, each of which may have several sub-divisions and each of which has specific regulations governing its use.

Express Mail Service

Express mail is a fast, reliable service for letters, documents, or merchandise. It is available in most major metropolitan areas and offers four major services.

Express Mail Custom-Designed Service is a 24-hour-a-day, 365-days-a-year service designed to meet a customer's particular needs with regularly scheduled shipments.

Express Mail Next-Day Service is available at designated post offices, each with its own list of destinations designed for those who occasionally need reliable overnight service. Two services are offered.

1. *Post Office to Addressee.* Mail left by 5 P.M. will be delivered before 3 P.M. the next day, including weekends and holidays.
2. *Post Office to Post Office.* Mail left before 5 P.M. will be available at the designated post office by 10 A.M. the next day the post office is *open.*

Express Mail Same-Day Airport Service offers service between airports within the United States. The mailer brings the mail to the airport mail office. There, the pick-up time at the destination is determined, and the mail goes out on the next available flight.

Express Mail International Service, like custom-designed service, is offered under a sales agreement to a limited number of countries. It is also available without a sales agreement, like Next-Day Service, to a limited number of countries. Mailing costs vary according to weight, distance, and types of service for all domestic and international services.

First-Class Mail

First-class mail includes items weighing under 12 ounces. This classification includes most written matter such as letters, checks, notebooks, bills, filled-out printed forms, sealed greeting cards, and business reply mail. Any other mail weighing less than 12 ounces can, at the sender's option, be mailed first class. New regulations now govern the size as well as the weight of first-class mail; a surcharge is added for any item over or under a certain size range.

Non-standard size mail is first-class mail weighing one ounce or less, that is higher than 6⅛ inches, longer than 11½ inches, and thicker than ¼ inch or that is less than 1.3 times the height or more than 2.5 times the height.

Many businesses doing large mailings prefer to use a postage meter. Such mail when bundled is processed faster as it bypasses postal cancellation. Postage meters come with a preset amount of postage in one, several, or all denominations. When the prepaid amount runs out, the meter locks automatically. Meter stamps can be used on all classes of mail.

Volume mailings of over 500 pieces may qualify for a special rate if they are presorted according to specific procedures. Other special first-class services are *Special Delivery, Registered Mail, Certified Mail, COD,* and *Express Mail.* Also available are certificates of mailing proving an item was mailed and large white envelopes with green borders indicating first-class mail.

Priority Mail

Priority mail is all first-class mail weighing over 12 ounces. Weight and zone determine postage. The maximum weight is 20 pounds, and size is limited to 100 inches in combined girth and length.

Mailgram service is offered by Western Union and the Postal Service. Sent via Western Union's network to 141 post offices, delivery is made by regular carrier the next business day.

Second-Class Mail

Second-class mail is used primarily for mailing newspapers and periodicals published at regular intervals at least four times a year.

Third-Class Mail

Third-class mail consists of circulars and printed matter, letters, booklets, catalogues, newsletters, corrected proof sheets, and such items as farm and factory products, photographs, keys, and other merchandise.

Items sent third-class mail must weigh less than 16 ounces; there is however no maximum size limit. Non-standard third-class mail weighs less than 2 ounces and is higher than 6⅛ inches, longer than 11½ inches, or thicker than ¼ inch, or is less than 1.3 times the height, or more than 2.5 times the height. Any non-standard third-class mail is subject to a surcharge.

Third-class mail does not have to have a specific name in the address but can be sent to Postal Customer, Rural Boxholder, Occupant, Householder, or Resident.

Fourth-Class Mail

Fourth-class mail includes Parcel Post, bound printed matter, and other special items. Packages mailed between large post offices cannot weigh more than 40 pounds nor be more than 84 inches in combined length and girth. Packages sent between smaller post offices cannot weigh more than 70 pounds nor be more than 100 inches in combined length and girth. Two or more smaller packages of similar size and shape may be tied together and shipped as one parcel if they do not exceed the weight and size limitations when combined. Fees are assessed according to weight and zone.

Bulk Rate Fourth-Class Mail rates are available for 300 or more pieces of mail of identical weight separated by parcel post zones.

Special Fourth-Class Mail applies to books of 24 or more pages of which 22 are printed, 16mm films or narrower, printed music, printed objective test materials, sound recordings, manuscripts, educational reference charts, and medical information. The address side of the package must be marked "special fourth-class rate."

Library Rate includes a wide variety of items such as books, music, and theses, for exchange between educational, religious, and scientific organizations, to name just a few.

Special Fourth-Class Presort rates are available for mailings of 500 or more identical pieces and so are the special services of insurance, special delivery, special handling, COD, and certificates of mailing.

Address Abbreviations

With automatic addressing machinery coming into greater use in businesses, the number of letters that can go into any one line is limited. The Postal Service has developed a system of approved abbreviations. There are three sets; one for streets, roads, and generalized institutions such as universities, institutes, or missions; one for specific cities, towns, and places, such as Petrified Forest National Park, listed by state; and one for states, territories, and possessions, which is included here. All three lists can be found in the *National Zip Code and Post Office Directory* (PUB 65).

Alabama	AL	Iowa	IA
Alaska	AK	Kansas	KS
American Samoa	AS	Kentucky	KY
Arizona	AZ	Louisiana	LA
Arkansas	AR	Maine	ME
California	CA	Maryland	MD
Canal Zone	CZ	Massachusetts	MA
Colorado	CO	Michigan	MI
Connecticut	CT	Minnesota	MN
Delaware	DE	Mississippi	MS
District of Columbia	DC	Missouri	MO
Florida	FL	Montana	MT
Georgia	GA	Nebraska	NE
Guam	GU	Nevada	NV
Hawaii	HI	New Hampshire	NH
Idaho	ID	New Jersey	NJ
Illinois	IL	New Mexico	NM
Indiana	IN	New York	NY

North Carolina	NC	Tennessee	TN
North Dakota	ND	Texas	TX
Ohio	OH	Utah	UT
Oklahoma	OK	Vermont	VT
Oregon	OR	Virginia	VA
Pennsylvania	PA	Virgin Islands	VI
Puerto Rico	PR	Washington	WA
Rhode Island	RI	West Virginia	WV
South Carolina	SC	Wisconsin	WI
South Dakota	SD	Wyoming	WY

Using the zip code does speed the mail service, especially when mail is sorted by scanner. A missing zip delegates the piece of mail to a special area to be sorted later by hand. All second-class, controlled circulation mail, third-class mail, and all fourth-class mail except parcel post must have the proper zip code clearly marked.

The expanded nine-digit zip was started in 1981 with use of the added four digits optional. Zip code directories can be obtained for a fee either from the post office or the United States Government Printing Office.

Addresses and Salutations for Special Groups

Federal Officials

The President of the United States   Dear Mr. President:
The White House
Washington, DC Zip

Senator John Jones   Dear Senator Jones:
The United States Senate   Dear Senator:
Washington, DC Zip

Representative Jane Jones   Dear Congressman Jones:
The House of Representatives   Dear Ms. Jones:
Washington, DC Zip

State Officials

The Honorable John Jones   Dear Governor Jones:
Governor of Rhode Island   Dear Governor:
Providence, RI Zip

Senator Jane Jones   Dear Senator Jones:
The State Capitol   Dear Senator:
Providence, RI Zip

City Officials

His Honor the Mayor, or   Dear Mr. Mayor:
The Honorable John Jones   Dear Mayor Jones:
City Hall
Providence, RI Zip

Clergy

Protestant Episcopal
The Right Reverend John Jones   Dear Bishop Jones:

Methodist
Reverend Bishop John Jones   Dear Bishop Jones:

Roman Catholic
Most Reverend John Jones   Your Excellency:

Protestant Ministers
The Reverend John Jones, or   Dear Mr. Jones:
The Reverend Dr. John Jones*   Dear Dr. Jones:

Rabbi
The Reverend John Jones, or   Reverend Sir:
Rabbi John Jones   Dear Rabbi Jones:

Catholic Priest
Reverend John Jones   Dear Reverend Father:

Brother
Brother John Jones   Dear Brother John:

Sister
Sister Mary Agnes   Dear Sister Mary:

* Use only if the addressee has a doctorate.

Index